THE WINGS
OF THE
MORNING

If I take the wings of the morning and dwell in the uttermost parts of the sea . . . even there shall thy hand lead me, and thy right hand shall hold me fast.

Psalm 139

THE WINGS
OF THE
MORNING

The life story of a very ordinary man
who proved that it is better to be lucky
than clever

Kenneth MacVicar

Foreword by Angus MacVicar

JOHN DONALD PUBLISHERS LTD
EDINBURGH

*This book is dedicated to my own
nearest and dearest*

ISBN 0 85976 4559

A catalogue record for this book is available from
the British Library.

Typeset by Pioneer Associates, Camserney, Perthshire
Printed and bound in Great Britain by
The Cromwell Press, Melksham, Wiltshire

Contents

Acknowledgements

I do not know whether thanks or blame is due to the members of my immediate family and to others who pestered me after my retirement, to 'get the story written down.' Three years ago last Christmas my sons and daughter gave me a Word Processor with the instruction 'get on with it!' *The Wings of the Morning* is the result for what it is worth and I would like to acknowledge the kindness and friendship of all who appear in the book. Without them there would have been little to write about.

I am most grateful to those who were kind enough to read extracts and who encouraged me to proceed.

My thanks in the production of the book is due especially to Lesley Beaney and Janet Dunn of Pioneer Associates who have been most generous with their time and expert advice, also to Russell Walker of John Donald Publishers, for his courteous encouragement.

Illeray,
Kenmore,
Perthshire.   Kenneth MacVicar

Foreword

by Angus MacVicar

Young Kenneth has always been a problem.

I am entitled to call my brother Young Kenneth because, as the fifth in our Manse family, he is thirteen years younger than I am. (And also because, as light fades behind the Perthshire hills, he can look like a teenager.) I say he has always been a problem because his opinions are held so strongly that some who choose to argue with him are often disconcerted and even intimidated.

He has now written the story of his life. I used to write what are called 'thrillers' in the trade but few of them are as full of excitement, both spiritual and physical, as is *The Wings of the Morning*.

Young Kenneth was the war-time pilot of a fighting Hurricane, and so his title is appropriate. In spite of its Celtic ring, it was first used by the Biblical King David, another adventurous and opinionated character, who, nevertheless, found God to be One he could not argue with. Young Kenneth has never been able to escape God, either.

After the violence of war (how sorely it affected our family he describes in this book) Young Kenneth found comparative peace in a happy family life and a long and devoted ministry in the Parish of Kenmore, where, by good fortune, he found it possible to combine busy pastoral work with play on the golf course. (About his life-long support of the Glasgow Celtic football team the less said the better.)

He became a Queen's Chaplain and also an active and sometimes controversial member of various committees of the General Assembly of the Church of Scotland. Here he makes some 'observances' about the Kirk and its government which are bound to be disturbing. With some of his conclusions I heartily agree. With others I, equally heartily, disagree. But I understand that in his own way – like King David – he is working for God.

FOREWORD

The Wings of the Morning is a human story, worth reading. It is a testimony not only to Young Kenneth's muscular Christianity but also to his courage.

Achnamara,
Southend, Argyll, 1996   *Angus MacVicar*

Introduction

It was a summer's day. Loch Tay was sparkling in the morning sun, and as I stood on the lawn outside the Manse at Kenmore, I was moved by the beauty around me. Yet, I was anxious. The postman had just delivered the mail and in my hand I held an official postcard which informed me that one of my parishioners had been admitted to the Bridge of Earn Hospital. Her address was given as Smiddy House, Acharn, and my worry came from the realisation that this intimation called for action on my part. The day before, the Presbytery of Dunkeld had ordained me to the office of the Holy Ministry and had charged me with the cure of souls in the beautiful parish of Kenmore in central Perthshire. During the service I had been so intent on making the correct responses and of doing the appropriate things at the right time, that I had given little thought to the enormity of the responsibilities being laid upon me. During the social gathering which had followed in the evening, I was aware of a great goodwill among many present, but also of a certain canniness on the part of others. They were obviously willing to give me a chance but would reserve judgement. My father, with more than forty years in the ministry behind him, asked the congregation to be patient with me and told them that I was not only soft-hearted but also short-tempered! My brother-in-law, the Reverend Johnston R. McKay, a man of clear vision and without illusions regarding the vulnerability of the ministry, asked them to treat me with respect and kindness, promising that if they did not, he would return to chastise them.

It was a good humoured if rather embarrassing affair. We all knew that the talking would have to stop and that, for good or ill, the congregation and myself would be left to get on with building the relationships which would make or mar my ministry. As I stood with the postcard in my hand, I knew that the talking had already stopped. Action was called for. I felt very alone. There was nothing for it, however, but to find out more about the situation. As luck would have it, the Beadle's wife, Mrs McGregor, had agreed

1

to help us get settled in the Manse and she had arrived promptly at nine o'clock. For the first hour she had felt it her duty to give to Isobel, my wife, a character sketch of everyone who had been in the hall on the previous evening. When I went into the kitchen, Mrs McGregor was in full flow and Isobel was looking at her in a somewhat bemused way. Our children, Angus aged three and Kenny, two, could not take their eyes off her.

'Oh, hullo, Mr MacVicar,' I was greeted. 'Great night, last night.'

I agreed, and produced my postcard.

'Who is Mrs McDonald and where is the Smiddy House, Acharn?'

We were swept away on a torrent of information.

'Steady on,' I said, 'Who is likely to be in Smiddy House?'

Mrs McGregor gave me the information I wanted and I left the house while she gave answers to unasked supplementary questions.

Acharn was some two miles distant. I mounted my bicycle and took the south road by the lochside. Beauty was all around me but I could scarcely appreciate it because of the anxiety that I felt. I was well aware that the first pastoral visit might be very important in the scheme of things.

I found Acharn a hamlet built on both sides of the road. The top village had been built in a square and I was to discover that all the houses in this square were condemned and were due for demolition, but in 1950 and for some years after, the tenants kept them warm, clean and cosy, drew their water from the single tap in the square and longed for the day when they would be rehoused.

Following the good Mrs McGregor's instructions I found Smiddy House and, with some trepidation, knocked on the low double door. It was opened by a fresh-faced and comely young woman who, when she realised who I was, welcomed me into the house. I asked about her mother and got the story of a rather delicate lady whose life had been punctuated by illness and pain. I confirmed which hospital ward the lady was in and promised to visit her as soon as possible. Isobel, the daughter, was most gracious and thanked me for my speedy response to the notice of her mother's illness. I began to feel more relaxed, found it easy to talk with the girl, and was generally pleased at how things were going. We commended the invalid to the care of Almighty God and asked for His blessing upon the household. With that the door was flung open and there entered a tall woman with a stormy countenance.

Isobel was a bit put out, but immediately made the introductions.

'This is the new minister, Mrs Fraser,' she said; and to me, 'Mrs Fraser, my neighbour.'

I proffered a hand in greeting and it was taken in a claw-like grip as she peered into my face.

'You canna be the minister!' she said with some heat.

'Oh, Mrs Fraser, like it or not, I *am* the new minister,' I countered.

'You are not,' she said. 'I saw the new minister at the induction last night, and he's naethin' but a wee bachle.' She laughed uproariously at the thought. Isobel was embarrassed.

'She doesn't see very well,' she offered in explanation.

'Well,' I said, 'this wee bachle had better get back to the Manse and see what's for lunch.'

Mrs Fraser called on the name of the Lord and looked at me more closely. 'Ye might be him, right enough,' she admitted and departed the scene without embarrassment.

When she had gone Isobel was full of apologies but I re-assured her that I had enjoyed my very first visit in the parish. I took my leave and went whistling down the path to be met by another middle-aged lady, her spectacles glistening in the sunshine.

'Somebody's happy,' she said.

I introduced myself.

'I met you last night,' she assured me.
'I hope you don't think I'm a wee bachle,' I said, and told her about my introduction to Mrs Fraser.

'My!' she said, 'is that not just like Mrs Fraser. Don't worry, she has been like that since time immortal.'

I could hardly believe my ears. I bade a cheerful farewell to the lady, and jumping on the trusty steed, pedalled back to the Manse. The sun was shining even brighter now, and Loch Tay was more beautiful. My heart was singing.

The love affair with the lochside and the people there had begun, but much had happened to bring me to that happy smiling day.

PART ONE

Early Days

I saw a stranger yestreen.
I put food in the eating place and drink in the drinking place
And music in the listening place
And in the Name of the great Triune
He blessed myself, my house, my cattle and my dear ones
And the lark sang in her song:
Often, often, often comes the Christ in the stranger's guise.

(Columba's Rune of Hospitality.)

CHAPTER ONE

In the Beginning

I was born on 25 August, 1921, in the Manse of Southend, near to the Mull of Kintyre, the fifth child of Angus John MacVicar, minister of the Gospel, and his wife Marjorie.

I cannot overstate the good fortune which attended me on that day. I have easy recall of happenings and people from a very early age, and I cannot remember a time when I was not completely devoted to my mother whom I regarded as the saintliest person in the world. I loved her with all my heart and could not contemplate life without her. I recognised my father as a key figure in my life but of such importance that he had little contact with one small child. My three big brothers also led a separate existence from me. They came and went on strange expeditions while I stayed at home with my sister Rona, who was much more a part of my life and, like my mother, usually within sight or sound. A further constant in my life was Maimie, the diminutive servant who had come with our parents from Duror to Southend. Her life was spent mostly between the scullery and the kitchen. Rona and I got among her feet and were chastised for doing so. We did not mind too much for we knew that in Maimie we had another guardian who would always stand between us and our foes.

I came through the infant years safely, watched over by the three most important people, my mother, Rona and Maimie. If there were any upsets in those first four years I cannot recall them, for my life was safe, happy and serene.

I went to school on my fifth birthday. Southend Public School was about half a mile from the Manse, and going there changed much in my life. I had no fears about going, for I had Rona to take my hand and I thought she would be with me all the time. I was wrong. On arrival I discovered that there was a playground for boys and one for girls and that the segregation was total. Inside the school we were allocated our desks and I shared one with a fierce redhead whom I had never seen in my life. It was obvious that school put a different complexion on life altogether. I hated it, and from Monday morning I longed for Friday afternoon. Often on a Monday morning I feigned sickness, but even the softest hearted mother is not so easily misled, and on several occasions I was faced with the stark choice of school or castor oil. My dislike of the dreaded laxative sent me unwillingly to school, but I never reached the stage of enjoying it.

I had no proper relationship with the teacher. She was severe, unlike any female with whom I had had close contact, and I disliked her. She seemed to have a sadistic streak, and I watched with fear as she passed between the desks overseeing our work on the slates. Where there were shortcomings she administered a sore clip on the ear with the back of her hard hand which was well-encrusted with rings. No knuckle duster was more effective. The slates were our work sheets and the slate pencil the tool of our trade, and when finished with our 'sums' or our 'letters' the class would be called out to form a semi-circle around the teacher's desk, the slates held up in front of us as a convict holds his number. Our work was scrutinised and we awaited judgement. If all was well we were allowed to return to our desks, but if there were flaws in the work we would be ridiculed before the class and made to repeat the exercise.

Punishment was meted out without emotion. My own great fear was in being kept in after the rest of the school had left, because I was afraid of being left alone with the teacher and I was further afraid of having to walk home alone. Early in my school career the fact that I had a long name was my undoing – I could not get Kenneth MacVicar into a single line on the slate. I was kept in and envied the John Smiths and the Neil Gows of this world.

The obvious advantage of the slate lay in the fact that it could be wiped clean once an exercise had been completed. For this purpose each pupil was instructed to have a damp cloth in his schoolbag. Needless to say, damp cloths were lost or pilfered, and were rarely available when required. Being without a cloth brought a torrent of abuse from on high. I was wide awake enough to notice that my new-found friends, Andy and Baldy, got over these small difficulties in the simplest way. Unconcerned by thoughts of etiquette or hygiene, they simply spat on their slates and wiped them clean with the sleeve of their jersey which, as often as not, doubled as a handkerchief.

I had unbounded admiration for my classmates; Alex and Andy, Baldy and Neil. They faced life with a courage which I did not possess and they had no fear of the teacher, no fear of bulls that might break out from the field, and no fear of the odd drunk whom we sometimes met on the road. They seemed to me to be free from care in spite of the fact that even at that early age I realised that they did not have the same material blessings which I enjoyed. They had an experience of life which had been kept from me and they also made use of a vocabulary which was denied to me. When, in innocence, I introduced some of their words to my own conversation at home, I was told that God would not be pleased if I continued to use certain words. Far worse than that, however, I was assured that it would cause my mother great grief if she ever heard me using these words again. It was quite obvious that my aforementioned friends were somewhat careless about pleasing God and were little concerned about their mothers' reaction.

When I look back on those early days at school, I wonder if my whole attitude was wrong. Was my dislike for the teacher due to an inadequacy in myself? How would I have got on if the teacher had shown more affection or kindness? Would I have learned more or less? Is it possible that I would have relaxed in a warm and affectionate relationship and learned nothing? If there is any truth in the text 'The fear of the Lord is the beginning of wisdom', I can also vouch for the fact that the fear of the school teacher was the beginning of any knowledge I acquired. Perhaps the teaching methods of the husband and wife who taught in my primary school suited me. Much of the teaching was by rote and I have to say that I've always had a strange satisfaction from learning things 'off by heart'. It was not long before I could recite the Shorter Catechism, although certainly I understood little of it. While to the first question, 'What is man's chief end?' I would vigorously respond 'Man's chief end is to glorify God and to enjoy Him forever', I was well on in life before I realised that chiefend was not a single word. At that period in my life the chief end of this wee man was not to understand but to recite without mistake.

After more than sixty years I still have nuggets of knowledge hidden away. I have the ability to recite the towns in each county of Scotland (old style), and how could I have got through life without knowing the wild life in the North West Territories of Canada, to wit: beaver, otter, ermine, bear, arctic fox and seal? I had almost reached manhood before I realised that there was no such animal as an ermine-bear!

I was relieved to be promoted from the 'wee' room to the 'big' room where husband was the teacher. He had a more expansive manner and seemed almost human on occasion. Most of the time, however, he treated us as poor deluded creatures without sense or grace, and from an Olympian height he poured scorn upon us: 'Why am I afflicted with such stupidity.' Once, when he had reduced me to tears by the administration of the belt, he observed, 'My poor boy, you hold your heart in your waistcoat pocket, ready to shed a tear at a moment's notice.' I have no doubt that they taught us in the manner of their day, with the 'three Rs' being dinned into us, and the number of pupils from that small school who went on to the universities and colleges is evidence of their success. I am sorry that so few of us remember our early teachers with any affection.

When, in later life, I visited primary schools and saw the cheerful and relaxed atmosphere in which knowledge was imparted, I smiled to think of the subject matter in the reading books of my own childhood. The stories were filled with gloom and disaster; the widows son carried off by the press gangs; the crippled child abused by his master. Our poetry lessons, in which we chanted the lines, were similarly full of death and destruction; the boy on the burning deck, the burial of Sir John Moore at Corunna, along with the real tear-jerker which began, 'A soldier of the legion lay dying in Algiers/ There was lack of woman's nursing, there was dearth of woman's tears.' There was no fear that we might escape the realities of life or death – 'Stitch, stitch, stitch, in poverty hunger and dirt.' Destruction, disease and death dogged our steps on every literary expedition. Life was nothing if not earnest.

CHAPTER TWO

Happy Days

This was, of course, in stark contrast to the life I led away from school, where all was warm, affectionate and safe. It never occurred to me that life could be any different. I would live forever and everybody about me would do the same.

There were crises of course, as on the occasion my beloved sister Rona became ill and Dr Niven had no hesitation in diagnosing scarlet fever. Suddenly there was a lot of activity about the place. The three elder brothers who, by this time were attending Campbeltown Grammar School, were all brought home. Doubtless they all thought that this was a splendid thing to have received an extra holiday, but my mother was worried and sad. I was sad too, for Rona was taken away. An ambulance came and I was told that she was being taken to hospital in Campbeltown. It was terrible to think of her all alone there, but she wasn't to be alone for long. In a fortnight's time I took the dreaded sore throat and before I got used to the idea of being unwell, I was in the next bed to Rona in the Calton Hospital.

I cannot remember being either happy or sad in that place, after all, being able to see Rona all the time made the place reasonably safe. I do remember two things from that six weeks in hospital. I recall vividly father and mother visiting the hospital and being allowed to look at us from outside the window. I would put my hand on the glass pane and my mother would press her lips to the other side of the glass. I also recall the great excitement among the nurses when units of the Royal Navy dropped anchor in Campbeltown Loch, with the leading ship in the Squadron being the battleship HMS *Benbow*.

It often appeared to us that we had been in the Calton Hospital for ever, but eventually Rona's six weeks of incarceration was at an end and she could get home. Poor Rona, someone decreed that she should wait for another two weeks to keep me company, but at last the day to go home arrived. We were in a fever of excitement and ready to go in the early morning, but it was afternoon before our parents arrived in the hotel car with our friend John McKay at the wheel. For some unknown reason John was known to everyone as 'Tow'. He was quite a character whose company we all enjoyed because of his boisterous good humour. By the time we were at Southend Manse he had worked us up into such a state of excitement that my mother was sure we wouldn't be able to sleep and we would make ourselves ill again. Maimie greeted us with warm affection, was amazed at how much we had grown, and promised to tell us a story before we went to sleep.

As we grew older we were to realise that our hero 'Tow' had, in common with all individuals, certain weaknesses. He was not keen on being alone in the dark and he had a fear of ghosts. This weakness became very awkward when Tow took a fancy to a girl who lived a few hundred yards to the south of the graveyard on the coast road at Southend. Our hero, it was reported, duly escorted his lady love from the dance in the village, bravely passed the graveyard where the stones shone disconcertingly in the moonlight, and having left the girl at her home, decided that discretion was the better part. He walked the six miles on the loop road around the back of the hill rather than the half mile to his home past the graveyard.

Now we were home we chased around to see what changes had taken place during our absence. Our little brother had grown but apart from that everything seemed the same. The time came for us to go to bed where the fire had been lit in our bedroom and the oil lamp gave a soft light. We got ready for bed and our mother hugged us tighter than usual as we said our prayers. Then she left us and Maimie came up with the promised story. Her story was in fact an account of all that had gone on during our time in hospital. No one had been allowed near the Manse for three weeks; men had come and had put disinfectant down all the drains and in the ditches near to the Manse, and much to the annoyance of the farmer from whom we got the milk, all his utensils had been inspected. Nothing had been found to explain why two children from one family should have taken scarlet fever while no one else took it, but eventually the scare of an epidemic had passed. Everyone had been very kind: Old Hugh had been over from the farm every day to ask for us, Donald the gamekeeper had brought a pair of rabbits the day before our return so that we could have our favourite stew, and farmers and their wives had come with eggs and chickens. We felt very important and, suddenly, very tired. Maimie blessed us in the Gaelic and we climbed into bed. For a little while I stared at the ceiling watching the fleeting patterns made there by the flickering fire. I felt an awesome happiness and an overwhelming contentment. It was like a knowledge of God.

Soon we were back at school and I felt a bit more secure. After all, I had been where neither Andy, Baldy or any of the others had been. I had been to a hospital and had survived! They were not impressed!

Life at home went on its own sweet way. We watched baby John grow and soon he was staggering about on his dumpy legs. In the spring and summer, after school, my father often took us on walks to visit the neighbours. We went up to Waterside to talk to the gamekeeper and his wife, across the bridge to Kilblaan to see Old Hugh and his nephew Archie, up the hill to High Machrimore to see Johnny and Rita, or down to the Smiddy to see the blacksmith. Sometimes when the adults got going on serious talk it was all a bit boring, but usually there was something interesting happening. Mrs McLean, the gamekeeper's wife, was a gentle soul who often hugged us to her apron, warm from standing in front of the black range in her kitchen. She was also generous with newly baked pancakes or with soft bread liberally spread with fresh butter and with sugar scattered over it. A dentist's nightmare, but greatly enjoyed. If we were really clever we would arrive at Waterside at the time when Mrs McLean would be feeding the hens. She had some on the other side of the river in a henhouse among the trees and this necessitated her taking the little boat across the water. If we were there at the critical time we always got a sail up and down the river, and it was magical looking down into the brown clear water and seeing the little trout dart away from the oars.

On one famous occasion we were thus engaged. It was a summer's evening and all was still except for the sound of the oars kissing the quiet water. Donald the gamekeeper kept bees and they were busy in the lime trees. Suddenly the calm of the evening was shattered by Donald himself, whose head had erupted from a skylight window.

'Helen!', he shouted at his wife, 'where'th ma thtudth?' (Donald had a lisp).

'Och, Donald,' she replied, 'they are in the left hand drawer of the chest of drawers.'

Donald disappeared and we continued our voyage. Out of the window came his head again.

'They're no' there,' he shouted, now red in the face. 'Come and find them.'

'I can't, Donald, I've got the children in the boat!'

'Chuck the little buggerth in the water and come and get my thtudth'. Everyone laughed, including Helen, as it was rather good to hear ourselves referred to in this way. Helen obediently rowed to the bank, got us safely ashore, and went to find the lost studs which had taken on the importance of the Elgin marbles. For our part we ran all the way home to tell the awesome tale and our mother didn't quite succeed in hiding her laughter.

Kilblaan was another source of interest and amusement. We often walked there with our father of an afternoon before tea. Down the brae to the riverside, lying on our tummies by the bridge to see if a sea-trout had ventured upstream; making sure that there were no bulls in the fields which we were to cross. If Hugh wasn't about he would be sitting in the kitchen, a room devoid of any kind of creature comfort, with a stone floor, a deal table, plain wooden chairs on one side and a wooden bench on the other against the window. Two armchairs which had seen better days were on either side of the black range. Every time I was in it I compared it unfavourably with the comfort which I enjoyed at home, and felt sorry for Hugh, his sister Flora, their nephew Archie, not to mention the maid Marion, a strong and large lady, who lived there with her two children, Annabel and Morag. We were always welcomed without fuss as everyone was too busy, except for Hugh, who always had time to discuss old times with our father. When we got fed up with listening to the adult talk we would amuse ourselves outside where Hugh had a whetstone wheel which worked on a treadle. This was a constant source of amusement. We often found Archie putting the horses away for the night in the stable or putting them out to the field after unyoking them, and if he was in good form he would tease us. Sometimes he would ignore us and we would feel deflated. We were well warned never to go near the dam.

One Saturday we were over at Kilblaan in the morning, for Hugh was threshing. We were not allowed anywhere near the threshing shed but watched the exciting proceedings from afar, with Hugh turning the sluice gate to direct the water on to the wheel which drove the threshing machine. The old boy with his bristling red beard was very busy and he shouted to us to bring various articles, but when he was excited he could never remember the name of the things he wanted. Thus it was that he would shout, 'Bring the whityecut' which being translated was simply 'what do you call it'. The morning passed and we played in the stackyard as the work went on, but eventually the threshing was finished and Hugh, now

14

very red in the face and with straw sticking to every part of him including his beard, went to turn the sluice gate open. It was at this point that the drama began. The top of the sluice gate was covered in green slime, and Hugh slipped as he turned the handle and fell into the dam. We were dumbfounded, quite unaware of the mortal danger the man was in. Hugh rose from the flood and sprackled his way to the dam side looking like Neptune without his trident. He was, however, greatly concerned and not about being soaked to the skin. He thrust his hand into his waistcoat pocket and with great relief took out his watch, put it to his ear and exclaimed 'It's a' right – ma grandfaither gi'ed it me.' We all rejoiced and couldn't get home quickly enough to relate the epic story as we had a great affection for Hugh.

We saw him practically every day, for his mail was left at the Manse for collection. I cannot recall much mail for Kilblaan but Hugh came anyway, read the *Glasgow Herald* sitting in the Manse kitchen, and departed bearing with him the previous day's edition for reading at leisure. He rarely fussed over us as children but was obviously interested in us. Often he sat with fingers entwined, his thumbs revolving around each other in a clockwise direction. Fascinated by this we would ask, to begin with in innocence, later, I regret to say, with some impudence, 'Do you always do that, Hugh?' 'No!', he would reply, putting his thumbs into reverse, 'I sometimes dae this.'

On the day of the Campbeltown Fair Hugh would return to Southend on the bus in quite good trim. Although he never drank to any excess he enjoyed a dram on occasions and coming into the Manse to collect his mail and paper we would be aware that he was redder in the face than usual, and more talkative. Rona, aged six, and myself, three, would be in the kitchen with Maimie. Much to our amazement Hugh announced that he had a poke of sweeties for us. 'They're for you,' he told Rona, 'when you give me a kiss.' Rona took a long look at the red, bearded face and made her decision. 'You kiss him, Kenny, and I'll get the sweeties.'

Without compunction I did just that. Honour was satisfied and Hugh went off laughing wheezily while we explored the 'poke' which contained fierce looking black-striped balls.

Our visits to the blacksmith were usually undertaken on a wet Monday in holiday time, but for a reason which was not at first clear to me Rona did not accompany us. I went with my father, who chose the wet Mondays because he knew that there would be many farmers taking advantage of the wet day to have their horses re-shod. He knew that the horses would be taken to the smiddy by the farm labourers and it was a good chance for him to speak with them. He always felt that on his pastoral visits to the farms he only saw the farmer's family and never the single labourers who were either consigned to the kitchen or a bothy. He looked upon the smiddy visits as part of his work and for me it was a great chance to watch Mr McCallum carry out his skilful art of shoeing the horses.

The mud-floored, high roofed blacksmith's shop was an Aladdin's cave of wonders. The smith and his son Dougie each attended to a horse, lifting the heavy hoof between their legs, their clothes and bodies protected by the leather apron which was split up the mid-dle. First the nails in the old shoe were extracted, the worn shoe flicked with the tongs into the corner to join all the other discards. During this operation a new shoe was being heated in the forge and if the smith was in a good mood I would be put on an old chair and allowed to work the bellows, until the fire and the shoe within it were white hot. With long tongs the shoe was taken from the fire and then shaped by the blacksmith on his anvil – I can still hear the rhythm of the hammer, clink, clink on the cold metal, clunk, clunk on the hot – the shoe 'tried on' the horse, with a flash of smoke as it touched the hoof; the all-pervading heavy smell of the burning hoof; more heating, more shaping until it fitted. Then the final exciting flourish as the hot metal was cooled in the water butt with the great hissing and escape of steam. It was magical. The careful nailing of the shoe followed and the whole operation ended with the application of a broad file which smoothed the hoof. When fitted with a full set of shoes I used to imagine that the horses set off for home with a new sense of pride and a new opinion of themselves.

Most of the beasts were docile during the shoeing but now and again one would take offence at the blacksmith's ministrations and would kick out and try to escape. There would be a great commotion while the blacksmiths plus the man with the horse tried to calm the animal and very colourful phrases echoed round the shop. I knew then why Rona had not accompanied us! When calm was restored there would be a lot of red faces both from exertion and from embarrassment. Apologies would be tendered to my father, but he was not concerned. Having been a padre to a mounted reg-iment during World War I he knew a thing or two about horses and, as far as swearing went, he had heard it all before. He never used bad language as far as we knew but on one red letter day when he took us all to see a shinty match at the opening of the Public park in Campbeltown, excitement got the better of him and when the Inveraray forward missed a 'sitter' in front of goal, a loud 'damn' escaped from the minister's lips. I think we loved him more after that.

It goes without saying that even as very small children, Sunday was a special day. I cannot remember a time when we did not go to church every Sunday if we were well. It has to be said that it was something to be endured as we had no idea of what was going on. In my early years I comforted myself by putting my face against the fox fur which my mother wore to church, and later I would try to count the number of panes in the stained glass windows which were opposite our seat. Later still I passed the time doing simple mental arithmetic sums – how many verses would we sing during the service and, importantly, when would we be halfway through the service? We were upheld by the thought that our presence was pleasing to God and that He would give us a just reward at some stage. When Celtic won on the Saturday I had the feeling that my church attendance had made a difference, but when they lost I could only think that some misdemeanour of mine had outweighed the righteousness of church attendance.

Sunday morning in the Manse was a time of great tension and my mother prayed that my father's digestive system would cause him no concern. We kept out of his way. We had our own problems for we had to get dressed in our Sunday best and for me the Sunday best was the kilt, tartan stockings, a suitable jersey and jacket, topped by an Eton collar. This latter was the bugbear for, having been newly ironed on the Saturday, its leading edge resembled the cutting teeth of a circular saw. Getting the thing on invariably ended in screams and tears and with her husband seething like a volcano downstairs and her children playing the fool upstairs, I am sure my mother often went to church wondering what religion was all about and wondering, too, what she had done to deserve it all. Before church the cry would go up, 'Where is my blasted soda?' It has to be explained that the 'blasted soda' was a mixture of milk and baking soda without which, my father had decided many years ago, he could not preach the Gospel. When the soda was downed we would all set out for divine service, none, including the minister, filled with the peace which passeth understanding. Still, the Lord had miracles to perform for we would return from church often with something of that peace and a restoration of the spirit.

Sunday afternoons were rather special, for we often went for walks with our mother and Maimie, our father having gone to bed to recover from his labours of the morning. The 'walk' was not of very long duration. In the summer time we climbed the hill behind the Manse to a sheltered spot where we could play, or sit on a rug and look down on the broad breast of Southend parish clad in its patchwork green. Beyond the land, the sea, the North Channel, shimmered in the sunlight and in the distance were the green hills of Antrim. On a Sunday afternoon little stirred. No one was working in the fields and few people were out and about – the 'solemn stillness' held. But about four o'clock there would be a stirring. The cattle would rise from their ruminating resting places and, on every farm, would begin to make their way to the gate of the field where they had been grazing. Milking time was near. As if by magic, tendrils of smoke would begin to rise from every farm where the kettles were being put on to make cups of tea. The afternoon siesta was over. We amused ourselves by imagining what was going on in one of the farmhouses – 'That's Mrs Barbour putting on the kettle; that's Mr Barbour lighting his pipe; Mrs Barbour is shouting to the twins to make the tea and to get the scones from the bread bin; Mr Barbour is shouting to his son John to get the dog and take in the cows; John's going to the barn to let out the dog. He's going through the yard and will appear – now!' We were very pleased when we got it nearly right. Sure enough all the farms would produce someone to go for the cows. We would watch them all streaming towards the various byres, for another milking time had come and on Sunday as on Saturday the beasts had to be seen to. As the cows went home it was time for us to go too, often to be met by our father, restored after his siesta and ready for his tea.

CHAPTER THREE

Growing Pains

The Manse at Southend provided a lot of space both inside and out for the adventurous play of young children. At the front of the house there was about an acre of level ground which could not truthfully be called a lawn but rather a large flat grassy space divided by a semi-circular gravel driveway, where it was possible to play all kinds of games from hide and seek to 'kick the can'. In the middle was a large copper beech tree, on a high branch of which had been hung a swing which was a constant source of pleasure to generations of children, but a constant source of anxiety for our mother who watched us, swinging high, from the window where she was wont to sit, expecting at least one of us to break our neck.

The vegetable garden lay at the back of the house and was of a similar size to the front. Our father was a keen gardener and longed for the day when his sons would be able to give a helping hand. In my earliest years the garden was delved in the spring by Hughie Stewart, a ruddy faced man from the village, whom we all liked enormously. Hughie had a good line in stories and, as he cleaned the blade of the spade in the toolshed, he would regale us with his experiences as a 'deep sea' man. He had been through such terrible storms, round Cape Horn on the sailing ships, and knew New York as the 'home village'. We were spellbound and refused to believe those who said that Hughie had never been further than Sanda Island in a boat. To us he was a hero and never more so than when he climbed on to the roof of the Manse to clean the chimneys, but it was nothing to Hughie – had he not climbed to the crow's nest more times than we could count?

Disaster, however, was to attend Hughie at the chimney cleaning. The dining room chimney had to be cleaned and the entire menage was moved into the drawing room so that preparations could be made. Dust sheets were put over everything and a heavy sheet hung over the fireplace to contain the soot which would come down. On the day we were up bright and early to watch the operation and

Hughie duly arrived with his brush and heavy ball and had a companionable cup of tea with Maimie in the kitchen.

'Ah well,' he said at last, 'we better get this chimney swept'.

'Do be careful, Hughie' said my mother.

'Don't worry aboot me, missus,' he replied, 'I could dae this wi' my eyes shut.'

So off he went, climbing the long ladder, over the slates, up the ridging and finally on to the chimney head. Then he stood on the coping and took the brush and ball from the bag which he carried on his back. As we held our breath he selected the chimney and with great precision, not to say some triumph, dropped the brush down the chimney. Inside the house breakfast was being prepared by Maimie on the kitchen range. She did not like the chimney cleaning as the house got cold and there was soot everywhere. She was muttering to herself, but the muttering soon ceased when she was suddenly enveloped in a cloud of soot! Meantime, Hughie was cheerfully pulling up the brush. The first we knew of disaster was when Maimie appeared out of the back door, black as an African – a very small African in a huge rage. 'You fool' she shouted at Hughie, 'you've put the brush down the wrong chimney!'

The brave Hughie knew when discretion was the better part of valour. He made sure that he cleaned the dining room chimney and departed silently. We made ourselves scarce too, as we knew that it would be a long day and that it would be some considerable time before we saw our friend Hughie again.

In remembrance, Saturdays were very special days. Not only were we spared school but there was always the hope of some excitement. This was especially true when our big brothers were at home from university, or, in Willie's case, when he was home from the sea. We looked upon these big men with the greatest admiration and awe, for they brought back stories from their travels which told of another world full of strange and exciting happenings. Our whole lives were brightened by their presence and I can still feel the joyous antici-pation of their homecoming, not to mention the real sadness of their way-going.

On Saturday we had our dancing class in the church hall which was situated in the back garden. This class was run by a family famous for their piping and dancing, the McCallums, presided over by the father who gloried in the nickname of 'beca'. This sobriquet arose from his habit of teaching the fingering on the chanter with much use of mouth music – 'beca, beca, beca'. He had been married twice and his sons from his first marriage had all become good pipers, the eldest, Ronald, eventually becoming piper to the Duke of Argyll. The two McCallum girls were the children of the second marriage and they became outstanding Highland dancers, well known at all the Highland Games. Rona and I were among the first to attend the classes and we were well taught, having modest success at the local Games. Sometimes with the big brothers at home and other distractions, it was something of a test of will to go to the dancing class. However, even from an early age, the thought of seeing the delectable Mary McCallum was an encouragement and there was always a promise of a game of football with the big boys when the dancing was finished.

Vans arriving on Saturday made for further excitement, with Hughie Smith's general store van and its wonderful smell of new bread, and later the baker's van with its tempting array of cakes. It was the only day of the week on which our mother bought cakes of any kind, but there is no denying that Hoynes's meringues were worth waiting for.

No matter what was being done on a Saturday however, some-one was constantly keeping an eye on the sea, for it was on Saturday that the great liners arrived at and left from the Tail of the Bank on the Clyde. The ships of the Anchor Line, the Anchor Donaldson, and often the really big ones from the Union Castle line, plied their timetabled voyages to and from North America. These timetables were published in the shipping news of the *Glasgow Herald* and we would calculate which ships we would see on the Saturday. We were especially knowledgeable about the Anchor Line ships: the *Transilvania* and the *Caledonia*, with their three funnels. How wonderful they were, thumping through the Sound of Sanda, so close that we felt we could almost touch them. If we were lucky and we were on the beach when they appeared, we would race to the top of Dunaverty Rock and get a grandstand view. Sometimes, on a still day, we could hear a band playing on board and we wondered at the luxury of it all. Even as a child I felt a lump in my throat as I thought of the joy of reunion which would be awaiting the ship's return, but as we watched those outward bound liners becoming ever smaller as they made their way to the Mull of Kintyre and the wide Atlantic, the sadness of farewell brought a coolness to the Saturday afternoon.

I did not know it then, of course, but these emotional feelings were to follow me all the days of my life and were to be a factor in a period in which I was to be a trial not only to myself but to everyone around me. If there had been child psychologists to hand when I was about ten years old, I would have been a godsend to them. I have often tried since that time to find reasons for my extraordinary behaviour. Life went on as usual of course, and I've no doubt for most of the period of about four years I was perfectly normal, but every now and then I became impossible, having almost hysterical outbursts of temper. Often these were brought on by defeat in some game. If ever there was a bad loser it was me, for although I loved playing the games I hated losing, and on occasion could not hide my feelings. The shame which I suffered when eventually normality was restored was hard to bear. Fortunately the older members of the family saw no reason why I should be allowed to win anything. I was not 'coddled' out of my weakness.

In the midst of it all, however, I passed the Qualifying exam which allowed me to enter what was known as the 'professional' class at Campbeltown Grammar School. At that time, 1933, alas, those attending the school in Campbeltown had to lodge in the town during the week and, although I had the kindest landlady in Mrs Rankin, the departure from home and the strangeness of the new school were all too much to bear. Hardly a Monday morning passed without scenes. I was cajoled, threatened, even bribed, but nothing made any difference. I would be thoroughly miserable until Friday. Needless to say, everyone who cared for me suffered, and although I knew that it did not help, nor did it give me any motivation to mend my ways.

The first year at the Grammar School eventually came to an end but I had not done well. This was before the time when teachers felt it necessary to consider the nasty remarks which they directed at the pupils in their classes. We had one who had been all her teaching life in Campbeltown and was known to generations of pupils as 'Wee Lizzie'. She thought nothing of libelling those under her. On the first day in her class I can recall a poor waif of a girl giving her name as Helen Victoria Margaret. 'Less would have done you,' snapped Lizzie. Later in the term a boy had handed in an exercise which had not come up to scratch. 'You're a fool,' announced the teacher. 'Of course you can hardly be blamed, you're father was a fool before you.' I wonder what 'damages' that would have been worth today!

While Lizzie had looked upon me with some kindness when I arrived at school, having had some success in teaching my older brothers and Rona, by the end of the Session she was not slow in telling me that I was a disgrace both to my parents and to the rest of the family. Perhaps she was right.

The second year began like the first, but salvation arrived in the guise of illness. The doctor diagnosed 'kidney trouble' and I was confined to bed. My parents were greatly concerned as my brother Willie some years before had almost died of the same disease, so my mother excused all my foibles on the dreaded kidneys. 'We should have known,' she said, 'that something was working on him'. No one was kinder than my mother! There followed weeks and months of rest and recuper-ation during which I cannot recall feeling very ill, but my mother and Maimie attended on me hand and foot. I was fed chickens by the dozen and the only real drawback was in having to drink gallons of barley water. Old Dr Niven came to see me, took my temperature and looked wise, but my parents had a backup in the young Dr McKenzie who tested my blood and my urine and prescribed my medication.

I was a model patient, read everything that was given me and fortunately began to think about what life was all about and what my role in life might be. By the early summer of 1935 it was evident that I was making a recovery, but would not return to school until after the summer holidays. Having missed most of the year it was obvious that I would have to repeat the second year.

My return to the Grammar school coincided with the institution of the school bus service, which freed me from coping with the problem of homesickness. This, with the more responsible attitude and more adult outlook on life which I had developed during my illness, meant that it was quite a new person who resumed his education. All was not lost. Other factors helped. The school had had an intake of younger teachers during the time I had been off, and Messrs Kaye, Crerar and Sturrock were encouragers. Jimmy Kaye developed in me a love of the English language and encouraged my interest in history. Mr Sturrock nurtured the almost physical pleasure in the working out of a mathematical problem, and while Mr Crerar could not make me into a linguistic scholar, he encour-aged me sufficiently to reach a modest standard in French. In the gym the newly appointed Jimmy Burgoyne made our physical devel-opment a meaningful and enjoyable exercise. I was sorry that Wee Lizzie had departed in my absence as I would have liked to have shown her that I had changed, but I did have one triumph in relationships with a teacher. The art teacher was a Miss Smith, known to all and sundry as 'Wee Dolly' who I had found short in temper and lacking in grace. She annoyed me too, for she found me unteachable in the arts and rightly, no doubt, gave me a derisory mark which always reduced an already modest average mark on my report card.

The medicos had decreed that I should have a solid mid-day meal to build me up, and, as there were no school meals, my father arranged for me to have a lunch in the Argyll hotel, which he and other members of the Presbytery often frequented. I was not too pleased at the prospect of entering the hotel dining room and was less than pleased when I found that the only other person having lunch there was Wee Dolly, so I sat at the table furthest from her place. There was, however, a most pleasant waitress on duty who fussed over us both. In the second week she announced that she was not going to wear her legs to the knees walking between our tables, that we would sit at the same table. There was nothing for it, but then I discovered what has been impressed upon me so often since, that if you talk to people, you understand them so much better; that it is lack of communication that destroys relationships. Miss Smith and I got on well. She told me about her garden and her pets, and on reflection I realised she was a lonely soul looking for someone to listen to her but unable easily to make friends. Soon I was to be given another lesson for life. It's not what you know but who you know that can count. Strange to relate, while my artistic impression did not improve one iota in the classroom, the marks I received were at a much higher level. My waitress friend was most impressed at the change that had overtaken Dolly. 'She's quite human noo!' she told me one day.

Her remark encouraged me to believe that there might be a place for me in the field of human relationships and that I found it easy, and at the same time very pleasurable, listening to and speaking with people. It was an unformed and hazy idea in my mind but in an experimental way I followed it up. I did find in one or two cases that I was able to make some people feel a little bit special, something which did wonders for their personalities. It didn't work every time of course, and often I was left wondering why I should try to be nice to anyone. However, I was able to put discouragement behind me because life was so good for myself. I was now much more aware of what my religious beliefs meant to me in my general attitude to life and work. From the age when I could think, I had believed in God. I was not very old when I was able to believe that I loved God in a highly emotional way. Now there was a growing awareness of the person of Jesus Christ and his sacrifice, but there was also the need to think more about His teaching. It was one thing to love God but what about loving one's neighbour?

Doubtless it was all part of growing up, but I developed a terrible responsibility for my neighbour. It could be difficult as I contemplated all the things which I might do for my neighbour. There was a great danger that I would become such a little 'goodie two shoes' as to be unbearable. Fortunately I believe an inherent selfishness probably saved me from an excess of zeal but there is no doubt that a sense of duty to God and man energised much of my life.

CHAPTER FOUR

My Place in the Family

With three big brothers and a sister, I was not allowed to get too far away from reality. They were all pursuing their careers by this time. Angus, who had been most kind to me during my traumatic first year in Campbeltown when he had been editing the local paper, had been given a year out to see whether he could make it as a writer. This meant that he was at home most of the time, bashing away on his little typewriter, making some pocket money with small articles to newspapers and magazines while he pounded out his first book, *The Purple Rock*. I can still recall the shared pleasure when news came of an acceptance from a publisher, and the awful hopelessness when the addressed envelope with the manuscript inside intimated a rejection.

Angus had by this time graduated as an MA of Glasgow University and had tried to satisfy his father's ambition by studying for the ministry, but he had a stammer which, in private conversation was barely noticeable, but which in public speaking became more and more acute. Having attempted a church service in Glasgow which should have lasted three quarters of an hour but which, in fact, lasted some hour and a half, even his father began to believe that perhaps Angus was not cut out for the ministry. Because of extramural activities, mostly to do with writing, Angus had found some of his degree exams difficult to pass. The results from Glasgow at that time were published in the *Glasgow Herald*, and as the day for these to appear approached, our mother made herself ill with anxiety. If Angus's name did not appear among those who had passed she would then attempt to keep the *Herald* from our father until he could be prepared for the worst. It made no difference. He who had never failed an exam in his life was not amused that he had produced sons of such stupidity. One degree subject which had caused Angus great tribulation was Political Economy, and on reflection his brothers and sister have always declared that, considering his political judgement (or lack of it), not to mention his lack of economic expertise, it was miraculous that he ever managed to pass!

In 1935 the crunch had come for Angus if he was to pursue his ambition to be a writer. His parents could not support him for long and he required a fairly quick success. We all willed it to happen and eventually the day came when he received word that the publisher, Stanley Paul, had accepted *The Purple Rock*. We all rejoiced, and when a contract was offered for the publication of three books a year we knew that he was on his way.

John and I benefited greatly from having Angus at home in that year. Being so much older, and engaged in the serious business of trying to make a living, he was not only a big brother but a kind of extra father to whom we might go with our problems without bothering the head of the house. Angus was always a man with an original and fertile brain, never short of ideas and with a great capacity for fun. He invented new games for us to play and fantasised with us in holding Olympic Games, Test Matches, and Open Golf Championships, all within the bounds of the aforementioned front garden.

He also had a sadistic streak. When John and I would be settling down in our beds there would suddenly come ghostly footfalls from the attic above our bedroom. We knew that it was Angus but nothing would have persuaded us to go up the attic stairs to prove the point. The sleep which had been so close to us was put entirely to flight. Maimie muttered darkly that it was a pity that some people did not grow up. The truth was that neither she nor anyone else in the Manse of Southend could be cross with Angus for very long because he, the eldest, always had a very special place with his parents and with the rest of us.

With the successful publication of his first book, however, we were about to lose him from the Manse. For years he had courted his beloved Jean from the farm of Brunerican – I cannot remember a time when he hadn't been courting Jean, as they had been sweethearts from schooldays. Now with the prospect of a few pounds in his pocket he would marry her. Long before their marriage of course, we all had a great affection for Jean and every now and then our mother and we younger children would be asked to Brunerican for tea. Not only did we love to visit the farm, we enjoyed the winsome 'crack' of Jean's father. He had lost an arm in an accident and we looked on in some awe at the method he used to light his pipe. He put the match box between his knees and holding it firmly there he could scratch the match along the emery paper. When the pipe was going to his satisfaction he would transfer the matchbox to his pocket and have the free arm to control the pipe. He was then ready to entertain us either with a story from the past or with a song. Every member of that McKerral family could sing, and Jean's brothers were the backbone of every concert held in Kintyre. Today they would have made their fortunes, but in the thirties farming was so depressed that two of them had to emigrate to Rhodesia and the sweet voices were lost to us. As young boys we did not enjoy being taken on visits to other houses, but Brunerican was an exception and Jean's sponges were beyond compare. Soon she was our sister-in-law. She and Angus were married in our father's church, St Blaan's, and Dr Kenneth McLeod assisted. I felt very important in my role as usher but remember little about the day except that the sun shone. One phrase from Dr McLeod's prayer remained with me: 'May the kindly eye of Jesus Christ follow them all the days of their lives'. I thought it was a lovely request and like to think that it was a prayer which to a great degree was answered.

Archie and Angus were very close to each other, but in my earliest recollections Archie does not assume the same import-ance in our lives as Angus, who always had a certain aura of authority about him. Archie was just a golden big brother who had a perpetual motion in him which drove us all into competitive games of every kind.

Suddenly Angus and Archie were no longer part of the household as they were at university. Our parents wrote to them every week, our mother on Sunday evening and our father on Wednesday and nothing was allowed to interfere with this routine. News came back from the big city and we were proud of their doings. Great excitement was generated when their photographs appeared in the Bulletin, showing them fearfully and wonderfully made up for the annual Charities Day parade. It was obvious too that they were holding their own in the athletic field. Both were fast over the shorter distances, but it was in the field events that Archie began to excel.

Archie was suddenly no longer the golden youth but a very complete man, working towards his honours degree in English, winning his 'blue' at soccer and representing the University in athletics, but for us he was very much the same Archie who would return on holiday ready for any fun and games on offer. Wherever he was there was noise and excitement and his obvious zest for life infected everyone in his company. In the long summer holidays Angus and Archie toured the various Highland Games to enjoy the competition and to make a little money. To do this, transport was necessary, and so cars were bought. The first car was an open tourer which cost seven pounds and ten shillings. She was Angus's pride and joy, and being ugly but dependable gloried in the name of Belle, a name which had nothing to do with her chassis but made for good alliteration – Belle the bullnosed Morris. She was followed by a ten pound car in the following year – this model was prettier but less dependable, and was named Kate for no good reason.

After Angus's marriage, Archie went into the car market and bought a saloon car of large proportions, purple in colour and 'square' in every dimension and sense. Such was the gravitas of this car that Archie immediately christened it John Knox. Many wonderful runs were made in these cars and my mother enjoyed various expeditions. The knowledge that the vehicles might blow up at any moment gave an added excitement! She loved speed and encouraged her sons to push the cars to their limit, and when one considers that the top speed of all the cars was in the region of fifty mph, her irresponsibility is put into perspective.

These were bright summer days. We bathed in reflected glory when our brothers won some of the events for which they were entered and they came back from the Largieside, from Inverary, from Dunoon and from Oban with great tales of success or failure. Their success, however, proved their undoing. The Scottish Amateur Athletic Association, under whose aegis they competed at university level, ordered them to stop competing in the Highland Games, indicating that their acceptance of prize money jeopardised their amateur status. When I think of the good fun and good fellowship which was enjoyed at the Highland Games and the paltry few pounds won at them, and set it all against the thousands of pounds given to so-called amateurs for appearing at events today which seldom pass without some scandal or disagreement, I cannot help wondering if the SAA could have employed their powers better. They were not to blame, however, for an accident which interrupted Archie's successful athletic career. Shutting a window at Jordanhill College with his natural gusto, his arm broke the glass and his wrist was badly injured. Although making a speedy recovery, his right hand was never as strong again. Life, too, was becoming a bit more earnest. He had decided on a teaching career and had met and fallen in love with a bright star, Mima, with whom we all fell in love, but the storm clouds of war were gathering.

My recollections of the three or four years prior to the war are very clear. As crisis followed crisis I became more and more of a British patriot. As each crisis built up there was the dread fear of war, but as each crisis passed there was the disappointment that war, with all its attendant excitements, had not come. I read the quality papers from cover to cover, spending every lunch time in the public library in Campbeltown perusing *The Times* and the *Scotsman*. The *Glasgow Herald* I could read at home. I discussed with my classmates the possibilities, but many of them were socialists and pacifists and so I got little encouragement for my conservative and patriotic viewpoint.

Archie had been to the Olympic Games in Berlin. He returned greatly impressed by the organisation of Germany but deeply perturbed at the overbearing totalitarianism which he noted in the country. All that was forgotten, however, as he started to train his young brothers to run in the way of Jesse Owens, but in this he had a very limited success. While all this was going on, brother William was riding the seven seas - at least he was plying to and fro from Glasgow to Bombay with the ships of the Anchor Line. Getting to this stage for him had not been plain sailing at all.

It was rumoured that in spite of the obvious cleverness of Angus and Archie, the teachers at the Grammar School had concluded that William was even brighter. He, however, seemed to lack application because his whole concern was to achieve his ambition of going to sea. His school reports dis-appointed both his teachers and his parents, and there were ructions at school, and at home. Matters came to a head one Wednesday, the day on which the Guild met in the Manse. At three o'clock in the afternoon the ladies of more mature age would gather to discuss the church affairs, knit or sew for the church sale and generally have an afternoon of pleasant chat and friendship. At seven in the evening the daughters and others had their meeting. Such meetings could not take place without tea, so our mother and Maimie made the sandwiches and the ladies all brought an offering of cakes. John and I looked forward to Wednesday for, though we had to be especially quiet around the house while the meetings were in progress, we had the pick of the leftovers when the ladies departed.

On the day in question the afternoon meeting was under way when suddenly the back door opened and Willie entered. As the boys lodged during the week in Campbeltown, his coming home in the middle of the week denoted a crisis.

'What's wrong, child?' asked Maimie.

'I'm not going back to school,' growled Willie.

Maimie made various remarks in Gaelic but eventually extracted the information that one of the teachers, Mr Gault, had been so incensed with Willie's inattention that he had belted him severely – Willie had great weals on his wrist as proof of this. Maimie was incensed.

'Just let me get my hands on him,' she said, 'I'll give him a piece of my mind.' With this mixed metaphor, however, she realised there were more pressing problems with which she had to deal immediately.

'What will Mamma and Dadda say?' said Willie, realising at last the implication of what he had done.

'Never mind that just now,' said Maimie, 'the first thing is to get you out of sight before these women come through for their tea.'

Willie was despatched to his bedroom with dire instructions that he was to stay there until the house was cleared of the visitors, and Maimie had time to prepare the parents. Threatened by the wrath of God were we to misbehave, John and I were sent out to the garden where, in the toolshed, we discussed the impending excitements. Doubtless we decided to keep a low profile so that we would not get in the way of any of the 'flak' that might be flying. We knew that our mother would eventually bring about a solution to the crisis but that there could be fireworks from our father before this was achieved.

We were not wrong. There were explanations and some tears, and both parents were offended by the severity of the beating. Our father however could not help raising his voice in anger: 'If God has given you brains, why can't you use them?'

However, by tea time the storm had blown itself out, Willie had agreed to return to school next day, his father would write to the rector, and, most importantly, he would also write to the Anchor Line to see if Willie could be taken on as a cadet when he reached the required age.

It wasn't long after this episode that Willie set off with his father to the big city. They returned in some triumph, for Willie had passed the physical tests and had been accepted as a Deck Officer

Cadet. In due time he was called to join his first ship and once again he and father set off for Glasgow, but only father returned. We all felt that Willie had taken a very big step into the unknown but we also knew that while we would all be special to our mother, Willie would have a very special place in her heart. He wrote from every port and we followed the meanderings of the MV *Tarantia* in the shipping news in the *Glasgow Herald*. Soon he was on his way home and we hoped that he would get sufficient leave to warrant a trip to see us. The anticipation of his homecoming was intense and his arrival a great joy.

He had achieved his ambition and had no regrets.

In the years before the war, with Angus married, Archie finishing university and getting a teaching post in Dunoon Grammar School, Willie being at sea and Rona in Edinburgh, John and I pursued our different studies with varying degrees of success.

Archie had achieved an Honours degree at Glasgow and soon Rona was to become one of the youngest graduates in Edinburgh. We were proud of them, but I knew that I could not emulate them. John, however, was showing great promise and the new teachers at Southend, Margaret Paterson and John Cameron, encouraged pupils towards their full potential. The school was an attractive place and John delighted in any praise which came his way.

I was now more relaxed at school and able to apply myself, but I had to admit that only hard graft would achieve anything as I was not a natural scholar. My father felt that I was unlikely to make the university grade but was willing to give me every encouragement. Archie McCallum, the blacksmith's son who had been to university and was awaiting a teaching job, was recruited as a tutor in French. His was a thankless task, but he was a very likeable young man and, in the end, I struggled through to a pass in French - in the lower grade. My French teacher, a decent man who was known to all as 'Big Graham' accosted me in the streets of Campbeltown some time after the declaration of the results. 'Well Kenneth,' he said, 'you have renewed my faith - miracles do happen.'

CHAPTER FIVE

Rumours of War

These were the final years of peace, but looking back, it seems as if the sun shone mockingly upon us. The summer holidays, with Archie and Rona at home, were times of great joy. Afternoons were spent on the beach at Dunaverty Bay and while in the past we used to undress among the sand dunes, we now had Achnamara, the home of Angus and Jean. To everybody's joy, Jean had produced a son – another Angus John – the fourth Angus in the line. As a new uncle I made much of him and often rocked him to sleep when all others had failed.

But the sands were running out. After a lovely summer holiday we returned to school in the middle of August, knowing that the crisis was near. As senior pupils we were recruited to unload emergency rations into a warehouse in the town. Everyone was getting edgy and I lived in an unreal world filled with fear and excitement in equal measure. Our mother looked more anxious every day, while our father got rid of his tensions by railing against all politicians.

By the time I got home from school on Friday 2nd September, news had come that Hitler had invaded Poland. There was little hope left. On the Saturday evening someone suggested that instead of moping around, we should go for a drive. It was a beautiful evening and everything in our little world was calm. As we made our way up the hill towards Glenbreckrie the sun was going down over the Mull of Kintyre hills, and as we came into sight of the sea again the purple light which is unique to the western seaboard had clothed the hills. It was breathtakingly beautiful. No one spoke until suddenly our mother said 'I don't think I've ever seen Southend look so beautiful,' and, after a little, in a wistful prophetic voice she went on, 'things will never be the same again.'

The next day we all sat around the wireless at eleven o'clock and listened to the Prime Minister telling us that we were at war. With fear gnawing at my heart and yet an awesome excitement within me, we then went to church to ask for the protection and guidance of Almighty God.

To use the trite phrase, life does go on, and we were back to school the next day. If studying had been hard before it was now doubly so. The Navy commandeered the Grammar School as Campbeltown became a naval base. Classes were held in the old school in Dalintober at the other side of town, and in an adapted drill hall just below the Grammar School. It cannot be said that we were concentrating on our studies as what mattered was the conduct of the hostilities. We all became chairborne generals, studying the maps of the continent provided by the newspapers, along with pin flags. What did studying matter when soon we would be part of the great design!

We were helped to come to terms with our lot by the fact that, while the days were punctuated by sharp crises such as the sinkings of ships like the *Athenia* and the *Hood*, there were no great battles being fought. For long periods it was all very disappointing, this lack of action. Would it all end before we were free to take part? How foolish we were was soon apparent in the following Spring when the Blitzkriegs started. One could hardly credit the ease with which the enemy cut through the Allies' lines.

While all this was going on we had to sit our Highers, but, as misfortune would have it, I was sick on the first day of exams. In former days I think I would have looked upon this sickness as a heaven sent excuse for ducking the exam, but now one had to show a stiff upper lip and I set off feeling very frail but brave! It turned out to be nothing but a passing upset and by the time I returned home I was more than ready for a plate of my mother's broth. At the end of the week I felt that I had done as well as I could. This did not fill me with confidence but it gave me a certain satisfaction.

With the Highers behind me and now eighteen years of age, I could seriously consider what I might do for King and Country. I scanned the posters and the adverts in the news-papers looking for volunteers for this and that but nothing appealed to my romantic soul. Dunkirk shook our confidence. Could the day come when Britain might be invaded? Up until that time the possibility had never entered my head. When the local Defence Volunteers were established I joined immediately and felt very important when drilling with the local company even though, to begin with, our weapons were broom handles, pitchforks, or any other implements that might come to hand. Maimie could not join the L.D.V. but she too was ready for any German that might be bold enough to invade Southend. Behind the front door she put Archie's training javelin and the axe. (Why did we assume that the Germans would come to the front door?)

We had our excitements too. Our father who was, of course, chaplain to the local force, had been called to an emergency meeting of the officers. He returned to announce that there was a general 'call-out', for a report had been received that a party of Germans had landed on the East coast and invasion was imminent. By this time it was beginning to get dark. Angus, who was still at home recuperating from a life-threatening illness, and I, were assigned the patrol along the shore road from Southend village to the graveyard at Keil. It was a perfectly still night and we talked in whispers lest we should miss any unusual sound. There was a low moon which gave some light, and out in the North Channel we could hear the thump of engines. Ships which we could not see were passing into the dread Atlantic or, filled with hope and relief, making for the safety of the boom in the upper Clyde.

Now and then we heard the drone of an aircraft engine. Friend or foe? We peered into the sky to see if parachutes were descending. To begin with we were strung up with the excitement of it all, but as time passed and weariness began to overtake us we spoke little. The moon rose higher in the sky and gave more light and we were walking towards Angus's house (with me hoping that he might suggest going in to make a cup of tea), when suddenly his hand grasped my shoulder.

'There's movement in the field behind Achnamara,' he whispered. We dropped down behind the wall which ran along the roadside and gingerly peered over the parapet. Sure enough there were figures moving towards the wall that surrounded the Achnamara garden. They seemed to go into conference at the corner of the dyke. We slipped behind our wall. By this time I was suitably terrified but Angus was in no doubt that our duty lay in tackling the situation ourselves. I was to crawl round the wall from the other side while he would crawl across the field towards the shadowy figures. When I was in position to jump the 'enemy' I was to give a great shout which would immediately distract their attention, upon which Angus would attack them from the other side. The plan worked like a charm. Angus and I nearly killed ourselves diving upon the unsuspecting foe. I think we got more of a fright than the three 'tups' which bounded out of their resting place!

We felt then that we deserved a cup of tea and, while drinking it, decided that the Mull of Kintyre would not be invaded that night after all. The early dawn was coming as I set off home and familiar things began to take shape in the morning light, reassuring me that all was not yet lost. I was, however, considerably shaken by the events of the night and had to confess to myself that my fear threshold was on the low side. Did I have what it took to face danger? If these figures had been trained soldiers instead of sheep, Angus and I would have come to a silent if painful end. As I wearily climbed into bed it seemed that suddenly all the romance had gone out of the war. After a good sleep, however, I awoke with a more positive attitude and scanned the posters and the adverts again. One took my eye. The Fleet Air Arm was looking for volunteers as pilots.

My parents, who wished me to go to university, were not impressed. My mother said little and my father shouted at my folly, but in the end they told me that I could apply. My father, though, extracted the promise that if I was not accepted I would go to university for a year. Being quite sure that the Navy could not wait to have me, I readily made this promise.

I was called to Glasgow for an interview and medical examination. Now it happens that my little toe on my left foot grows over its neighbour, which has never caused me the slightest inconvenience, but the doctor examining me seemed to think that it would interfere greatly with my flying. I was turned down. At the time I was shattered. How often, however, do the things which seem such misfortunes turn out to be the opposite. I returned to Southend with my tail between my legs, where my father was sympathetic but reminded me of my promise. By this time the Higher results had come out and I had achieved the necessary passes, so with no enthusiasm I made application to the University of Edinburgh. I was too late to be accepted for Medicine but there was a place in Pure Science. That would have to do.

The summer of 1940 moved on. Shattered by the defeat of France and by the events of Dunkirk, we waited for Hitler's next move. What happened, of course, developed into the Battle of Britain, and as we watched with mounting excitement the gallantry of the Few – and their ultimate victory – I knew that it was with the RAF that I would want to be. But would they turn me down too? Achilles might have his heel. I had my wee toe!

August and September that year found me in gainful employment. For the first time in my life I was paid for working. I went to work during harvest at Kilblaan, the farm across the river from the

Manse at Southend, where as a child I had had so many happy visits with my father and others. Kilblaan, the first place in Southend with a wireless which one could listen to without earphones. Kilblaan, where we went on the occasion of the Scotland versus England international football match listening in the kitchen, while old Hugh snored in his chair. When the match was over we would rise either in despair or ecstasy according to the result and Hugh would waken and ask 'Who won?'

I was to work at Kilblaan for the great sum of £1 per six and a half day week. My mother bought me a stout pair of boots, and on the first of August I set out for an eight o'clock start. The farm was really worked by Archie, old Hugh's nephew, a sister's child born out of wedlock. After his mother's marriage he had remained on the family farm. There was no great affection between uncle and nephew. Hugh had not married, nor had his sister Flora who kept house for him. They had a servant, Marion, a buxom young woman whose generosity with her favours had landed her with two daughters, one a little older and the other a few years younger than myself. The outdoor farm servant was John, an ex-soldier who, on his return to civilian life had been bewitched by Mary, a harum scarum sonsy girl. They married when it seemed prudent to do so and, annually, for some twelve years produced yet another child. My father beat a path to their cottage door for the yearly christening.

It was a strange mixture of people, uncle and nephew bearing with each other but without any closeness, John wishing he was younger and back in the army, Marion without bitterness but knowing that she had 'burnt her boats' and had lost the chance of a stabilising marriage. Into this strange mix I came with the unconcern of youth, and by a great good fortune they all took to me and were glad of my company.

Hugh looked upon me and upon my lack of farming skills, with some amusement. He had a dry laugh – Hi, Hi, Hi – and I was pleased that some of my antics made him laugh. Archie looked upon me as an 'intellectual' like himself, the only person in the team worth talking to. Marion treated me as an extra child to be chastised or encouraged according to circumstances. John enjoyed my company because I could be instructed by him on the ways of the world. Some of his stories amazed me, some appalled me, none bored me.

Years later my mother told me that all four had separately confided in her that the two months that I had been with them had been among the happiest times of their lives. As Marion had said, 'There was more laughter at Kilblaan when Kenneth was there than there was before or since.' I have often wondered how that should have been. In so many ways each of those with whom I had worked were prisoners; Hugh because he had wanted to do something else; Archie because his illegitimacy had tied him in with his uncle and aunt; Marion because of her own folly, and John because of his family responsibilities. I came among them, free as the air, with the whole of life before me. I think the four of them each found some freedom through association just as each of them taught me a good deal concerning life and the crosses which so many people bear. Although it was of short duration, my time at Kilblaan was important to me too. It was part of the learning process and it was the beginning of understanding. I began to understand that, not only did I want to be liked by people, I wanted to be important to them as well.

So the summer days passed and we hoped that by working hard to secure the harvest we were helping the war effort. This effort was concentrated in the south and east of Britain where, daily, the pilots in their Hurricanes and Spitfires were taking on the might of the Luftwaffe. After so many reverses everyone was cheered by the efforts of the RAF, as for once the enemy had met his match. Some days were better than others. We did not know how close the contest was, and it was a strange optimism we had. I for one never doubted that the Battle of Britain would be won by us. We had faith in the pilots, their courage and their skill, although at the time I do not think many people could have had any idea of the cost in young life.

While they fought it out with the enemy we gathered in the harvest at Kilblaan. The weather was ideal and in the beginning I learned to cut the 'roads' for the binder. John and I scythed down the standing oats round the border of the field and later in the day gathered up the swathes and made them into sheaves, putting them against the fences to dry. Now we awaited the decision from on high, the decision to begin cutting with the binder. The day duly came and with great excitement the binder which Hugh had been getting ready for days was wheeled out of the shed and its canvas rollers put into place. John and I got great amusement listening to Hugh talking to himself whilst all this preparation went on. When all was ready the machine was taken to the field by a single horse, where several more adjustments were made, Hugh arguing fiercely the while with Archie and himself. The second horse was then brought out and yoked in with its neighbour and, at last, with a smacking of his lips Archie would jump on to the metal seat. A final look around and a slap on the horses' hocks with the reins and we were in business.

John and I followed the binder as it flung out the sheaves with a turn of its 'grape'. We collected two at a time and stood them up in stooks, two against two. As the binder went up and down or sometimes right round the standing corn I was amazed that such a rickety looking thing could be so efficient. As the day wore on and my back got more and more tired from bending to pick up the sheaves, I have to admit that I longed for a breakdown. These came at regular intervals, and were of course the cause of great annoyance. Everybody knew that a spare bit should have been purchased from the Smiddy long before the harvest had begun. Everybody knew also that it was somebody else who had failed to take the precaution. Everybody knew also that a new bit had to be got now and that there was likely to be half a dozen other farmers at the Smiddy on a similar mission. Johnny and I would finish the stooking and await developments. Hugh would set out for the Smiddy carrying the broken piece in his hand, and conversation with his hidden self could be heard until he disappeared out of sight.

These occasions however brought no great respite, as Archie had other things for us to do. Off we would go either to cut bracken for the base of the stacks or rushes to be used later in the thatching of them. Loud 'halloos' from Marion, who could make herself heard over six fields, would bring us back to the farm for our tea. While it was always welcome, the tea in the house or in the barn was never the same as the tea which was brought out to the field. There, with one's back to a stook and the sun on your face, the warm scones with the butter melting within them and sweet tea by the gallon, one experienced a physical pleasure which was almost frightening in its intensity.

When Hugh came back from the Smiddy with the repaired part, there was gossip about who else was there. The similar or even greater misfortunes of others was a source of shared amusement to us all, but soon we were stooking again and wondering if the day would ever end.

Each day, of course, had an ending. In the early days I would drag one foot after another as I returned home up the hill from the river bank, with my boots feeling as if they were made of lead. I soon toughened up however, and the time came when I could whistle as well as any farm hand as I made my way home, taking some pride in looking at the fields which we had worked, seeing the waving corn turn into the regimented rows of stooks marching across the fields.

Far away over the south of England, the Battle raged day by day. We could only look on and wonder. Our mother talked quietly of the 'dear brave boys' and thought of their mothers. In the meantime I was learning. On the way over to the farm in the morning I would inspect the stooks near the river and when the discussion was taking place between Hugh and Archie as to whether the oats were ready for stacking, my opinion would be sought. I felt very important. The weather was glorious and soon it was September. The Battle was being won in the air. We began to secure the harvest.

We worked as a team. In the morning, once the morning dew had dried on the stooks, John and I would throw down the sheaves so that the damp base was exposed to the sun. The carts were readied and Archie and John took charge of one each. Marion and I forked the sheaves up to them and when loading was complete the two ropes were flung over the sheaves from the back and secured to the trams. Off went cart after cart to the stackyard where Hugh built the stacks. It was as well that we were well off the main road, for while many of the neighbouring farmers took great pride in building stacks of symmetry and beauty, Hugh gave no place to artistry. When those who were forking to him gave a cry of warning as the wall of the stack took an incline inwards, 'You're going in Hugh!', he would reply without looking up, 'I'm putting the head on!' The result was that we had far more stacks than anyone else but of half the size. The days wore on, the fields emptied of their store and the stackyard became full. The Germans had had enough and the Few had put us all eternally in their debt. The harvest was almost complete.

In the last week of September the last cartload was led to the stackyard. Hugh finished off an even smaller stack and jumped down.

'Well,' he said, 'that's it'. Looking at us fiercely he gave more of a command than an invitation. 'Ye'll stay fur yer tea'. With that he went off into the house while the rest of us attended to the horses. Everyone was in good form because we had done what we had set out to do. We washed our hands at the outside spicket and, led by

40

Archie, who was by this time smacking his lips like limp castanets, we filed into the kitchen which had been scoured for the occasion. The deal table, scrubbed white, was laden with baskets of scones, potato scones and oatcakes, and a whole cheese stood on a large plate. We had soup which was solid enough to stand on, followed by stew of a similar consistency. Potatoes were available by the half hundredweight. The 'crack' was good and, very favourably, we compared our own efforts with those of our neighbours who had not yet finished. Marion and the girls screamed with laughter at some of my stories of schooldays past, while John made ribald references to his own past in and out of school. Hugh allowed himself a satisfied 'Hi, Hi, Hi' before departing the scene and returning from some nether regions bearing a bottle of whisky. He put a good tot into the glass of the adults present and looked at me quizzically before putting a thimbleful into my glass. 'Well,' he said, 'here's fortune,' and we drank the toast before laying into the scones and cheese with lashings of tea. Hugh allowed himself and the two men another dram. Soon it was time to go and Hugh gave me what was my due in an envelope, 'And a wee thing extra for yerself.'

They all accompanied me to the door and when I got to the top of the knoll I looked back and they were still there, waving me off. I found myself getting quite emotional. It was the end of a very small chapter but I discovered that I didn't like partings of any kind. I made my way down to the riverside, looking at the fields in which I had expended such energy, which were now bare but for the pale gold stubble. I crossed the bridge and ascended the hill, but before I went into the Manse I looked over to Kilblaan and thought again of how Hugh, Archie, Marion and John were tied to the place by circumstances which had overtaken them all. I had greatly enjoyed my time with them and we had created relationships which would affect us one way or another, perhaps for always. Unlike them however, I was not tied. I was free but where would that freedom lead me?

PART TWO

The War

David was in the stronghold and a Philistine garrison held Bethlehem. One day a longing came over David, and he exclaimed, 'If only I could have a drink of water from the well by the gate of Bethlehem!' At this the heroic three made their way through the Philistine lines and drew water from the well by the gate of Bethlehem and brought it to David. But David refused to drink it; he poured it out to the Lord and said, 'God forbid that I should do such a thing! Is not this the blood of these men who went in jeopardy of their lives?' So he would not drink it.

(*The book of Samuel*)

CHAPTER SIX

A Promise kept

My freedom was conditional as I now had to fulfil the promise given to my father, that I would spend a year at university. I had been accepted as a student in the Science faculty of Edinburgh, and to the capital city I set out at the beginning of October. In no way was I happy because I wanted to get into the armed forces and I hated leaving home. Once again Rona was my strength and stay. She had a final term to complete at the Moray House teacher training centre and her companionship and pragmatic view of life's circumstances made it possible for me on the day of departure from Southend to say the farewells without tears. We travelled by bus into Campbeltown, from there caught another bus which took us to Glasgow and from Glasgow took the train to Edinburgh. It was a journey which seemed endless. Having been in school in Edinburgh as well as at university there, Rona was a seasoned traveller and I followed her every move. We took a taxi from the station to our lodgings in a terrace house in the St Leonards district. Here we were met by our landlady, a Miss Isbister from the Northern Isles who, we discovered, had a heart of gold and a tongue which went like the proverbial babbling brook. She soon presented us with a splendid tea which was more than acceptable after a long day on the road. I didn't dare think of what was happening in the Manse at Southend as such thoughts were too near to tears.

Next day, getting dressed, I looked out of the window on to the Queen's Park. Looking down at me was the bare face of the Salisbury Crags and beyond that towered Arthur's Seat. It was a magnificent view from a city house, although at that moment I thought nothing of it. I felt utterly desolate and even had thoughts about abandoning the whole project, but at breakfast Rona soon sorted me out. She would take me to the office of the University where I would matriculate, after that I could have a look around the place on my own. She would go her own way, but she would be

45

back for tea to hear how I had got on – perhaps we would go to the pictures at night.

Thus instructed and encouraged I set out with her and, having matriculated, launched myself on a tour of discovery. Rona had told me to be sure to read all the notices on the notice board to see what clubs or associations I might like to join, so half-heartedly I went to the archway under which were the notice boards. Certainly there was every kind of invitation and although I didn't think that the Philosophical Society was for me, there was a sheet for names of those wishing to play football. I knew that I wasn't very good but I could play, so I put my name down. Having done something I felt that I could go back to Miss Isbister's house to report to Rona. I quickly scanned the rest of the notices and, in that moment, my whole future was changed. On a notice larger than the rest was the heading ROYAL AIR FORCE. What could this be? It was in fact the announcement that Edinburgh University was to have an Air Squadron of its own, and all interested were to meet with one Squadron Leader Penfold. The time and place were noted and I sped home to tell Rona and to get her opinion. She was her usual level-headed self. 'Half the University will want to join,' she said, 'and they will only want so many. However,' she went on, 'you get down there early and get yourself a front seat. If they are taking names get yours in as soon as possible.'

As on so many occasions Rona had judged the situation aright. I went early to the meeting to find quite a number already there, and by the time the Squadron Leader appeared, the hall was crammed. There was the Squadron Leader, neat in his RAF uniform, bearing on his chest below his flying brevet, the ribbon of the Distinguished Flying Cross, which he had won in the Battle of Britain. The way most of us looked at him he might have been God. When he started to speak, however, we discovered that he was an easy going young man not much older than ourselves. He explained that the Air Squadron gave the chance to those who wished to take up flying duties in the future, of doing their ground training while still pursuing their studies. Those who passed the course would go straight on to flying training on entering the Service.

The more he spoke, the more I knew that this was a chance not to be missed but then came the dread information that only fifty would be accepted. I looked round the hall where there must have been close on two hundred men, every one looking more capable and much more mature than myself. We were asked to fill in forms which would be the first step in the selection process, and then further tests, including medical, would follow. I didn't feel hopeful.

I started the University classes in Physics, Chemistry and Mathematics. The first two subjects I could cope with, finding them an extension of school work, but the third I found quite bewildering. Perhaps my mind was not completely on the Calculus.

The weeks passed, punctuated by tests and interviews and then, finally, came the personal interview with the Squadron Leader. He asked me about my home and my family; what made me want to join the Air Force; had I flown before? Little of what he said or my replies seemed to have much to do with the matter in hand. I did notice, however, that he never took his eyes off me and they seemed to be looking into my soul. Suddenly he stood up and came round the table. 'Well MacVicar', he said, 'if you are absolutely sure that you want to be part of the Royal Air Force, we will be glad to have you.' He smiled and shook me by the hand. 'Send in the next one' he said, and dismissed me. I walked out of the room feeling about ten feet tall, and ran home to tell the news to Rona.

Eventually the fifty 'chosen' were assembled in the gymnasium which was to be our headquarters. We were given a 'pep' talk by the Squadron Leader and introduced to our Adjutant, a Flying Officer, and our two instructors, two very smart looking sergeants. There followed measurement for uniform, discussion of the timetable, and the assurance that, if at any time it was felt by anyone that we weren't putting our backs into the Squadron training, we would find ourselves replaced by others waiting in the wings.

I seem to remember that we had two training evenings in the week, various afternoon sessions, and the odd project on Saturdays. It was hard going in every way. We were given basic drill, taught the Morse code, instructed in aircraft recognition, studied engines and taught the theory of flight, all in time stolen from our University studies. We were given a strict programme to enhance our physical fitness and the initial sessions left me exhausted, but into the spring session things were beginning to come together. I felt that I was keeping ahead of the work on the Squadron while becoming more and more doubtful about the Calculus and all its implications. By the time the Easter holidays came round I couldn't believe how fit I was feeling. Every morning before breakfast I ran round the Queen's Park, and with the evening physical training sessions we were now a group of very fit young men. In some of the team games, in fact, it was very obvious that we were fighting fit. No quarter was asked or given, but we were also becoming a close knit brotherhood with but one ambition – to become pilots as soon as possible. We were indeed in great form.

On the day before departing for our Easter holidays, the blow fell. Our father was never able to give us more money than enough to meet our immediate needs, but when providing us with our 'dole' he always assured us that if we were short at the end of term, he would always send enough to get us home. It was in this impecunious state I found myself and so I 'wired' my father to send me the fare home. I was therefore expecting a telegram with the remittance, and in about two hours I was delighted to open the door to a telegraph boy. I quickly opened the buff envelope, but there was no promise of money. Instead it contained the news that Willie was missing after the sinking of his ship the *Britannia*. Up to that time I think I always believed that in some way we were proof against the tragedies which happened to other people, but here in my hand was the evidence that, after all, we were not immune. Although I told my landlady the news, and she was more than ready to be sympathetic, I found that I didn't wish to speak to anyone. I took myself off and climbed to the top of Arthur's Seat and found myself a place to sit out of the wind. I looked down to the Forth and out to sea, wondering where Willie might be in the vastness beyond the horizon, refusing to think that he might be lost in the deep. I tried to imagine how our mother felt and what was going through her mind and that of our father. I wanted to wake up and find that it was all a dream but nothing helped and eventually, chilled, I started down the hill, willing God to do something about our tragedy. When I got home a second telegram awaited me. Hoping against hope that this was more and better news, I tore it open, only to find that it was the money order. I felt worse than ever thinking of how, in the midst of their anxiety and grief, my petty needs had intruded.

Next day I made the sad journey home to Kintyre, hoping that my presence might do something to strengthen our parents. Needless to say, it was their courage which strengthened me. My father's refusal to allow anything to upset the even tenor of his ways had reasserted itself and he was making optimistic noises. My mother knew that she had to keep up if the whole family was not to disintegrate in self-indulgent sorrow, so she put a brave, if tremulous, face on things. Maimie railed against the Germans and wished that she could get her hands on them.

The days passed. Rona as always was a tower of strength, being sensible, and avoiding swings of optimism or pessimism. The days passed and hopes faded. Life went on, of course, and Hugh still came every day to read the *Glasgow Herald* and to enquire. To begin with he would ask, 'Any news?', but as the days passed he didn't need to ask. One day he had parked himself on the bench at the window, behind the kitchen table where our mother was baking and getting vaguely irritated by Hugh spreading the *Herald* over her baking board. Suddenly to her consternation, Hugh pushed the table back and in high excitement shouted out, 'That'll be them!'

'What on earth are you talking about, Hugh,' said our mother.

'That'll be them!' he repeated, pointing out a small paragraph in the paper. By this time the commotion had brought others into the kitchen, Maimie muttering 'has the man gone mad?' Everyone strained to see what had taken Hugh's attention. He pointed it out with a hairy and stained finger: 'A lifeboat with survivors from a British merchant ship has been picked up on the coast of Brazil. The survivors have been taken to a local hospital.'

'That'll be them!' repeated Hugh. 'The trade winds would have taken them across the Atlantic from where they were sunk.'

Nobody spoke. Suddenly Hugh was embarrassed. Our mother said, 'Oh, Hugh, I doubt it is too good to be true.' 'You'll see!' said Hugh, and turning on his heel, left to tell the folk at Kilblaan. We had mixed feelings. The snippet of news certainly gave a new optimism but was it, in fact, merely raising false hopes? With the passing days it certainly seemed so.

My Easter holidays ended and the leave taking was even worse than usual. I travelled to Edinburgh with my heart in my boots and made my way up the street to my lodgings. In front of me was a telegraph boy on his bike and I wondered what dread news someone else was about to receive. He waited at the gate of Miss Isbister's house and when I came up he said to me 'Do you happen to know if someone by the name of MacVicar stays at this address?' 'That's me,' I said and he handed me the message. I opened it. 'Willie safe in Brazil' it said.

The boy looked at me and asked, 'Any reply?' 'No reply,' I said, 'but thanks.'

It was a great beginning to the summer term and, in spite of the Calculus, everything in my life went fairly well. Crunch time was coming however, in all fields. I was fairly sure that I had satisfied all my instructors at the Air Squadron and it was not long until this was confirmed, and with the other successful candidates I was sent for the final medical examination which would allow us to fly. Having failed before because of my wee toe I went to the medical with some trepidation. Standing in a line, stark naked, we awaited the MO, and I screwed my little toe below its neighbour and stood on it. We endured the critical inspection when he came to me and surveyed me dispassionately from head to feet. Suddenly, the little toe escaped and jumped into its normal position. 'Good God!' exclaimed the MO, somewhat unnecessarily I felt, as I was thinking that perhaps God had deserted me. However, after asking me if I had any other tricks to display, he moved on. I passed the medical and knew that I was now clear to enter the RAF. In my University exams the Calculus defeated me and I had a hard earned draw with the Chemistry and Physics.

I returned to Southend to await the call. What a difference in atmosphere from my last visit. Willie had eventually returned from America and was none the worse for his twenty-three day ordeal in the lifeboat. He and Nina had fixed their wedding day for September. The anxieties of our parents, however, were increasing, as Angus and Archie were both in the army, Willie was about to go back to sea and I was on the verge of going into the Air Force. It must have been hard to bear.

My time came in August and I was asked to report to a building in St John's Wood in London. We were to report on a Sunday evening, ready for parade on Monday morning. There was no way that I could get from Kintyre to London in one day and so I had to leave on Saturday morning and spend half a day in Glasgow, before taking the night train to London. It was some experience for one who had been sheltered all his life. Arriving in London, I made my way to the appointed place and, naturally, early on a Sunday morning, found nothing but empty buildings. Eventually I unearthed a somewhat disinterested clerk who told me that I was not expected until five o'clock and that I'd better go away until then. I was not pleased, but managed to persuade him to allow me to find a bed on which I could lay my weary head. Having had no sleep for twenty-four hours, I slept like a child and when I awoke was able to view the situation with some amusement. There were, by then, a few more permanent staff about and I chatted them up sufficiently so that, when the intake started arriving in numbers, I was already processed, had my allotted bedspace and was generally able to give the impression that I was an experienced campaigner. We discovered that the place where we would be fed was the restaurant of London Zoo. As the days passed we were to believe that it was not an inappropriate location!

On the Monday morning we were paraded. We had dis-covered that the intake of which we were part consisted of the University Air Squadrons from Edinburgh, Oxford and Cambridge. The corporal in charge looked at us with a jaundiced eye. 'The cream of British youth,' he said with heavy sarcasm, 'gone sour' he added as he made us understand that any privileges we might have enjoyed in our sheltered existences would now be withdrawn. We were kitted out with the usual predictable remarks. Tunics which were far too big were foisted upon us. 'Fits you like a glove – it covers your hands.' We were given our inoculations and injections. I was amazed to see some of the 'tough' characters flaking out before being offered the needle. We were kept busy. I had one crisis – while struggling to get ready for parade, I discovered that I had no cap. As every serviceman and woman knows, it is almost better to go on parade without trousers than without a hat. Our friend the corporal called me many names and I was sure that my career had been deeply damaged. The final blow came, however, when he told me to wait behind to see him at NAAFI break. I couldn't imagine what dreadful punishment awaited me, but instead, I was to find that the corporal was, somewhat surprisingly, a fellow human being.

'You think you have lost your cap,' he began.

'Yes, Corporal.'

'You haven't lost your cap, it's been stolen. Don't you realise that you are now living among thieves and robbers? You will only survive if you are ready to steal somebody else's cap.'

I was appalled.

'Just make sure it's the right size,' concluded my mentor as he strode off, leaving me to contemplate the new moral climate into which I had strayed.

The thing which made me most homesick though, was the porridge. Made without salt, it was tasteless and practically inedible, and I longed for some of Maimie's breakfasts.

CHAPTER SEVEN

Wings over America

Every new day brought another rumour to keep us on our toes, and at last there came the hard news that University Air Squadron types were to be trained in the United States. Needless to say this caused great excitement, but I wasn't so sure. The United States was a long way from the Mull of Kintyre. To confirm this piece of news we were issued with a suit of civilian clothes, and it was explained that we couldn't wear our uniforms in neutral America.

It was all very confusing but we were not allowed to vegetate. In two or three days time we were on our way to West Kirby in Lancashire, and as the train sped northwards the clever among us were sure that we would be sailing from Liverpool. I was, however, learning that those who pretended to know everything were often mistaken! After a couple of days in West Kirby we were told to have all our kit ready for a move that night, and so we assembled outside the guard room just as darkness was falling – about eleven o'clock – to await the transport. None came, and when darkness fell we were paraded in column of route and, carrying all our worldly goods, kit bags and suitcases, we marched away as best we could, knowing not where we were going.

To begin with there was quite a lot of good natured banter, but as time went on and the kit became heavier, an awful silence befell the squad, broken often by terrible oaths. We did not know where we were going, but it soon became apparent that it was some distance away. Men wept with fatigue and some actually fell out, unable to proceed. To our great relief we eventually arrived at a station and found a train waiting for us. As soon as we were all aboard it started, and again we knew not where we would arrive. As daylight came, it was soon apparent that we were heading north and into Scotland. After many delays and stoppages we began to recognise the environs of Glasgow and great discussion took place as to which station would be our destination. Wrong again! We were taken straight to a dock. As we were paraded on the dockside, we had time to look up to the great ship which towered above us. It was the *Duchess of Atholl* and we boarded her on my birthday.

This was real excitement at last. We were allocated our mess decks and received our first shock. We were issued with hammocks and given instructions as to how to swing the same. It became evident that we would eat, sleep and generally have our being, all on the same deck. It was indeed quite horrendous and, although we were pleased when we sailed down the Clyde that afternoon, it was evident to all that the ship was something of a death trap to those who were consigned to the lower decks. If we thought at all, we accepted it as our lot, and as we anchored off Greenock we were amazed to see the number of ships which were assembling inside the boom at the Cloch lighthouse.

As the good book says, 'the evening and the morning were the first day'. I swung my hammock, but fell out of it two or three times before mastering it. After two nights without sleep, two or three of us sneaked up on deck in the darkness, finding out of the way corners in which we might sleep. We did sleep too, until the morning, when the sailors hosed us down as they swabbed the decks, with dire warnings that if we were found thus again we would be reported, if not thrown over the side.

The days passed and we still sat in the Firth of Clyde. On one memorable day I looked over to Greenock, knowing that Willie and Nina were being married that day, that most of the family would be there some hundred yards away, and I might as well have been on the moon. On Saturday afternoon there was a great scurrying of little boats going from ship to ship and it was evident that something was afoot. An evening mist came down on the Cunbraes as our great ship began to tremble quietly. About six o'clock the leading ships began moving through the boom gates. The fog prevented us seeing as much as we would have liked of the stately procession, the destroyers like sheepdogs getting their charges into position. I did not know whether to be glad or sorry that we would pass the Mull of Kintyre during the hours of darkness, however the great adventure had started and with some excitement and not a little trepidation we got into our hammocks, rocked in the cradle of the deep.

I slept too, and on awaking, dressed quickly to get my first view of the wide Atlantic. Everything was strangely quiet and when, with some companions we got out on deck, we were amazed to see Greenock still two or three hundred yards away and the *Duchess of*

Atholl becalmed inside the boom. The know-alls could tell us why all this had happened but the bottom line was that the good ship had broken down before getting to the Mull of Kintyre, and had been sent back because she could not keep up with the convoy.

We were disembarked, put into trains, and by nightfall were back at the transit camp – this time at Wilmslow. Everyone was deflated but then, out of the blue, we were given three days leave. This meant of course that with luck I might have twenty four hours at home. Was it worth the hassle? I took two seconds to consider this and set off back up the line to Glasgow. By dint of various lifts I arrived home at the Manse of Southend about tea time and, having been unable to give any prior warning of my coming, I must have given my parents the fright of their lives when I passed the dining room window. As far as they were concerned I was somewhere in mid-Atlantic. Suddenly there I was, more or less, in the flesh.

The two days at home, however, were well worth all the trouble. Once again I said my farewells and returned to Wilmslow where all was hustle and bustle to get us back on to a troopship. This time is was a ship named the *Stratheden* and we were no sooner aboard than we sailed. We passed the Mull of Kintyre about mid-afternoon, and there was the place of my heart looking very strange from the different perspective. I could hardly believe that I had been there forty-eight hours before, and I wondered when, or if, I would ever see it again. The convoy ploughed on. Our accommodation on the *Stratheden* was much superior to that on the *Duchess*, and we felt reasonably safe sitting with the other troopships in the centre of the convoy, while the cargo vessels took their chance around the edges. We were quite heavily escorted too.

About the third or fourth day we came up on deck in the morning, and the convoy had vanished. Later we were to learn that it was carrying troops to Singapore. We were alone except for two destroyers and it was obvious that, free from the convoy, our ship was able to increase speed to its maximum. We were making our dash for the American coast. About ten o'clock in the morning the alarm bells started ringing and we were summoned to the lifeboat stations. One of the destroyers made a mad dash to starboard while the other closed in on us. This I felt was getting a bit earnest, and while we all tried to be funny as we mustered at our stations, I, for one, felt very frightened, wondering when the first torpedo would be sighted. The spouts from depth charges dropped by our escort made us realise that the enemy might be a bit frightened too, which made us feel better. In less than an hour the panic was over, the destroyers took up their normal station and we returned to the shipboard routine of reading, playing cards, the odd PT session and sleep. On the sixth or seventh day after leaving Glasgow we sailed into the port of Halifax and there received a rousing welcome from all who were waiting on the pier. Men and women leant out of the office windows and cheered our arrival and we felt as if we had already won the war.

We entrained for the transit camp at Toronto, and on the journey were again feted by the Canadians. Whenever we stopped at a station there were ladies standing besides pyramids of apples to distribute among us. It was all very touching. Although the food on the boat had been quite adequate, after the rationing of home, the food on the train was beyond belief. The camp at Toronto, however, was just about as soulless as any other transit camp, but once again the tremendous hos-pitality of the Canadians made sure that we had little time to be homesick. The outstanding memory of our time there was a Sunday trip to the Niagara Falls in a fleet of cars, with one kindness heaped upon another.

By now, however, we had been allocated our places at the various flying schools. This meant that we would be losing some of the University people with whom we had begun in Edinburgh. Sixteen of us, along with a similar number from Oxford and Cambridge became the latest course to be sent to the No 5 British Flying Training School at Clewiston in Florida, and on the appointed day we were put on yet another train and despatched to the deep south. The train stopped on the US border, with great hilarity we removed our RAF uniforms and donned our civvy clothes, then the train started up again. Once more we were amazed at the variety and amount of food available. I enjoyed sleeping on the train as we sped south. Waking one morning we found ourselves halted at no less a place than Chattanooga. It came as something of a surprise to me that among the many hundreds of people milling around at the station I had difficulty in seeing a white face.

We arrived at Clewiston and were taken by bus to our camp. It was quite a strange set up for, while within the camp we came under the military discipline of the RAF, the flying instruction was provided by the Riddle McKay Aero College. All the instructors were American civilians. Accommodation was sensible if a bit spartan – eight of us slept in bunk beds in each unit – but our mess was beautifully clean and the food beyond belief, although I found the waffles and syrup which were served at breakfast time a good deal too sweet. Wing Commander Rampling and his staff provided the service back-up and supervision and we were left in no doubt that if we did not behave ourselves there would be no second chances. We would be returned to Canada and consigned to whatever litter bin might be available.

After a day or two in which we were again given a hospitable welcome by the people of Clewiston, and during which we were threatened by a hurricane, the training began. We were given our instructors and once again my great good luck held. With a few others I was assigned to a Mr Ellis, who turned out to be the quietest and, we thought, the nicest of all the instructors. There was nothing aggressive about him. He issued no threats and as we gathered around him he said, 'All I want to do is to make you good pilots. Life will be dangerous enough for you. I want to see to it that you will always have the best chance.'

The flying training began and it was a wonderful feeling to take to the air. We flew Stearman biplanes for our initial training which were sturdier than Tiger Moths but not difficult to fly. Mr Ellis took me through the various exercises: the effect of controls; straight and level flying; medium turns. After a day or two we were doing glides and gliding turns; climbs and climbing turns. The first two weeks passed without incident and then came the tales of those who were about to go solo. Soon there was confirmation before our eyes of pupils flying alone. When would we do it? Rumour had it that if you did not go solo within thirteen flying hours, you were out. Tension mounted. Then on the 28th October, after numerous takeoffs and landings, Mr Ellis eased himself out of the cockpit, patted me on the head. 'Do it yourself,' he said, and jumped to the ground.

'Dear God!' I thought. 'This is it. There is no place to hide'.

I did all the cockpit checks, looked around, got the green light from the end of the runway, opened the throttle and, before I knew much about it, I was in the air and on my own. The feeling was good except for the knowledge that I had to get the thing back on the ground without assistance! Needless to say, the training I'd had was sufficient, and soon I was coming in over the fence, stick back, throttle closed. I wouldn't say it was the best landing ever but it was good enough. 'Go round again,' signalled Mr Ellis, so I did. I was signalled into the parking place and got out. The good Mr Ellis shook me by the hand and congratulated me. By this time the adrenalin was running strong and I was quite euphoric. In a superior and patronising way I was sorry for those who had not yet gone solo. Remarkably, and for the first course ever, everyone did in fact go solo.

We were kept very busy as the weeks passed into months. At the start of our stay in Florida earnest attempts were made to interest us in the flora and fauna of our new 'home'. The Everglade swamps were close at hand and while we were never allowed to fly over them and they were out of bounds at all times, we were lectured upon the wonders to be found there. I do not think that we appreciated this educational thrust and it all came to an end when an elderly lady came to lecture us about the various plants, especially the fern variety, which were to be found in the vicinity. When she told us of the wonderful 'poifume of the foins', it became rather much for her restive audience. As we fell about laughing, she departed in high dudgeon. Needless to say our commanding officer paraded us the next day and told us how ungrateful and un-gracious we were, but there were no further botanical tutorials.

We had plenty to do, flying either morning or afternoon, the remainder of the working day being taken up with lectures on airframes, engines, aircraft recognition, wireless procedures and Physical Education. Time passed quickly and with a swimming pool on camp and a pleasant mess with the inevitable soda fountain and juke box we didn't weary. We were able to leave camp most weekends but being paid the going rate for Leading Aircraftsmen–General Duties, we were not very 'flush'. In fact when our pay was turned into dollars it became even more derisory. Still, with the help of various friends among the locals who more or less adopted us, we did manage some weekends to Miami where an Englishman with a small hotel on Miami Beach gave us very special rates during the off season. Whether we liked it or not we lived very temperate and simple lives because we could not afford to do anything else – after all, we were not there for a holiday. Letters from home were the joy of our lives although it was evident from them that the war was not going very well. When we thought of the food rationing we felt rather guilty that we were living, quite literally, off the fat of the land.

Our flying instruction went on apace, and soon we were doing simple aerobatics. The instructor would take the pupil up for an hour and then the pupil would be despatched by himself to practise the various exercises. My own course was marked by two crises. The first concerned the test which every pupil had to pass at the end of the primary phase of training which was carried out by one of the senior instructors. In the folk lore of the flying school there were some instructors named who were better avoided. My luck gave out on the day of my test and I drew the most dreaded of all. His fame had gone before him and it was not long until I realised that everything which had been reported about him was true. I could do nothing right. Eventually he told me to land, and while I was trying to do so he kept telling me that I would never make a pilot. I taxied in feeling utterly miserable and became aware that in the dispersal area there was something of a furore. I wondered if there had been some kind of accident but was so miserable in myself that I wasn't all that interested. There had, however, been one of the biggest accidents of all time. The Japanese had sunk a goodly part of the American fleet at Pearl Harbour. It was amazing to see the reaction of the Americans, grown men wept, others swore volubly, all were prepared to leave then and there in their unarmed planes to rectify the wrong. Even my adjectival tester was so upset that he failed to file the report on my test and two days later I was tested again by a gentleman by the name of Johnstone. After half an hour he drawled down the intercom, 'You'll do!' and I landed with a high heart.

We passed on to a heavier monoplane for our basic training which I completed without mishap. During this time we were introduced to night flying which was frightening to contemplate but turned out to be quite easy, as with the amount of town and road lighting the night was practically as bright as the day.

My growing confidence was about to be tested. In February we passed from the basic to the advanced course of training and now we were flying AT 6s, the plane which was affectionately known as 'The Harvard'. It was a real aeroplane with speed, sweet control and its own idiosyncracies. If you did not give it all your attention, it was inclined to have a mind of its own, especially on landing. Everything went well, and on the night of 18th February we were doing night flying. My advanced instructor, the very pleasant Mr May, took me up and I did a couple of landings. We were then sent out on solo patrol. I was the first off and was told to climb to 8000 feet. The remainder of those flying were then sent off at intervals and were patrolling at 500 feet intervals below me. This was called 'stacking' and I was on the top of the stack. It was very pleasant sitting up there in the moonlight, as I could see for miles. Suddenly I saw something which jolted me out of my pleasant thoughts. The Everglade Swamps had the nasty habit of producing a ground mist which in the prevailing westerly wind could envelop our airfield. I saw it forming over the swamps and immediately called base. Everyone was recalled, the ones at lower level going in first and the rest of us reducing height to take our turn. Being on top I was in a position to give a commentary on the progress of the ground mist. It was progressing much too fast for my liking and I held my breath as one after another my colleagues got down safely. By the time I had got down to 1000 feet however, I knew I wasn't going to make it. The landing lights disappeared under the mist and I was informed by the flying control that I was to proceed back up to 5000 feet and resume patrol, to await further instruction. I felt deprived, thinking of all the lucky ones who had landed while here I was marooned in the sky.

My instructions duly came. I was to maintain height and keep up the patrol over the base until my petrol ran out, at which point I was to bale out.

Couldn't be more simple. As far as I was concerned, it was simply awful. I willed the mist to clear and perhaps that was a mistake. After about half an hour I was elated to see the landing lights and I called up the flying control and told them that I could see the flarepath. They told me that it was very thick on the ground, but if I could see the lights I was to come in. I lost height very quickly and made my approach. The lights were clear enough to me and as I came down between them, I levelled off with a great sense of relief. Suddenly everything was out of my control as with a splintering crash the aircraft cartwheeled its way down the flarepath. I was thrown hither and yon, but eventually the nightmare came to an end and there was an awful silence. I couldn't believe that I was still alive, then I realised that I was hanging on my safety harness, I was upside down and petrol was running up my nose. Fire, I thought, and turned off the magneto switches which were still there. Then there was noise – bells ringing, men shouting, the fire engine and the blood wagon had arrived. A voice shouted 'Take your time you guys, nothing will come out of that alive.' Much put out by this I yelled 'Get me out of here!' The original voice called upon the name of the Lord with more fervour than devotion, and they began lifting what was left of the cockpit and eased me gently out and down. I was driven at high speed to the local hospital, tightly strapped in the stretcher to save further damage, then I was wheeled into an operating theatre where various doctors were waiting, ready and willing to give their all in putting me together again.

I began to get worried. 'I don't think I'm hurt at all,' I said. They smiled with some pity upon me. 'You'll be OK son,' they said without conviction. Each took a turn in examining me as they were obviously afraid that any movement would bring further injury. I was getting quite annoyed. 'Look,' I said, 'I can feel all my fingers and toes. I don't feel any pain at all. Let me try to walk.' After further consultation, two men eased me off the trolley and, taking my weight, set me up on my feet. With them holding me I was allowed to take a step or two. Eventually they let go and I walked smartly across the room. 'Well I'm darned' they said, more or less in unison.

In the end they were all convinced that I had suffered no injury. It was all something of a miracle, a fact which became even more apparent on an inspection, in the daylight, of my shattered Harvard. It was utterly destroyed but I had survived because the crash bar behind the pilot's seat had held firm. There was an inquiry of course and the general opinion was that as a trainee pilot I was blameless. I *had* seen the landing lights, but they had been shining through the mist. I had made a good landing, but some thirty feet off the ground, and the plane had then spun in. No one could remember anyone who had survived such a circumstance. I was allowed to sleep until midday but, after an interview with the Wing Commander, was told to report for flying duties that evening. Mr May said how glad he was that things had turned out the way they had and then said quietly, 'Let's go fly'. I was reassured when he got into the rear seat and we took off. We did one circuit and landing and he got out. 'Take it easy,' he said, and I was signalled off. I did two landings and was then waved into the dispersal point where Mr May signalled me to shut off the engine, and I got out. 'You'll be alright now,' he drawled, 'but if you hadn't flown tonight you might never have had the nerve to fly again. Get away to your bed now.'

This was the last crisis in training. The crash increased my confidence rather than diminishing it. I was never going to be a crack aerobatic pilot, but it appeared there were three things I was good at: I could take off and land with the best, I could find my way around on a map, and I could fly an aeroplane close to the ground better than most.

The great day came when we got our wings. I could hardly believe it when they were pinned on my chest. Wing Commander Rampling shook me warmly by the hand and then quietly, so that I was the only one who could hear, he said, 'Keep your eyes open – especially at night!'

CHAPTER EIGHT

Wartime travel and Training

It was with high hearts that we left Clewiston where all but three of the original fifty had achieved what they had come to do. Now it was time to get back home to play our part in the conflict. We came back to Moncton via New York where our RAF uniforms with wings gave us free access to all the places we wanted to visit. We viewed the city from the top of the Empire State building, we wondered at the romance of Times Square and we even visited Jack Dempsey's bar. And so to Moncton where we soon realised that we were back with the herd. We got our sergeants stripes however, and soon we were off back to Halifax to join the *Capetown Castle* which was to take us back to the UK. Our accommodation was splendid and the food well up to that to which we had grown accustomed. The convoy which was of troopships only, made good speed, and one morning as the dawn broke I saw again the Mull of Kintyre. It was a moment to savour.

We disembarked at Liverpool and were whisked away by train to an unknown destination which turned out to be Bournemouth where, in the Grand Hotel, we had a day or two pretending that we were living an elegant life. There was little required of us. Our Commissions came through and we busied ourselves getting measured for our uniforms. I chose Hector Powe as my tailor and wondered at the ridiculous nature of the whole exercise. Once the uniforms were ready, however, we stepped out on the town quite sure that we were the centre of attention! The days passed pleasantly and we took coffee and tea in a restaurant which boasted a palm court orchestra where all the musicians were in the geriatric class. On Sundays we listened to a band playing at the bandstand. Then came the great day when, with all our postings settled, we were sent on leave. It would be difficult to describe the joy of that homecoming. It was good to return having achieved the initial goal, but it was better to return and be a member of that family at the Manse of Southend.

We had to go back of course, and it was to a conversion course at Hullavington where we flew Miles Masters. This short course was to familiarise us with flying conditions in the UK which indeed were much different to those we had experienced in America. This was especially true at night. Night flying in America had been very little different to flying in the daylight, but now with Britain in blackout it was a shock to the system to take off from a dimmed flarepath into a blackness with little point of reference. Below, there was a multitude of flarepaths, to confuse the enemy raiders, and if they were half as confused as I was then the exercise succeeded. On my first trip up at night I was accompanied by my instructor, a Warrant Officer Green, who, after a tour of duty in Fighter Command was not all that happy trying to teach greenhorns like myself. He was a man of few words. Our times in the air were long periods of silence interspersed with taciturn instructions, but we really got on quite well until the night flying. We took off quite reasonably and W.O. Green suggested that I land. With the multitude of flarepaths below me I made my choice and proceeded to make my approach to land. About a hundred feet from the ground there came the sepulchral voice from the back: 'You're going to kill your bloody self.' I overshot and came round again, made my second choice of flarepath and came into land. Again the voice, 'You're still going to kill your bloody self,' and as I opened up to go round again he added, 'this I don't mind except that you will kill me as well.' Eventually I began to understand how one picked the right landing spot and Warrant Officer Green was quite expansive when I left for pastures new: 'You'll do - I hope.'

It was on then to our operational training, and once again we were separated from quite a number of our colleagues, as some had gone to train on twin engined machines and some had gone to Transport Command. The best pilots - much to their annoyance - had been sent to Training Command to act as instructors. My group was sent to Crosby on Eden near Carlisle, to be trained on single engined aircraft with a view to us being sent to Fighter Command. We were delighted.

After a few hours of flying with an instructor in a Miles Master, the day came when I was to make my first flight in a Hurricane. Being single seater aircraft there was, naturally, no chance of any familiarisation with the comfort of an instructor. It was like the first 'solo' trip all over again. There was no one to fall back on - nowhere to hide. So, sitting at the end of the runway waiting for the green light, there was little to do but pray. I will never forget the shock I got when I opened the throttle as the engine was so much more powerful than anything I had been used to. I felt that I had received a huge boost in the back and before I knew it the aeroplane was dashing to the end of the runway and wanting to take off. Easing back on the stick, there I was in the air, travelling faster than I'd ever gone before. I remembered to retract the undercarriage and with a huge sigh of relief found that the aeroplane was flying like a bird. There was a great exhilaration. Here I was in charge of a Hurricane – the legendary Hurricane. It was the beginning of a great association, for the Hurricane never would let me down.

Our training was concentrated and varied. After getting used to the plane we started flying it the way we would have to in conflict. We practised air to ground firing, formation flying, air to air firing, altitude flying, and low level flying. It was all very exciting. A touch too exciting one Sunday morning when we were doing a little gentle formation flying over the Lake District. I was complimenting myself on the closeness of the formation when suddenly there was a loud bang and I lost all power. Of course I dropped quickly out of the formation, and when there was no response from the engine I began to wonder if I should perhaps step over the side. By the time I had considered this however, I was below three thousand feet. I looked for a field in which I might make an emergency landing, but there was little but sloping hills and high tension cables. I was now below the safe height from which I could jump, but I could see a small hamlet which had on the outskirts the encouraging sight of a graveyard. What took my eye though was a piece of ground which was obviously an extension to the graveyard. It was the only place. The training which I had received for such an emergency stood me in good stead and I took the Hurricane, wheels up, in through the hedge surrounding the graveyard and placed her on the green sward which was the extension. I'm sorry to say that I made an awful mess of the place and disturbed a few of the dear departed, but I stepped out unscathed and made my way to a nearby farm, where the lady of the house allowed me to use the telephone to tell them at base that all was not lost, that one of their most valued pilots had survived. I was put out when the first question from the Flight Commander was 'And what is the Hurricane like?' Then I was fed with scones and coffee and the little farm servant kept asking me – perhaps in hope – 'Are you feeling any worse now?' I was quite sorry to leave them when the truck arrived to take me back to the station.

It transpired that the engine of my Hurricane had split because of lack of oil. A very tearful little WAAF admitted that she had failed to fill up that morning, and the naughty girl had signed the 700 form that she had done so. I did not enjoy the proceedings when she was brought to book, as the Station Commander did not spare her feelings. 'If Pilot Officer MacVicar had not landed safely, his death would have been on your hands.' By this time there were uncontrollable sobs. We were all glad to get back to the flying lines. I heard later that the poor girl had been admonished and posted somewhere else. Our training went on apace and we transferred to an airfield in Northumbria where we did a lot of low level flying over the border hills. I was in my element and enjoying life.

My companions included Boris and Ian who had been on the same course in America. Boris from Weybridge was a gentle soul and had been studying classics at Oxford. He had a wonderful sense of humour but suffered from a dreadful speech impediment. He found this Scotsman a constant amusement and we became firm friends. Ian was a botanist studying at Cambridge; another gentle man who could study his botany while all hell was going on around him. He was the bane of his instructors because of his absent-mindedness. Another companion was a hell raiser by the name of John Baldwin. He had joined us from some other course but was immediately recognised as a superb flyer, a born leader and a bonny fechter. Boris, Ian and myself from somewhat sheltered backgrounds took to Baldwin with his greater experience of life.

Our course came to an end in August of that year and we awaited our postings. The training was over and we all knew that the next move would be to the sharp end. When our orders came through I couldn't believe my luck. I was to join No 1 Fighter Squadron which was flying Typhoons. Without doubt it was a plum posting and I was the envy of so many, especially of one John Baldwin who had distinguished himself so much in training that he was to be retained on the station as an instructor. He was not pleased.

Home we went on leave and I enjoyed ten days of being spoiled by the family. There was no doubt in anyone's mind, however, that I would be moving into very dangerous country. We might joke about it but we all knew that the future could be a very black joke. I had about three days leave left when a telegram arrived recalling me to a transit camp at Padgate. I couldn't make out what this was about but, not reasoning why, off I went. On arrival I found all those who had been on OTU with me had been brought in. We were gathered together in one of the messes, where we were told that all previous postings had been cancelled and that we were all being sent to India to re-equip the Squadrons which had been decimated in the retreat from Burma. None of us was enthusiastic but realised that we had no say in the matter.

I was never to know how I would have performed in aerial conflict over the South Coast, though I heard later that my posting to No 1 Squadron had gone to one John Baldwin. It couldn't have gone to a better chap. The Germans suffered at his hand, for as everyone knows Group Captain Johnny Baldwin became one of the aces of the war.

For the rest of that course it was to be a different tale. Within days we found ourselves aboard a troopship sailing from Liverpool. The *Empress of Russia* was on her last legs and we were told that she was the largest coal burning ship left. Watching the clouds of thick smoke which belched up from her funnels it appeared as if she was failing to burn a good deal of the coal in her furnaces. Her smoke displeased the Commodore of the convoy and we all felt that our ship was letting the side down. She had a permanent list too, and there were many jokes about arriving in India with one leg shorter than the other. Apart from the bad jokes however, the *Empress of Russia* was not a happy ship. Rumour had it that there had been difficulty raising a stoker crew for her and that those who had been persuaded were not of a trustworthy nature. Every now and then there would be flash rumours of trouble below decks but mostly day followed boring day and the sun got hotter. We had been issued with the fundamental kit needed in the tropics, including pith helmets, and as we got into the tropics we all faithfully took them out and wore them *a la* Dr Livingstone. We took on coal at Freetown and were amazed to see the coal being loaded by hand from barges which lay alongside, with the black men toiling in the heat, filling their huge baskets with coal and carrying them to the ship. It took days.

We entertained ourselves as best we could and had a party most nights. On one very merry occasion we had amused ourselves by swinging from the halyards which were hanging from the lifeboats. Out over the side of the ship we swung like monkeys. We had as much sense. We sobered up in the morning very quickly when Ian did not make it to breakfast. He was not in his cabin either. His bunk had not been slept in and the awful possibility began to dawn upon us that Ian had gone over the side. We spent some miserable minutes discussing who would tell the CO Troops. We decided that we would first make another search of the ship and to our great relief we found Ian asleep in one of the toilets. He was stiff but unharmed.

At last we reached the Cape of Good Hope and our spirits rose with the hope of some time ashore. With what majesty that was left to her the *Empress of Russia* sailed into the bay at Capetown along with the other ships of the convoy. We then sailed out again without anchoring. The wiseacres told us this exercise was meant to fool watching enemy submarines. It fooled us anyway and we had to settle down to further days at sea until we came to Durban where, as she always did, the white lady on the quay welcomed us by singing 'Land of Hope and Glory'. In a strange way it was very moving.

We went ashore and were royally entertained by the white community there, whose kindness to us was quite spectacular. Our departure from Durban, however, was marked by a mutiny. The stoker crew, which had always been troublesome, refused to stoke as they claimed they had been promised that they would be home by Christmas. Knowing that we were going to Bombay they downed tools. Those of us who did not know how many Christmases we would be away from home were in no mood to be sympathetic. Eventually the stokers were put into detention on board ship and a party of naval ratings took over the unenviable job of stoking the vessel. Our troubles continued and eventually the convoy Commodore lost patience with us, and we were directed to Mombasa and left with a couple of destroyers to escort us. As it turned out there were excitements in Mombasa too. As junior officers we were detailed to patrol the downtown district to make sure that no 'other ranks' wandered out of bounds. There had been some trouble locally before we arrived and the atmosphere was tense. I have no happy memories of Mombasa although it appeared to me to be more western than I would have expected.

At last we made our dash for Bombay, although the *Empress* was beyond dashing anywhere. It was with great relief that we arrived and viewed the Gateway of India, a noble structure and worthy entry point to a mysterious land.

Before we had left the UK I knew that Angus had been commissioned in the Royal Scots Fusiliers and was on his way to some unknown destination, Archie had been commissioned in the Argyll and Sutherland Highlanders and was in the Middle East, and Willie as usual was on the high seas. I wondered what news would come of them when I got to India. En route we had heard of the Battle of El Alamein, and Madagascar had been taken. Nothing good was happening in the East. So much had occurred while we had toured the oceans in the *Empress of Russia* that it was with some trepidation I opened the first letters which were awaiting me. As it transpired, all the personal news was reasonably good. Archie, though wounded, had survived Alamein; Angus had been in Madagascar and had survived unscathed; Willie was coming from, and going to, various ports throughout the world; everyone at home was well and wondering what on earth had happened to the other wandering boy.

By this time I was becoming a bit bemused myself. One thing, however, impressed me. After all these weeks and months of wandering on the high seas, we paraded in our transit camp and there were people there who knew every one of us in great detail. It was proof, if proof was needed, that in the services you couldn't get lost. Somebody, somewhere, would have your records. They might stop short of numbering the hairs of your head but, in most other aspects, the Powers that be had an Almighty aura about them.

CHAPTER NINE

Wings over India and Burma

India was a culture shock. Although the number of coloured people in America had come as a surprise to me, the social environment was much the same as I'd been used to. The language was the same, in content if not in delivery. India was different. The language, dress, and appearance of the people were all different and there were different sounds, sights and smells. Yet upon it all there was the veneer of western civilisation, which misled one into thinking that perhaps the differences were not so great as they appeared. They were, in fact, greater than we could have imagined. As was my wont in a new and strange situation I was a bit apprehensive of the Indian and his strange ways, but it was not long before I felt an affectionate sympathy for him. Life seemed to be such a struggle as it appeared that every man's hand was against him. Everybody seemed to be shouting at somebody else, the rickshaw wallahs struggled through the traffic, others pulled ridiculous loads, nothing was done with any kind of efficiency, and the caste system made it appear that even those of the same race were all seeking the exploitation of the caste or castes below them. I think I was wise enough not to make judgements after a few days or weeks in the country but there is no doubt that I was amazed and sometimes appalled at what went on. We of course were apart from it all, leading our own lives without understanding of, and I suppose quite uncaring of, what went on in the country which was to be our home, we hoped, on a very temporary basis.

Within a few days of getting to Bombay we were on the move again, this time to Ranchi in the province of Bihar. It took us days to get there by train, and on arrival we found ourselves attached to No 28 Squadron, an Army Co-operation Squadron which had been in India since the early twenties and had battle honours from the campaigns on the North West Frontier. The Squadron had lost many aircraft during the retreat from Burma when it was equipped with Lysanders. Now it was to be re-equipped with Hurricanes and be given a much more offensive role. As a new and fresh intake of pilots operationally trained on Hurricanes, we came to strengthen and augment the pilots who had had such a bad time trying to help the army in retreat.

We were billeted in a fine country house. The senior officers had rooms in the house while the juniors slept in tents in the garden. The large dining room of the house which opened on to these lawns was the officers' mess. We were each given a 'bearer' who attended to all our needs. This, I thought, was really the kind of life I had been born to. No matter in what state the bed was left, no matter in what state of chaos the tent, when I returned all was in order, fresh clothes were awaiting; everything needed for ablutions was at hand and a clap of the hands or a shout brought the bearer running, ready to meet the smallest request. Except for the fact that it gave employment locally, it was almost obscene. My 'bearer' was a middle-aged man of ample proportions whose white robes and turban were always immaculate. He had an unpronounceable name but soon answered to 'James'. I became very fond of him and encouraged him to talk of his wife and innumerable children in the village and I often wish that I had been more relaxed at that time. I could have gone to see James in his home but the received wisdom was that one did not get too familiar with the natives. The time was to come when I ignored the received wisdom. It was a very pleasant time at Ranchi. We usually flew in the morning and our exercises included a lot of low flying which I enjoyed. After a light lunch, a long siesta, followed by a further flight in the cool of the late afternoon. Dinner in the evening was followed by a visit to the Ranchi Club or a party session in the mess. On these occasions all the bearers would sit on their hunkers on the verandah outside the mess awaiting the call of their 'masters'. In retrospect I sometimes feel that we repaid them somewhat with the amusement we afforded them with our antics. At a certain stage of the evening there was always a call to go round the room without touching the floor. This exercise was often attended by breakages or by near disasters. When there were 'Grand National' races over the furniture, the bearers could not contain themselves as they came nearer and nearer to the door hoping their young master would be victorious. Often they had to put the said 'Young masters' to bed. In the morning when James would wake me gently with a cup of 'Char', he would give me a report: 'Boris sahib not good', or 'Ian sahib very sore head'. Often his own young sahib felt less than robust.

The aforesaid Boris and Ian were the only colleagues left with me from the Clewiston days. Naturally we supported each other and were known to the rest of the pilots as the 'three prunes' . There were two Flights, and we were indeed beginning to 'gel' as a Squadron. Our Flight Commander was one Henry Larsen, a friendly extrovert with a good opinion of himself and a burning desire for promotion. He immediately christened his only Scottish pilot 'MacPorridge' and took great delight in (badly) imitating my accent. He had, however, a great loyalty to his own Flight and would stand up for his pilots on all occasions. The daily flying and the settled nature of the personnel meant that we got close to the ground crews in a way which had been impossible in training. Soon the morale which had been sorely dented in the retreat began to be rebuilt. We got a new adjutant, Eric Adams, who was a delightful man, a friend to all ranks. Being older than the pilots he tried to look after us like a father. Often, like God, he had great pity for his children, especially when they were unable to contain the same volume of gin as himself. Two Army officers – Liaison Officers – Major Loveless and Captain Matthews, were also assigned to us. They had to stand a lot from the irreverent young pilots – 'Bloody brown jobs' was the least offensive epithet applied! They soon integrated very well, however, and became part of the team. Major Loveless looked like a cartoon army officer, suave and moustachioed. He became more and more stylish in his speech the more gin he took, but there was a cut off point when he reverted to his Yorkshire accent. Matthews was from Lancashire and was known from the start as the Admiral. Both could be very good fun, and put up with us very well. For a short time we had a training officer, a Flying Officer Kenneth Gillies, who had won a DFM in the Battle of Britain. He was a hell raiser of the first order and usually flew over to a neighbouring squadron for lunch if he knew some of the pilots there. One could tell how good the lunch had been by Gillies' flying display on his return, when he would give an exhibition of aerobatics and low flying which was usually both dangerous and impressive. Once on the ground, however, it was touch and go whether he would get out of the Hurricane. He would retire to his bed to recuperate and to be ready for another party in the evening.

The New Year arrived and during the following weeks we wondered if we would ever get into the action. I came close to ending my particular war, however, without interference from the enemy. Boris was to blame. We were doing air to ground firing and the target was a canvas sheet strung between two poles. Boris was the range officer and sat in his bunker with a radio. He called us in turn to attack the target and when we had done so he would inspect the target and tell us how successful we had been. Range orders decreed that we should not descend lower than two hundred feet in making our attack. My turn came and I went down in a shallow dive, loosing off the eight Brownings, then circled to hear how I had done. With stammering ribaldry Boris announced that I had missed the target altogether and would I get my finger out and try harder. Stung by all this, I made up my mind that whatever happened I would hit the target second time round. I brought the aircraft round about half a mile from the white sheet and approached it, flying very close to the ground. I was amazed to see the target disappear altogether when I opened up, but was more concerned to see the trees behind the target rushing towards me. I pulled hard back on the stick and the Hurricane, as usual, responded valiantly. I was, however, rather close and clipped the top branches with the propellor. I was shaken and amazed that the machine was still flying, but the engine sounded and felt very rough indeed. Boris came on the radio. He too was shaken. 'Are you all right?' he asked. 'You've destroyed the **** target!' By this time I was making tracks for home, for the engine had begun to overheat rather alarmingly. With great relief I landed and inspected the damage. The prop blades were shortened by some six inches and the overheating had been caused by the radiator nascelle being filled with leaves. There was no way I could claim that I had not been below two hundred feet. I was not popular – not with the ground staff who had to change the prop; not with the Flight Commander because it was a black mark; and not with the CO for it was an aircraft out of commission. All my colleagues thought it was helluva funny and made sarcastic remarks about me driving a truck for the rest of the war – close to the ground.

In truth I was very miserable for I knew that this disobedience of range orders would not be ignored. I was grounded, and next day formed up in front of the Wing Commander. He asked for an explanation of my conduct and when I told him the tale, he lashed me with his tongue for about five minutes, leaving me in no doubt that the RAF could well do without idiots like myself. He was in the middle of this tirade when an orderly clerk came into the room and handed him a signal. The Wing Commander looked at the signal and then gave me a long look. 'Perhaps, MacVicar,' he began, 'you're born lucky. Your flight has just been posted to the Imphal front and you'll get plenty of flying below two hundred feet there. I will put a red endorsement in your log book, but try not to be such a bloody fool again.' When I had saluted and made for the door as fast as I could he stopped me. 'And the best of luck' the nice man said.

So that was it. After feverish preparation for the transit of the ground crews overland to Imphal, the flight took off on the last day of February. We were flying in pairs, but I had barely got my wheels up when I noticed a wisp of Glycol smoke streaming from the exhaust. I made a hurried return to base hoping that a quick repair could be made, but the flight went off without me. It was well after midday before I was ready to go. I flew from Ranchi to Jessore and after refuelling there set off for Imphal. I knew in my heart that daylight wouldn't last and as Imphal had no night landing facility at that time, I had to decide to put down on the landing strip at Silchar, hopeful that there would be a ground crew there to give me a start in the morning. When I got down the place was deserted. Darkness came swiftly and I was coming to terms with sleeping in the aircraft when suddenly a car appeared and out jumped a middle-aged man who addressed me in a Scottish accent.

'I saw you come in,' he said, 'and I wondered if the boys had gone back to their camp for the day. Come to my bungalow and I'll give you a bed.' I felt that he had been heaven sent. He was a tea planter in the district and we had a very convivial evening, consumed some decent scotch, and talked of home. I slept the sleep of the just.

Next morning he took me back to the Hurricane. The skeleton crew had turned up and within minutes they had checked the machine, I was in the cockpit, and started up. Waving goodbye to my erstwhile saviour, I took off in the bright morning light and climbed up over the Assam mountains, setting course for Imphal. The country was so beautiful, with the mountain tops shining green in the morning sun while the mist still lay in the valleys. Soon I could see the break in the mountain range which was the valley of Imphal. I made a circuit of inspection of the north end of the valley, picking out the airstrip running parallel to, and beside, the road. I made a lower inspection of the dispersal areas and found the Hurricanes which had flown in the day before. I could see some of the ground crews and the pilots coming out from their huts to see if it was 'Mac'. I made a further circuit and made a very low pass over the squadron's dispersal point so that they would be sure who had arrived. With that folly complete I climbed into the landing circuit and made my first approach and landing at Imphal. I was more than glad to be back with them all.

Everyone was glad to see me. They had wondered what had happened and gathered round to hear my tale. Already there was a new atmosphere among the flight personnel with the feeling that we were all in this, and now, at the sharp end, we had to pull together. My kit was unloaded from the aircraft and I was taken by jeep to our new abode – a vacated native settlement with the usual bamboo 'duftahs' or 'bashas'. These had mud floors and the beams and sides were coated with soot from generations of fires. In each of our rooms there were two 'charpoys', a simple bed frame with interlaced ropes to hold the mattress. No interior springs were in vogue. I looked around my new abode with some distaste and wondered how it could be made more habitable. The one consolation was that I was to share this basic habitation with Boris. I flung my bedroll on the charpoy and set out for the mess which again was a long hut with a plain table and some chairs scattered about. In true RAF style, however, work had already begun in creating a bamboo bar at one end. Other necessities would follow – but first things first!

Our Squadron, having been based in India or the East for all of its existence, had 'camp followers' attached to it. These were native Indians who, while they were not part of the services, carried out all the menial tasks on the Squadron – not only for the officers but for all ranks. They were the sweepers, the 'char' wallahs who looked after the tea, the dhobi wallahs who did the laundry, and India being India they had their own hierarchy. Any class distinction which was within the RAF membership of the Squadron was nothing compared to the caste system among the followers. All and sundry were shouted at and sworn at on a continuing basis, but in the best of humour. To hear the British airmen talking to the followers was nothing if not hilarious. There was quickly established a new language which was something between English and Hindustani, all interspersed with Anglo Saxon swear words which, of course, were the first assimilated by the Indians. I like to think that a certain affection existed amongst us all.

It was difficult to understand the relationship of the followers to the services. Certainly if they misbehaved they could be punished and the biggest punishment was to be dismissed and sent home.

Everyone was aware that in spite of all the shouting and swearing, the lot of a follower attached to the services was much to be preferred to the poverty he might endure at home. However, there was no way that they could be made to go anywhere and when the Squadron was moved into the forward areas some just melted away. Here today, they were gone on the morrow, but there were others who welcomed a more aggressive posture. Among the followers were some Pathans from the North West frontier. Much taller than the Bengali or Madrasi, the Pathan's only regret was that they were not allowed to carry weapons, though who they would have used them against was an open question.

On arrival at Imphal, I was allocated one of these as my bearer and I transferred the name of James at Ranchi to James at Imphal. No one could say that this James had the domestic skills of the former. He did his best however, and James being bigger than any of the other bearers, I knew that I could always leave my belongings safely in his hands. He was a very big man and in many ways quite handless, but he looked after Boris and Mac sahib with great loyalty, bringing us our tea in the morning to wake us, seeing that we had clean clothes to wear each day, waiting on us in the mess and generally being at our beck and call. James however had a weakness. Every time he came back from his day off he was very lethargic and clueless. I spoke to the doctor about this and he consented to see him the following week on the morning after his day off. Sure enough, James failed to appear with the tea and when enquiries were made I was told that he was sleeping. Poor James wasn't sleeping for long and, hauled before the MO, it was established that James's weakness was the hashis, the smoking of which was a fairly widespread habit. I would not say that we cured James of the habit, but we made him think. The doctor prescribed for him what can only be described as a more than adequate dose of castor oil. While I had to do without a bearer for another couple of days, he was a sadder and wiser man when he surfaced again and did not fail with the tea for a long time afterwards.

James, though, was a man of his word. The followers got leave to go home every now and then; some took this leave and did not return, some had no homes to go to. James however wanted to go back to see his people and so arrangements were made to get him back into India, and a pass was issued to take him to the railhead nearest to his home. After that it would be up to himself. When he knew he was going, he began to persuade me that I needed a new pair of 'chuplies', the native leather sandals. He knew a man in his village who could make the best in the world 'very cheap'. After long discussions regarding what constituted 'very cheap', I agreed to having the outline of my feet drawn on a piece of brown paper. This was to be the template for my chuplies. Next day I said good-bye to James, and to my money, as he set out for his home village on the North West Frontier. Considering this journey of so many hundreds of miles, the fact that he was under no great obligation to return to the Squadron, the likelihood that we would be moving to some other location and, even if he wanted to return, he would have difficulty in locating us, I began to wonder if I would ever see James again. I got used to the ministrations of a small Bengali who had taken his place as our servant, and as the months passed I became more sure that James had decided that east or west, home was best. I wronged the man. True, much had happened and we had been in various places. Somewhere, however, James's radar was working well, his intelligence service did not let him down and one morning he appeared with the tea as if he had never been away. At the side of my charpoy was a pair of new 'chuplies' – the best in the whole world. There was much backslapping and laughter.

But that was in the future. For now the 'B' Flight was in for a disappointment. It has to be said that at that time the army did not know what their reconnaissance Squadron was capable of. It was soon evident that what they wanted us to do at Imphal was beyond our range. The Hurricane, flying at ground level, was capable of staying in the air some 90 minutes but the sorties which the army wished us to undertake would take well over two hours. There we were at Imphal and feeling useless. The decision was made to fit the machines with additional fuel tanks which would double the range of the aircraft. Pilots were selected to fly the aircraft to the maintenance unit outside Calcutta, but I was not among those selected and expressed my disappointment to Henry, the Flight Commander.

'Oh, MacPorridge', he jeered, 'greater things are expected of you. You are going to be commanding officer at Palel.'

He thought this a great joke but, in fact, it was no joke at all. At the other end of the valley from Imphal, there was a grass strip at Palel which was to be used as an emergency landing ground for aircraft in trouble coming back from operations in Burma. Nobody knew anything about Palel, except that it had the highest incidence of malaria in the country. With a rigger (airframe) and a corporal fitter (engines), I duly set off to take over my first command. It was an extraordinary week in many ways. There was nothing to do except await emergency landings. We had one Lysander come in but he wasn't in much trouble. The boys and I played pontoon and rummy, told each other about our homes and friends, made friends as far as we could with some of the natives in a nearby village, and were visited by some army types from a gun site. The time began to lie heavily upon us and we were glad when the news came that we were to be relieved by a more permanent unit. We wished them luck. It was not wasted time, however, as it taught me a lot about how to get on with people in strange circumstances.

Returning to Imphal we found the aircraft had come back with their ugly tanks slung underneath the wings. A test flight soon indicated that with these tanks the Hurricane became a lot less manoeuvrable and we knew that if we happened to be 'jumped' by Zeros we would have no chance. Fortunately the pilot had the facility to jettison the tanks in such an emergency.

It was on the eleventh day of March that we began operations out of Imphal. When we came down in the morning from the mess to the operations room, Henry was already there in conference with the Admiral, our Army Liaison Officer.

'Well,' said Henry, 'this is it. Major Matthews will brief you.' We giggled nervously at the talk of Major Matthews. We realised however that Henry was signalling to us that we were now on serious business. My stomach turned over. After all the ups and downs of the past years - after all the training, the alarms and the escapes - this was the real business. My panic did not get any less as I awaited my turn for briefing. Much to my dismay, while we had been trained to fly in pairs, it had been decided that the longer range tasks would be undertaken by single aircraft.

'Right, Mac,' said the Admiral, 'let's see what delights we have for you'. I didn't laugh. With that he produced the maps which I would require and began detailing the route I was to take down into the Cangaw valley. The further he indicated down the valley the less impressed I became.

'But that's bloody miles', I protested.

'Ours not to reason why', said the Admiral smugly. He went on, 'And here, and here, and here' - he pointed to about a dozen places - 'you will take nice oblique photographs, to please the General'. He concluded by telling me 'If you see any sampans, don't leave them for the Japs to use!'

That was that. All very simple, and I was so scared I could hardly speak. The thought of going forth with the possibility of being killed was almost unbearable. However, all the training paid off. I folded the maps so that they could be used on my knee-pad; I went down to the dispersal point and gave the orders for the oblique camera to be fitted to my aircraft; I went to the makeshift and draughty 'loo', and realised that whatever other medication I might need in Burma, laxative would not be required while operations lasted. I found myself signing the 700 form, collecting my parachute, climbing into Hurricane IIB HV775, strapping myself in with the aid of LAC George Kew who gave me a pat on the top of my head, almost bringing tears to my eyes. Thumbs up – 'Contact'. The engine burst into life and I taxied out from the dispersal, across the road and up to the end of the runway. I tested the engine again, both magnetos gave solid readings, the green light from the control tower shone and I was off down the runway and on my way. With wheels up and everything working properly, the absolute panic began to settle down. I was just very scared, but not so scared that I couldn't concentrate on what I was doing.

The next big moment came when I knew that I was over enemy held territory. I knew that my best hope of survival was in flying as low as possible so that I could surprise any of the enemy who were about. If they *were* there, I couldn't see them. As I went further and further down the Gangaw valley the thought struck me that if I turned round and went home, no one would know but myself – after all, there was no movement anywhere. I knew that there was no 'mileage' in thoughts like these, and anyway there were photographs to be taken. Taking them, of course, increased the danger because I had to rise to a hundred feet and get the angles on the wing right. There was nothing for it but to get on with it, so I found the locations and took all the pictures. Feeling a little more settled, I got to the end of the recce and was amazed to find that I had been about an hour in the air. Again I felt the rising panic thinking of how far I was into enemy territory. I set off on the return journey, and finding some sampans drawn up on the bank, I took my spleen out on them and then wondered if it would be the Japs or the natives who would suffer. Keeping very close to the ground I did my return recce, again seeing little movement except in the villages where the natives looked up before scuttling away into their houses.

Whilst I was doing my recce the time passed quite quickly, and suddenly I realised I was over friendly territory. The relief was immense and I began to enjoy the trip over the mountains, slipping into the Imphal valley and proceeding home with a high heart. I called up the control tower and got permission to land. Before I did so however, I had to engage in a little bravado, so I 'beat up' the camp, pulled up into the circuit, wheels down and made a good landing. I taxied back into the dispersal, noting that I had been over two hours in the air, and when I took off my flying helmet I found it drenched in sweat. Jumping down from the Hurricane, my knees almost gave way and I began to realise how much nervous energy I had expended. But I had done it. Perhaps I hadn't seen anything of him but I had faced the foe and had survived. My nerves couldn't settle completely however as we waited until the photographer brought the prints.

As the Admiral and I looked at them and discovered that they were what was wanted, he said, 'I'll take these over to the Divisional ops room. They'll be pleased to get them. God knows why.'

'Ours not to reason why,' I said before accompanying Boris back to the mess.

CHAPTER TEN

Hurricane:
Low level Reconnaisance

In the following month I did about a dozen similar operations, interspersed with long sorties to the East where our aim was to contact the men of the Wingate expedition. Much has been written about General Orde Wingate, not all of it complimentary, some of it unkind. The fact remains however that this man was of such a powerful personality that he was able to persuade some two thousand men that they could take on the Japanese at their own game. When one considers that at that time there was an aura of invincibility about the Japs; that they could survive in conditions which were beyond a western soldier's capability, and that no mercy could be expected from them, one begins to understand the miraculous nature of Wingate's achievements.

He infiltrated his column into Japanese held territory and of course the column had to be supplied from the air, and the transport aircraft had to know where to drop. It was our job to find the column. All would be well if it suited Wingate to reveal himself. Naturally this depended on circumstances of which we knew nothing. What we *did* know however, was that we had to fly a very long way from base and, at ground level, some three hundred miles into enemy territory. A certain loneliness descended, but there was a feeling of great elation when the coloured ground markers were found and one was able to take down an accurate map reference. Too often, however, Wingate and his men were as elusive as the Japanese. That of course was the secret of their success, but as I turned for home and knew that there was a comfortable charpoy and a drink awaiting, I was filled with the greatest admiration for the two thousand brave men who were the first to show that the Japanese soldier was not a superman. While we often swore at their invisibility, there was no pilot on 28 Squadron who did not take off his hat to Wingate and his men.

During this spell of operations we became more and more

attached to our Hurricanes, so ordinary looking compared with the sleek and beautiful Spitfire, but so dependable and so well-suited to our operations. There were, of course, bad moments such as the day when, at the very extremity of my mission, over the railhead at Wuntho and some two hundred miles behind enemy lines, I found that the oil pressure gauge was registering zero. I knew enough about aero engines to know that if the gauge was correct, I had about a minute's flying time left. It was a long minute before being fairly certain that it was a faulty gauge. When I returned to Imphal I was still in a highly nervous state, ready to tell anyone who would listen about my awful experience. No one was interested, however, for news had come through that we were to be withdrawn from Imphal and would be returning to Ranchi.

Ours not to reason why, but rumour had it that we were to be deployed on the Arakan front. For once the rumours proved correct and a fortnight later 'B' Flight with Flight Lieutenant Larsen at its head flew off on the long haul to Chittagong. After refuelling at Calcutta I had my first view of the Bay of Bengal with its myriad of islands in the delta of the great rivers. It was not productive to wonder what your chances were should the Merlin engine fail. On this occasion none of them did and we landed in good order at Chittagong where we were given orders to fly to a mud strip at a place with the code name Lyons. When we got there the strip appeared mighty short but after Henry, the flight commander, had tested it and had landed safely we all took our turn, and bumpy though the landings were, we all got down without mishap. We were relieved to have completed the long haul from Ranchi and soon found the tents in which we were to live. The advance party which had been there for a few days included some followers who helped us to put up our camp beds, and some 'bully' and biscuits were produced for supper. We were back in business and when the ground crews arrived the next day we were ready for operations.

It was obvious that our operations on the Arakan were going to be much different from those we had been carrying out at Imphal. We had got rid of our long range tanks. We were much nearer the fighting and the situation on the Arakan was much more fluid than that on the Northern front. Broadly our task was to be the eyes of General Lomax, the commander of the 15th Division. I am glad to say that 'B' Flight and the said General were to become very good friends.

As a Flight we were actually based on two strips. The HQ and most of the ground crews were at Lyons, but each morning the operational aircraft flew down to a strip code named Sybil where they were refuelled, ready for longer sorties down into the Arakan. Most of the enemy contact was along the Maungdaw to Buthindaung road, on either side of the Naf River and the Mayu mountain range. While the Japs were still practically invisible there was more movement, and every now and then we could have a shot at them. It was not long before we realised that things were not going very well for our ground troops. A week after starting our operations, on a morning sortie, Ian Gibson and I found Maungdaw village in flames and knew our troops had had to abandon it. We now flew in pairs, the leader doing the recce while his number two kept a weather eye open for enemy fighters and other unfriendly gestures, of which there was an increasing number. Aircraft were returning damaged by ground fire – the Japs realising that our recces were to their disadvantage put their inventiveness to bear on the problem. One day I was horrified to see ahead of me a few little parachutes floating down in my flight path. Pulling smartly up and over them, I was appalled to see that they had grenade-like objects attached to them. Hit one of them – pull the string – goodbye, for your wing would be blown off. Other pilots reported hawsers being strung across rivers and chaungs to catch the unsuspecting low flyer. As we lost a number of pilots in inexplicable circumstances, it must be assumed that some of these lethal weapons worked on occasion. On the other hand, such was the strength of the Hurricane that once, when a pilot hit one of the hawsers, while the wire cut into the wing to the depth of about a foot, the aircraft returned safely. The pilot was shaken but the hawser had snapped.

We had our little successes too. On 17th May, Sergeant Pilot Baker and I were doing a twilight sortie on the Maungdaw to Buthidaung road. This road ran under the Mayu range through a series of tunnels, and it was obvious that the Japs, who now controlled the road, kept their transport and troops hidden in the tunnels during the day and moved them at night. It was hoped that the twilight sortie might catch an impatient Jap. We popped over into the Buthidaung valley at Bawli Bazaar and keeping close to the ground, made our way down to Buthidaung. Up the road we came towards the tunnels, rising with the ground, and as we swung past the tunnel mouth I thought I saw the nose of a truck inside the entrance. I called up Dickie, told him, and suggested that when we completed the recce, it might be worth another look. Night was beginning to fall when we came back over the mountains, hoping that the Japanese had concluded that the danger was past. Sure enough, there was a truck moving off with another on its tail. Needless to say the Japs were not pleased to see us and began firing with everything at hand. I came down the mountain side with the eight Brownings spitting, but I couldn't get a steep enough angle and I pulled away disappointed at seeing the bullets overshooting the vehicles. Dickie Baker, however, had been further out to the left and when he came in to strafe, he got the angle needed. As I turned to come in for a second run I could see the tracer bullets from Dickie's guns clip the side of the leading lorry, now reversing back into the tunnel. Suddenly there was an almighty flash which lit up the whole valley. Explosion followed explosion. Dickie came on the radio in a high state of excitement. 'We got the bastards – bloody hell, Mac, look at that!' He went on in this vein while we 'mopped up' the Japs who were running around the tunnel mouth trying to escape the flames. With adrenalin pumping we returned to base, well pleased with ourselves.

The enemy got something of their own back the next time Dickie and I flew together. It was another sortie in the same area but over Buthidaung Dickie reported that he had been hit by ground fire and that the cockpit was full of petrol fumes. I immediately ordered a return to base. When we had cleared the Jap positions I asked Dickie how things were, and suggested that if he was afraid the machine would go on fire he should either crash land close to some of our ground positions, or bale out. He replied that the smell of petrol was very strong but that everything seemed to be functioning. We flew on but I got no answer from Dickie to my subsequent calls, so I called base and asked for emergency landing procedures to be put into force. The strip was cleared and I called Dickie to say that we would land without doing a circuit. No reply. I told him to put his wheels down – he did that and I assumed that his transmitter had packed in. I flew up beside him and told him to put his flaps down and to throttle back – he did all that. He went in and landed, but as I was coming in behind him I expected him to taxi off the runway. He didn't do anything, but sat in the middle of the strip, so I did a quick overshoot. When Dickie did not taxi off the runway, the ground crews immediately ran to see if he had been hurt. They found him completely unconscious, anaesthetised by the spirit fumes. How long he had been flying in this state we could never establish for he could remember nothing of my instructions.

Near the end of May I was told to lead the Flight on a strike against a Japanese column which had been reported in the Kaladan valley. If we found them we were to take them out. Our secondary target was Buthidaung village. To our dis-appointment we did not find the column, and so we proceeded to Buthidaung. We gave it a good going over without seeing any evidence of anyone. Later reports however, from the V-Force (Burmese agents) in the area told of the killing of some twenty Japs and the wounding of many others.

Day followed violent day. Something of a stalemate developed as the Monsoon came racketing in to drive us off the mud strips. We moved to Cox's Bazaar where a Summerfeldt track strip had been laid out on the sand. This track, which was little more than heavy wire mesh stitched together with metal rods, gave a surface on which we could operate in all weathers. It had its own dangers, however, as the metal rods could become buckled and spring up out of the mesh, ready to catch the unwary. Sad to say we lost one of our best pilots, Sergeant Gray, a most popular Australian, when he overturned on hitting one such obstacle. Aussie's death affected us all – other pilots had been lost, but it had always been a case of going out and not returning. Here now we had Aussie, still with us and dead. The medical orderlies sewed him into his blanket and we all proceeded, with an army chaplain borrowed for the occasion, to a little hillock above Cox's Bazaar. There on a still morning, in a most peaceful place overlooking the Bay of Bengal shimmering in the sunlight, we laid him to rest and thought of his parents. No one said very much as we made our way back to the airfield – even George Kew, my most talkative rigger, was lost for words. 'Bloody hell, Mac' was the sum of his conversation for the rest of the day.

All these happenings, of course, helped to bind the Flight into a tightly knit unit where everyone worked together for the common good. We had hilarious bathing sessions on the beach at the end of the day's operations, with splendid football and rugby matches on the sand. Being separated from Squadron HQ we felt ourselves to be very special, and the kind remarks of the army commander regarding our role in the campaign helped greatly in the building of morale.

When the monsoon passed, operations became more hectic and also more dangerous as the Japanese gunners on the ground were getting better. In August, September and October most of the pilots were on operations at least every second day. Life was becoming a bit earnest as more pilots failed to return and more aircraft returned damaged. It was not the Japanese who ended my first Arakan tour, but the dreaded malaria. On 3rd November I was carted off, semi-conscious, to the 72 IGH. My ambulance was a sampan and I arrived in the hospital with a temperature of 105. I was not so far gone that I could not appreciate the real bed into which I was put, and after being given a draught of quinine I fell asleep. When I awoke I felt such a new man that I immediately tried to get out of bed. Only the quick action of a nurse saved me from crashing to the floor. Everything about me was soaked in sweat but the quinine had done its stuff – my temperature was down. I was not ready, however, to do anything but lie there and appreciate the clean sheets.

By the time I had recovered, 'B' Flight had been withdrawn from the Arakan and had been replaced by the first Squadron of the Royal Indian Air Force. The army was sorry to see us go but when I came back from sick leave in Darjeeling it was to rejoin the Squadron in Imphal. Once again the Squadron was to operate as one unit. Henry Larsen was the Squadron Commander and with a year's operations behind us we felt ready for the New Year of 1944. Hungover I might have been but, on the first day of the year I was back in the Hurricane and sliding down the Yu river hoping to 'first foot' a few Japs.

It was while we were at Cox's Bazaar that the dread news came that Archie had been killed. It came in a letter from my father. The coming of mail was an occasion for rejoicing especially in the forward area. Everyone excitedly tore open the precious letters. I was no different. But there was the first sentence, 'dear Archie has been killed in action in Sicily'.

I took myself off, finding it impossible to share this news with anyone. I lay on my charpoy and thought of the great grief which my parents would be feeling. They would be wondering why they should lose 'the brightest and best.' For there was no doubt that Archie was an extraordinary personality. While the rest of us might do our duty and get by, Archie would be going a second mile for someone. From Alamein to Gerbini, he had never been in action but he had been wounded. At Gerbini he was wounded again and could not recover. It was the first break in the family and it was hard to bear. Realising that something was wrong my friends came one by one and expressed their feelings in different ways. They were kind and their support was invaluable, but I was to find then, as on so many occasions, that work is the greatest therapy. The war went on and there was work to be done. Archie would never be forgotten by his nearest and dearest or indeed by anyone who had known him. He left behind the beloved Mima who became a bright star in her own right and was to prove the greatest support to us all. I cannot tell the number of times during my life that I have been approached by total strangers who have asked me if I was Archie's brother. Their comments were always the same: 'there never was anyone like Archie!'

Over fifty years after his death, Isobel and I were able to visit his grave in the War Cemetery at Catania. We brought heather from the garden to place on it. He lies there with three thousand of his comrades including Bobby Hutchison from Bolfracks, the brother of one of my senior elders. Remember-ing all the happy days at Southend, the fun and the laughter and the brightness which seemed always to surround Archie, we wept the tears we could not shed when he was killed.

I was to get to know parts of the Yu river quite well in the next few days. While the army liaison officer tried to keep us in the general picture, it was never policy to let us into any secrets regarding the plans of the High Command. This used to annoy us somewhat, for we felt that we would be much more useful to the army if we knew exactly what the situation on the ground really was, or was likely to be. On reflection of course, it made very good sense that we should not know too much. Each one of us was in danger of being taken prisoner, and as everyone knew, the Japs had ways to make people talk. So I recced the Yu river once or twice, took some photographs of a section of it from various heights and obliquely. I wondered what it was all about. On 13th January I was asked to form up before the General who was flanked by his Chief of Staff and Intelligence Officer. The photographs I had taken were behind them on a map board.

'Good pictures, Flying Officer,' said the General rather stiffly.

Modestly I murmured thanks and knew that there was more to come. The Chief of Staff then explained that there was a heavy concentration of the enemy dug in on the bank of the river Yu. It had been decided to try to dislodge them by an 'earthquake' air strike by Bomber Command. However, as our own troops were also dug in by the Yu river some four hundred yards away, the greatest accuracy was essential. He went on to explain that the bombing would be carried out by the American Air Corps in daylight, and concluded, 'to be quite sure, we want you to fly with the mission.' And so it was that I flew down to Pandaveswar where the B24 Liberators were based. For five days I enjoyed the comforts and hospitality of the American set up, and could scarcely believe the difference between their lot on an established base, and our lot on a forward strip. For their part they could hardly believe that anyone would risk life and limb in the oil-stained and patched little Hurricane which sat rather pertly at the dispersal point alongside the big bombers.

I think the crewmen of the bombers thought that they could have done the job perfectly well without me. Three Squadrons were taking part in the raid. Eventually we arrived over the target at the third time of asking and from 10,000 feet delivered the bombs on the Japs. Lying in the bomb bay with the leading bomb aimer and looking down on the country below was a strange feeling for one used to being much closer to Mother Earth. The bombs hit the target area and I felt quite satisfied that in one operation at least I had been in on it from its inception to its conclusion. After six and three quarter hours in the air we landed, stiff and sore. One more night of luxury and I climbed back into my little Hurricane. The Americans saw me off with much shaking of the head, however, two and a half hours later the object of their derision delivered me safely to Imphal.

The rest of the month passed with a series of operations and alarms and it was evident that the ground operations were not going as well as we would have wished. On the northern front where we were operating, there seemed to be something of a stand-off as there was little movement anywhere. On the Arakan the enemy had made a move and were pushing up the peninsula. It was at this point that General Messervy with the 7th Division was overrun by the advancing Japanese, and so began what was to become known as the Battle of the Admin Box. The 1st Royal Indian Air Force Squadron which had replaced us in the Arakan, had taken severe losses due to the increased activity of the Japanese Air Force, and it was decided that it should be reinforced by six aircraft of 28 Squadron. I was ordered to lead this contingent back to the Arakan. It was all very exciting, for by now everyone knew that a vital stage had been reached there. If the Commonwealth troops were routed again on the Arakan there would be little to halt the Japanese from pouring into Bengal via Chittagong. Everything was very tense as we swept down from Imphal to throw our little weight in the balance. With great bravado we had provided ourselves with the packets and streamers used for message dropping, and as we passed over those units in the Arakan which we had known well from our last visit, we dropped the messages with the arrogant claim: 'All is well, 28 Squadron is back.'

I'm sorry to say the Squadron Leader of the Indian Air Force Squadron was not so pleased to see us, as he took it as a personal affront that we should be required. We operated independently during the fateful week and during our reconnaissances of the forward areas it was horrendous to see the conditions within the Admin Box where the division was being squeezed on all sides by the rampant enemy. For the first time the forward troops were being supplied by the Air Force Transport Command and we were all filled with admiration for the Dakota pilots operating at low level in hilly country under constant enemy fire. My own best moment of this short campaign came on the 12th February. I had just returned from a sortie along the main Japanese supply route between the Kaladan and Kalapanzin valleys, when the Air Commodore rang from Chittagong to say that there had been an urgent request from the Admin Box for some of the new sulphono-mide drugs to treat wounded who would certainly die without them. The Dakotas could not guarantee an accurate drop on the Field Dressing station where it was required. Could we do it? There was only one answer to that and I undertook the mission myself. The drug arrived in a small package some hours later and we wrapped it in the streamered envelope. Circling over the Admin Box I eventually located the red-cross marker at the entrance to the foxhole dug into the mountain side. Either an MO or an orderly, realising that we were the bearers of the necessary medicine, waved encouragingly, but it was difficult terrain and it was not easy to get as low as I might wish. After a dummy run or two however, I decided that I could get pretty close, so I made a steep turn in, opened the cockpit hood, came in as low as I dared and threw the precious drugs out. It was a miracle. They landed within feet of the red-cross sign, and coming round again, I was more than recom-pensed for the effort when the waiting figure held up the coloured streamers in triumph.

By the end of that week the situation in the Arakan had been stabilised. The army had refused to yield this time and the Japanese had been made to pay a terrible price. Their Air Force had been virtually destroyed by the Spitfires of Fighter Command. That particular excitement was over for us and we returned to Imphal unscathed showing how clever and how brave we had become by landing in formations of two on the narrow Imphal strip. I was brought back to earth when Henry, the Squadron Commander tore me off a strip for risking aircraft in such a stupid display of bravado. Later in the day however, a signal was received from Group Headquarters congratulating the detachment on their contribution. Henry accepted such commendation as a feather in his own cap and was comforted enough to forgive and forget.

As February came to a close and March came in, our reconnaissance was beginning to show that the Japanese were planning something big. With terrible rapidity the Japanese advance seemed to take everybody by surprise. They were pouring up the Manipur valley from Tiddim and along the famous chocolate staircase came our 17th Division in retreat. Out of the Kabaw valley they came, over the hills into the Imphal valley. My old friend Palel was soon in enemy hands. Worse from our point of view, we began recceing to the north into territory which had always been looked upon as friendly. Across the Somra Hills the Japs came, striking at Kohima and the only road into Imphal, closer and closer each day. Our patrols became shorter and shorter. The evacuation of non-essential personnel began and the Headquarters of our own Squadron and 'A' Flight were pulled out to Jorhat where they could cover the operations in the Kohima area. There we were, the gallant 'B' Flight, left behind to carry the banner. Everybody was very jumpy and as each sortie brought back news of further Japanese advances, everyone wondered if they could be halted.

It was certainly exciting. Imphal became the landing ground for all supplies coming in, as everything had to come by air. Why they bothered bringing the soya link sausage no one could tell. Dropping them on the Japanese might have been more effective! It was a great boost to morale when the airlift began and the 5th Division was flown in to our strip from the Arakan. Everyone felt then that there would be one helluva fight before Imphal was surrendered.

There were of course difficult times, such as the afternoon I was discussing plans with Admiral Matthews. We'd had some of our own guns set up beside the airfield and we were getting used to them firing off at the enemy. On this occasion however, after the Admiral and I had ducked at the explosion, the Admiral said, 'You know you would almost think these shells were coming rather than

The Beloved Parents

Where it all began – St Blaan's Manse at the Southend of Kintyre

Three of the Best – Briefing Session for Pilots of 28 Squadron: Robert Farquharson,
Earl Ross and Ralph Hunter

IN MEMORIAM ('Farquy' – missing over Burma 1945)

You were too young to die. I can recall
When first I saw your smooth-skinned face, and eyes
As innocent as new-born babes, I said:
'Another child for Martian sacrifice.'

But you were man enough, when in the sky
You plumbed the depths of fear with those of us
Who, older, hid our terror from the world,
And helpless, watched the deathly exodus.

You were too innocent to share this sham
Of empty bravery. – Your quivering smile
Showed what you felt, and in our hearts we prayed
The fates to bring you back. – They did awhile.

But now you're gone. You are the youth of heaven,
Bright spirit of the dawn, so fresh and true.
We will throw off the worldliness of years,
When we look back and we remember you.

C.O., Pilots and Ground Crew of 'B' Flight celebrate the award
of the D.F.C. to their Flight Commander

Cast of pantomime performed by Kenmore Church Youth Club – late 1950s

Members of Youth Club and school children as extras in Pageant to mark
400th Anniversary of Kenmore Church – 1979

Kirk Sessions with Beadle at 400th Anniversary – 1979

Kirk Session of Kenmore with Organist at the time of the Minister's Retiral

The Great Day, 4th September, 1946

Kenneth and Cameron accompany their parents
to Buckingham Palace
when father receives the M.B.E.

Jean graduates at St Andrews

Presentation to Lady Douglas Home by
little Jean after the Prime Minister's wife
had opened the women's guild sale of work.

Angus joins the Merchant Navy as a Cadet

On day of retirement after 40 happy years at Kenmore Manse

The whole clan at our Golden Wedding celebrations

The Four Lovelies
Fiona – Susan – Aileen – Emma

going'. With that there was another earth moving bang. We flung ourselves to the floor and agreed that indeed the shells were coming in. After the initial shock I went outside to find out what was going on. Sure enough, the Japs had got close enough to lob shells to within a short distance of our runway. To protect the aircraft I ordered pilots to take off for a mud strip a few miles west of Imphal. They all got off safely and we breathed a sigh of relief. I was aware, though, of an uneasiness among the ground crews and I tackled my own rigger, George Kew.

'What's the matter?' I asked him.

'Well you see' he said a bit shamefacedly, 'the pilots can take off and get out of here when the Japs come, but what will happen to us?'

'You poor souls will be left with me,' I said, sounding a good deal braver than I felt.

'And you'll not be going?' he questioned.

'Don't be daft!' I said, and George went off to spread the news which seemed to give them all some reassurance.

The Japanese did get very close but we had a grandstand view of the courage and stamina shown by the forces on the ground, around the valley and especially at Kohima. Too many gave their tomorrows for our todays.

We had our own little battles. Some twenty miles north east of Imphal was a strategic place called Ukhrul and each day one or more sorties were despatched to find out what was happening there. There was a machine gunner on a hillside who seemed to take a personal dislike to me, and every time I was anywhere near he would start blasting off with his heavy machine gun. It was a challenge which could not be passed over. My number two and I would give him a going over before returning to base but next day he would be at it again, pumping the lead. For days this went on, but one day we went back and there was no sign of him.

One of our most exciting trips was quite unscheduled. The Flight had been 'stood down' for the day and many of us were having a wash in a makeshift shower that had been rigged up behind the mess. Suddenly there was a commotion and the Admiral appeared, to tell me that the army had had intelligence that the Japs were moving on Imphal at Pukhao. All available aircraft were to be scrambled to strafe the area where they were. Throwing on shorts and shirts we all piled into jeeps, collecting ground crews as we went. On the way down to the strip the Admiral gave me the map he had marked with all the information available. The others were simply told to follow me. With skeleton ground crews to see us off, I was in the air before I realised that the Pitot head cover was still on and that I had no indication of speed. Normally I would have aborted the sortie but I was the only pilot in the air knowing exactly where we were going. We pressed on and emptied our cannons into the Pukhao valley. We were certain that we had got the right place and were aware of a good deal of movement on the ground. Back we came, satisfied that we had done what we could. Landing without an air speed indicator is not funny, however, keeping plenty engine on, I got down safely. When the rest of the flight saw the streamers from the Pitot head cover rippling under my wing, they thought it the funniest thing they had ever seen. Reports from intelligence next morning spoke of 213 Japanese killed. The advance on Imphal in that quarter had been halted.

So the war raged around us day after day, with the Flight involved every day. In March I flew fifteen sorties, 25 in April, 21 in May. Others I am sure flew even more. It was very hectic and, with the loss of fellow pilots, too often very sad. By the time June had arrived, it was obvious that the Japanese had been fought to a standstill and were about to get their comeuppance. On 11th June I did my final recce of that campaign which was to take photographs of Ukhrul. They showed that the Japs had left.

The following day we left Imphal. It had been a scary and difficult six months, but the Flight had held together in a most remarkable way. The ground crews had been magnificent, keeping obsolescent aircraft flying long past what would become known as their 'sell by' date. In spite of all, everyone had kept their sense of humour and there was a tremendous spirit among all ranks. All of my fellow pilots had proved themselves to be quite outstanding individuals, showing great courage and tremendous resilience. During the siege I had received word that I had been decorated with the Distinguished Flying Cross. While I looked upon it as a great honour, I was in no doubt that it was given to the Flight which had the privilege of being among those who had borne the heat of the day in the valley of Imphal, and had played its part in the crucial action of the war in South East Asia.

And so we came back to join the Squadron at Jorhat prior to being taken out to rest in India.

CHAPTER ELEVEN

Action, Disaster, Evasion

I would have stayed at Jorhat for a few days but my fellow pilots were set on making early acquaintance with the fleshpots of Calcutta. Against my better judgement, and in spite of a very hairy weather forecast, I was persuaded to lead them down the Bramahputra river instead of going directly over the mountains. We calculated that we would make Alipore with some fuel to spare but the weather was so poor and the cloud ceiling so low that we had to fly at a lower altitude than we would have liked. This resulted in an increase in fuel consumption and by the time we started across the 'bund' from the confluence of the Ganges, I was getting a little jumpy. The weather got thicker, so we had to fly at about two hundred feet. The fuel gauge was hitting the zero with no Alipore in sight. I felt that my navigation had been good enough and that we must be very close to our destination, so putting the formation into line astern, I made a wide sweep. There below my wing was Alipore airfield and without more ado I led them in. We landed safely and I think it was the sighs of relief from eight young men which gave us the power to taxi to the dispersal point.

There is no need to elaborate on the next few days. Meeting up with Nicholson VC didn't make for a quiet life. Having got our wind out, however, we departed with our aircraft to a place with the unlikely name of Dalbumgarh, where we met up with the ground crews. We were on rest and with many going on leave to the hills, life was fairly quiet.

We kept our hand in with air tests and the odd cross country flight, but if truth be told, those of us who had been on 'ops' thought the whole thing a waste of time. Henry was sent back to Britain on a course, and for a brief spell I was in charge of the Squadron. We moved up to our old stamping ground at Ranchi. Replacement pilots came and some of the 'old and bold' left us for pastures new. I took another attack of malaria and spent a couple of weeks at the hospital in Ranchi. On discharge I found the Squadron preparing to move back to the front line. We hoped that

91

the new boys were ready for the fray, and the old sweats pretended that they were glad to be going back into action.

By December we were ready to go and many were the rumours regarding our future deployment. Some of us went down to the Bazaar at Ranchi to find out from the traders there where and when we were likely to go. They were frighteningly accurate sometimes with their information. At last the order came and for the first time the Squadron was to be moved entirely by air. On the 8th December the aircraft with the advance party and their equipment took off for Tamu in Burma. The next day the Squadron aircraft took off from Ranchi for the final operational tour. We all landed safely on the mud strip at Tamu and, by late afternoon, the Dakotas had brought in the rest of the personnel and equipment. By next morning 28 Squadron was back in business.

We were all glad to be back at the sharp end. We had needed a rest but the final weeks at Ranchi had been something of a drag. Now there was work to be done. Everyone moaned about the lack of facilities but it was good natured moaning. We all took off at various times to recce our new sector. For many of the pilots of course, it was all new, for some of us it was merely a revision of what we had known. On the 11th I did my first serious recce in the area of Pyingyain and Kanni. The former was very naturally pronounced Pink gin by everyone. The Japs of course were now in retreat. It was good to see our army on the ground pounding after them with so much confidence. For so long there had been the awful feeling that the Japanese were in some way invincible in the jungle hills. The Imphal campaign had shown that this was not the case. The Allied troops had taken them on and had defeated them. They were of course still a very dangerous enemy, made even more vicious by the fact that they were in retreat. Now that they were being pushed down towards the Schebo Plain we looked forward to seeing more of them in the open country. However, we were still searching for the small clues as to their movements; the dust on the leaves by the roadside; the movement of cattle from the villages. From the reaction of the Burmese we could tell whether the Japanese army were still in the vicinity.

Earl Ross was now the 2i/c of 'B' Flight, and he and I had a very good relationship. He was a brilliant pilot, thought little of my abilities in the air and was the greatest comrade. With drink taken, he was ready to fight with his shadow, but would never resist my correction. As the early days passed we were beginning to find out more about the pilots who had been posted to the Squadron while out on rest. They were a mixed bunch, some so young looking that at our age of 23, some of us were thinking that they were too young! One of these was the first Scotsman to join me and Henry now chortled over two MacPorridges. Young Farquharson was a 'character' in no time. He looked about sixteen, found his older colleagues a constant amusement, and smiled his way into everybody's heart. He was a good pilot too, and soon settled down to the operational flying although, it has to be said, Ross and I tried to break him in gently.

Another of the new intake was something quite different, an older man who had done a tour as an instructor. Some of us felt a little in awe of his flying abilities but in the first week of operations I began to get reports that he was finding it difficult to adjust to our type of flying. Ross and I had a conference and it was agreed that Ross would take the chap as his number two on the following day.

Ross was a very cheerful individual and nothing seemed to upset him. It was all the more remarkable therefore when on returning from his flight he stormed into my office, flung his parachute to the ground, and announced with great feeling, 'Right, Mac, if you want to kill your bloody self, you fly with B. . . . . . . – just don't ask me to fly with him again!' He was obviously serious, and he catalogued the poor chap's failings. We agreed that before reporting the matter to the CO, I should fly with him. It was the 21st December and I was down to fly the next day but my aircraft had been giving me some trouble. Down at the dispersal the ground crews were working on it. While awaiting their report I agreed with George Kew that I would come to his Christmas Eve party. About four o'clock Hurricane 2C 299 was ready for testing, so I took her off into the clear evening air and enjoyed myself throwing her around the sky. She seemed fine. I did what I thought was a very low pass down the airstrip before landing, where Ross was waiting for me. 'Were you using oxygen?' he asked, and gave his dark brown chuckle. 299 was refuelled and prepared for the morning.

B. . . . . . . and I had our briefing from the Army Liaison Officer, during which, it seemed to me, my number two was less than attentive. Now it has to be said that during briefing sessions, I was never the soul of patience. 'For God's sake pay attention,' I snapped at the man. The strain on his face worried me. With the briefing over and the maps marked and prepared, we were ready for the trip down to a place called Yeu, a town north of Schebo. It was a simple enough task to recce the road, the only road which ran down the centre of the country. It was also recognised as reasonably dangerous as it was well-known that the Japanese retreat would be following the line of the road. We were to look out for signs of troop concentrations and could expect plenty opposition from small-arms fire.

We took the jeep down to the dispersal to be met with the usual banter from the ground crews. Sergeant Iles our chief fitter tried to keep matters on a rational level – he was a man who took life seriously and thought that most of the pilots and the ground crews in his care were bordering on the insane. He might well have had a point! Having both signed the 700s, B. . . . . . . and I made our way to our planes. George Kew helped me to get strapped in.

'You're not forgetting the party in our dufter on Christmas Eve?' he questioned.

'Not likely' I replied. He jumped off the wing, having patted me on the top of my head in his usual fashion.

'Contact' we shouted, and wound up the old Merlin. It sprang into life and George removed the battery connection. I looked across at B. . . . . . . and he too had got started.

'Chocks away', and with thumbs up to those seeing us off I taxied out of the dispersal with B. . . . . . . coming behind.

Up the taxiing track, getting settled into the harness, checking everything in the cockpit and seeing that all the dials were working, we paused at the runway and revved up the engines, checking that both magnetos were operating. Nothing to keep us now! Clear for take off and with a final thumbs up to B. . . . . . . I opened the throttle and took off. While fear was always sitting on my shoulder it was at this point that training and experience took over and I just got on with the job. The sooner it was over the better, so I didn't bother making any circuit of the airfield but called up B. . . . . . . telling him to get weaving a little above, behind, and to my left. I settled down close to the tree tops and followed my flight plan towards the Kalewa to Yeu road. Before we got there, B. . . . . . . was already giving trouble. 'Regal Blue One, I have lost you'. I would rise some hundred feet and he would come back on: 'See you now.' This was fine as long as we were over friendly territory but I had no intention of rising any higher than was required once we began the recce.

'Regal Blue Two – keep your eyes open!'

We hit the road right on the nose and immediately began

searching for signs of the Japanese army. Thick dust on the roadside leaves indicated troop movements during the night.

'Regal Blue One, I've lost you' came the plaintive cry again.

'Regal Blue Two - just follow the road, I can see you'.

I was annoyed that my concentration was being broken and I was also aware that I was on my own as far as warning of ground fire, never mind any aerial interference, was concerned. However all was going well with the recce. I zigzagged back and forth, over the road, picking up scraps of information. Suddenly I swept over Yeu itself. No one was more surprised than a little son of Nippon who had been relieving himself. He made a dash for cover as he pulled up his trousers. He didn't make it to his slit trench.

'Regal Blue Two, I'm strafing Yeu, join me.'

'Regal Blue One, I've lost you.'

By this time B. . . . . . .'s fate was sealed. He was not fit to fly with us and I would be recommending his instant posting when I returned to base. I took some of my anger out on Yeu, emptying some half of my ammunition into it, before beginning to recce the road again on the way home. I actually 'picked up' B. . . . . . who seemed to be going round in circles. I gave him my position and told him to follow me up the road. There was, however, a machine gunner waiting for our return and I was suddenly aware of tracer bullets flashing around me. In a way this was splendid, for it gave me an indication of a Japanese position. I noted it on my knee pad and proceeded to give as good as I was getting. He must have been a brave boy for while I was giving him the benefit of four twenty millimetre cannons, the tracer still kept coming at me. The really dangerous time was not coming into the target but exiting from it. The secret was to exit low, with plenty of rudder, so that the gunner could not get a straight shot at you.

I did all the right things and it was not the machine gunner that brought about my downfall, but a single tree somewhat higher than its neighbours. I saw it before I hit it head on and pulled the Hurricane into a steep climb. 299 almost made it. I slid over the top of the tree, but like the mouse in the story of the farmer's wife, while I didn't leave my tail behind me, I did leave the radiator. As can be imagined, an aeroplane does not fly long without a coolant system. I knew that I had less than three minutes before the whole thing went on fire. I called B. . . . . . and gave him my position and his course for home. His last call to me was one of near panic.

95

I was not as cool as a cucumber myself. The engine temperature was going off the clock. I had three options. The first was to keep going until the plane caught fire, secondly I could try to climb to a height from which I could bale out, and thirdly I could try to crash land while I had engine power to give me some control of events. I knew that there was no mileage in the first two options and immediately started looking for a likely place to put her down. There was nothing inviting. There were open spaces but they were filled with paddy fields which had earthen 'bunds' or walls enclosing them. None of them was big enough to take a Hurricane even with the wheels up, but there was nothing else for it. I picked my spot and flew her on to the ground at the extremity of one paddy field and switched everything off. We went careering towards the first bund and I knew that what happened there would be critical. If the bund stopped the plane dead, or turned it over, that would be that. We hit the bund and, momentarily, the Hurricane took off again, before falling back to the ground and, in a cloud of dust, juddering to a halt.

I could hardly believe that I was safely down. I got out quickly, and finding that nothing was broken, ran away from the aircraft fearing it would burst into flames. I found a thicket in which I hid and watched for the fire to start. It didn't, and into my mind came the voice of the instructor: 'It is the duty of the pilot to destroy his aircraft to avoid any of it falling into enemy hands'. To hell with that I thought, nevertheless I found myself walking back towards the plane, removing the explosive device from the side of the cockpit, hitting the nose of it on a stone and throwing it into the cockpit. I then returned to my thicket. Such is the power of training.

I started to feel very sorry for myself, hoping that I might awake from a bad dream. I thought of my parents receiving the message that I was missing. The 'why should this happen to me?' syndrome had taken hold of me when, suddenly, I was not alone. Into the thicket had come a wild-looking Burman. This development helped to calm me. I got out the phrase sheet and began the conversation.

'I am a British airman. I will give you money if you help to hide me from the Japanese.' He screeched with laughter, and I tried again.

'What is the name of your village?' More giggles. 'Will you take me to your headman?' This was the funniest thing of all. He went into hysterical laughter and ran off. I felt my flesh crawl for I realised that the poor man was mad. Here I was, a fugitive in a strange land surrounded by enemies, and the first contact I make is with a man who is insane. It was surely a bad omen. I felt I couldn't stay there any longer and began to make my way towards more wooded country, trying to keep a low profile as I went from one thicket to another. All of a sudden I stumbled on an old lady sitting in the shade of a bush and watching over some scrawny cattle below her. She was calmly smoking a green cheroot. She showed neither fear nor surprise when I came on her. I pointed to the remains of the Hurricane some half a mile away by now, and then to myself. She nodded. I got out the phrase sheet again, and this time I was able to make some progress. I was near to the village of Kinbin. There were quite a number of Japanese in the area. She couldn't help me but she gave me directions to the village. While we were talking our eyes seemed transfixed by the ruined Hurricane. Suddenly a stream of people came out from the woods and made their way towards the machine. There were villagers and there were also Japanese soldiers. The old lady turned to me and for the first time she had something of a light in her eye.

'Go!' she said.

I went.

I knew now that the Japanese would be looking for me. They would know that I would be within a certain radius of the plane and I felt that I had to get help so that I might be hidden. I made my way through some woods until I came to the outskirts of a village. From a hiding place I watched while the villagers worked in their fields. They were engaged in some kind of community project like making hay. I waited until one of them was close to my hiding place and then, much to his astonishment, I revealed myself, drew him into the woods and put the big question to him – would he find the headman and bring him to me, or alternatively would he ask the headman if they would hide me? Off he went and I waited. He came back to tell me that it was too risky for them. While the Japanese were not in their village, they were all around. I started off again in the general direction of the British lines and found a path which the villager had told me should be safe.

For a mile or so I crept along the path listening intently for any sound that might indicate other human activity. In the early afternoon the path led me into a dried up river bed and then on to a little hillock which gave me quite a good field of view. I heard the sound of aeroplanes and there, some miles away were two Hurricanes obviously looking for me. I felt that they were bound to have found my plane, for I had been close to my recce track when I put her down, and then I remembered that my escape kit contained a mirror which could be used for attracting searchers with flashes of reflected sunlight. By this time of course I had abandoned the parachute, but was carrying the box of escape equipment which we always sat on in the Hurricanes. So that the medicines and foodstuffs and cigarettes would keep indefinitely in the hot damp climate, this box was hermetically sealed. There was a pulling grip in one corner and when pulled, the lid was supposed to strip off. I pulled with all my might but the metal refused to budge. I got tearfully frustrated, but eventually lost patience, took my kukhri and, using it as a tin opener, smashed my way into the box. I located the mirror and started signalling but to no avail. Soon the searching Hurricanes disappeared and I felt utterly alone.

I wasn't alone for long. Suddenly, along the path I had followed, came three young Burmese. One of them I recognised as the man I had spoken to in the village. They told me that they had thought about what I had said and, if there was enough money in it, they would see me back to the British lines. I was not convinced, but encouraged them by showing them my belt with the hundred silver pieces. I also showed them my revolver, in case they had any ideas about taking the money belt from me. We then got down to details. The spokesman, who obviously had a good idea of the country, drew a rough map in the sand.

'Tonight – this village, tomorrow night – this one, third night – here, fourth night – British Army.'

'Bloody good' I said, beginning to feel much better.

Before we started, however, he did something which in the event was to save my life. Much to my astonishment he began digging down into the dried up river bed. About eighteen inches below the surface, water began to appear and soon he had a little pool from which we all drank. We then set out on the great escape.

In the master plan, the first obstacle would be the main road – the same main road which I had recced a few hours before. About three in the afternoon we came to it and two of my companions crossed nonchalantly without any response from any quarter, so I then crossed with my other guardian. Half an hour later we came to a track which obviously led to some habitation. By this time we were getting very confident, but then I spotted a boot mark in the mud which I brought to the attention of the Burmese. They were unimpressed. Fortunately however, I was put on my guard, for as we rounded a bend in the track we came in sight of the village, and marching away from us, a Japanese soldier. I took off at high speed and dived into a thicket, followed by my companions. The spokesman said, 'Wrong village!', which must have won some kind of prize for the understatement of the year. They then had a conference and concluded that the 'right' village was some mile and a half away. We set off through long elephant grass and eventually surfaced on the perimeter of another village. I was getting a bit cagey by this time and sent one of the Burmese in to find out whether the Japanese were about. He came back beaming to tell us that the coast was clear, and I was escorted to the headman's house.

I began negotiations but did not get much helpful response. I remembered the escape instructors voice: 'Always try to get on the right side of the children.' I dived into the escape kit and produced the barley sugar sweeties. The children of course had all gathered round and one by one they took the sweets and found them the greatest thing. They were all drooling at the mouth and looking for more. The whole exercise worked like a charm. The headman agreed to hide me for one night and then sent a young girl to fetch food. I sat on the steps of the verandah of his hut and suddenly felt completely exhausted. Surrounded by the eager children and the impassive looking grown-ups, I felt that I had come to a sanctuary and thought that I could sleep for a week.

It was not to be. The young girl who had been sent to fetch the food appeared and came into the square around which the village was built. Suddenly there was shouting and screaming. The girl with the plate of food was sent spinning into the dust by rushing soldiers. The Japanese had arrived. There was nothing I could do. With a great sense of foreboding and complete weariness, I got to my feet and put my hands up. The response of the soldiers was to get down on one knee from which position they started firing their rifles.

The accepted wisdom was that the Japanese were very good with their rifles at anything over two hundred yards, but at close quarters they could not hit the proverbial barn door. I cannot vouch for the truth of this, but I was certainly missed by quite a few at a range of some twenty yards. Not by much however, and it was not long before I took the decision that if I was to die I might as well die running. I got off my mark and made use of the maze of houses which constituted the village. It was a deadly game of hide and seek, punctuated by the shouts of the soldiers and the screams of the

99

villagers who were doubtless suffering for my unexpected visit. Eventually I got to the perimeter hedge which surrounded the village and, not being able to find any opening, I went headfirst through it and set off across an open bit of ground which would bring me to a thickly wooded area. The further I got from the village the more accurate became the shooting of the soldiers. Bullets were pinging around my ears and thudding into the ground about my feet as I zigzagged like a frightened rabbit. Eventually I got to the woods, but by this time the soldiers were close behind and I knew that I couldn't outrun them for long. Drawing on all my native wit I went to ground and crawled in a direction which took me back towards the village. By this time the daylight was beginning to fade. The shouting of the soldiers became less, and eventually it was clear that the search had been called off for the night. I lay in the gloaming in my hiding place, thinking that the age of miracles had not passed. Suddenly I was aware that there was someone coming towards my hideout. Someone grumbling to himself and crashing about in the undergrowth. Then he was above me. It was a Japanese NCO prodding the undergrowth with his bayonet. The blade entered the bush beside me and passed within inches of my face. Withdrawing it, he went stumbling and grumbling on his way. Darkness came and there was a blessed silence. I lay shivering with nerves and fright and in an hour or two a beautiful moon rose. In the moonlight I crawled out of my hideout and began to assess the situation. In the melee I had lost all my escape kit and now I had one revolver, one kukhri, one compass and a money belt. I found a dried up river bed and crossed over to the other side. I would have liked to have gone further but I was now utterly spent, so I found a place where I could hide in the long grass. I pulled some of the grass on top of me and fell into a deep sleep. When all was said and done it had been a tiring and a trying day.

I was awakened by the crowing of a cock, an indication that I was not far away from human habitation. I crawled out of my resting place and tried to think rationally. I was still alive and I was still uncaptured, but I had now been 24 hours without any real food and I felt that this was something which had to be remedied, But how? As I made my way along the bank of the dried up river, I saw two men working in a field. I approached them and asked them about food, but they did not want to have anything to do with me and I went on my way. About half an hour later I heard whistling behind me, and investigating, I discovered that it was the two I had spoken to and they were carrying plates of rice with some green stuff on top. I took a handful of the rice and was then conscious of further movement. The men with the food had not come alone. I flung the plate in their faces and took off into the thick woods. It was so thick that I felt if I went to ground and remained silent, they were unlikely to find me. I made a hiding place under a fallen tree and willed myself to stay quiet. While there I concluded that I had been foolish making contact with the natives – that my best hope was to steer clear of everybody.

Knowing the country well, as I did, I knew that my best bet was to go due north into the sparsely inhabited regions north of the main road. I knew that the Japanese were bound to be mostly around the routes to the south-east, down which they were retreating. What would I do about food and water? In the event, the pangs of hunger didn't disturb me too much, but water was a different matter. I knew that I needed a regular supply and later that day when I started on the move again, I was indebted to the man who, the day before, had shown me how water could be obtained in the dried up river beds.

My new plan worked well. For the remainder of that day and for the whole of the next I saw no sign of life at all. By this time however, I had little idea as to where I was. I had obviously got quite beyond the fighting zone. By the end of the third day, though, the lack of food was beginning to make itself felt. I wasn't able to make the same headway and the rest periods were becoming more frequent. I had tried marching by moonlight but, bright though it was, I discovered that even the brightest moonlight is not like the day. I stumbled over fallen branches and fell into holes which I had not seen and generally became demoralised. Strangely, I slept for a few hours every night and awoke refreshed.

It was now Christmas Eve. I was very sorry for myself. I thought of the Manse at Southend and the previous Christmases we had had together there. I wondered how George Kew's party was getting on. The record of Bing Crosby singing 'Silent Night' would be getting well worn. Perhaps it was thinking about this that gave me my first nightmares. The 'Silent Night' theme kept recurring and I awoke in the night and thought I heard voices. I couldn't get to sleep again and the dawn of Christmas Day brought me no encouragement.

I felt now that I had travelled so far to the north that I could start going in a westerly direction, eventually coming to a point behind the fighting. Not being too sure of my position, however, I settled for a north westerly course and early in the day got the first bit of encouragement. Some Dakotas passed overhead with their fighter escort and began dropping supplies some miles to the south of my position. I began to think that I had made it and that the fighting had passed me by, and I wondered if I should try to go south to the position of the 'Drop'. I rejected that idea, concluding that sooner or later I would meet up with some army units. Once the Dakotas had gone I began to feel less sure of things – if supplies were being dropped from the air, was this a detachment holding ground behind the enemy lines? Suddenly I heard voices and from a position of hiding I saw a settlement of Burmese in the forest. I drew my revolver and went down to them. They seemed very demoralised. It appeared that they had left their village to avoid the fighting and were staying in the forest until the armies had passed. They'd had enough. There was a pot boiling on a crude fire and I pointed to it. Inside were some sweet potatoes, their only sustenance. I took three from the pot, ate one, and put the other two in my pocket. The natives knew nothing of any army position and they were neither for me nor against me. All they wanted was that the warring armies would get on with it so that they might return to their village and resume their struggle for survival.

I left them. The contact had done nothing for my morale. I felt instinctively however, that I had to take more positive action if I was to survive, and so I turned due west. Instead of walking along the 'grain' of the country I was now walking across it. This meant going down into deep chaungs and climbing up the other side and it was all very hard going. On each climb I would encourage myself by thinking that when I got to the top I would see more open country and know where I was. The day wore on and I became more and more exhausted. Climbing up a particularly steep bank I caught a sapling and pulled myself over the edge. The sapling uprooted and I went crashing down the bank onto the rocks at the bottom. As I gingerly moved arms and legs to see if anything was broken, I was conscious of the sound of running water, and sure enough, under the stones, there was a stream. I drank my fill and felt a little better. Once again the voice of my instructor came to me: 'If you ever have the chance, wash your feet. You have no idea what that will do for your morale'. I duly took off the boots and the socks which were now sticking to my skin, put my feet into the cool water and for a brief moment gloried in the sensuous pleasure. It then struck me however, that it was one thing to die with my boots on but it would be absolutely fatal if I was 'jumped' by the Japanese with my boots off. I got socks and boots back on and, as the instructor had said, felt much better. Nothing could persuade me to try the steep bank again and so I set off following the stream, which soon petered out. The stream, however, led me to a dried up river bed, and as I was becoming more convinced that I was on the right side of the British lines, I followed the bed of the river still keeping very much to the verge in case a hurried withdrawal was necessary. Before me I saw khaki clad figures approaching. I'd made it! I quickened my step. I hadn't made it – the soldiers were Japanese. I faded into the undergrowth on the river bank and felt completely defeated.

Nothing moved and there was no sound. The patrol had passed and I concluded that they had not seen me. But what now? My thoughts could not have been more rudely interrupted. I had never experienced such noise or general mayhem. Everything seemed to be crashing around me. There were loud explosions followed by whistling shrapnel with bits of trees filling the air. It was obvious that the area I was in was under heavy bombardment and that the fire was coming from the British side. I was appalled. This meant that I was within striking distance of safety and yet stood a very good chance of being killed by my own side. There were no decisions to be made, however, as there was nothing left for me to do but to lie doggo. There is nothing more difficult.

After about half an hour the firing stopped and, soon after, night fell. When darkness came, the hill under which I lay came alive, not with the sound of music but with Japanese soldiers who were obviously dug in in their foxholes. They crashed around the undergrowth babbling excitedly. They relieved themselves, they gesticulated, keeping up a constant chatter. As the night wore on however, they settled themselves to rest, and I lay still, petrified, frightened to sleep and yet afraid to be awake. I reckoned that it would be fatal if I was to cry out in my sleep. I dug my nails into the palms of my hands in an effort to stay awake. I couldn't, of course, and I drifted in and out of troubled sleep. Remarkably, the night passed in fitful dozing, and eventually morning came and movement started again. Quite early in the day new noises began to be heard. At first I couldn't make out what was going on but soon I realised that the whining noise was of tank engines revving. I was fairly sure that they had to be British tanks and was encouraged, but not for too long, for the tanks began to rake the hillside with their fire. Once again I was on the wrong end of our own forces. Even the longest day has an ending and, eventually, darkness fell. Without food now for six days and no water for twenty four hours I knew that I could not last out for many more days. I was confirmed in this when I realised that there was a very thin line between my dreams and hallucinations. That night I played football on the lawn at the Southend Manse, and it was so real that I could hardly accept my situation when I came to. But daylight came and to begin with I felt nothing had changed. Soon, however, I began to realise that many of my yellow companions on the hillside had departed. Suddenly the tanks appeared in the dried river bed. They gave the hillside a further going over with their guns and proceeded past my position.

I was tempted to reveal myself, but knew instinctively that if I did I would be shot, either by the snipers whom the Japs had left behind, or by trigger happy tank crews who would not be taking any chances. I stayed in my hiding place. I heard voices and motor engines and, shifting my position, saw that the British army were advancing up the road which ran along the hillside on the opposite bank of the river. This was the moment that I had waited for but how was I to make contact? I knew that they would all be very jumpy and sudden movement could easily bring a hail of bullets, yet I knew that I could not bear another night in the wild. I crept to the very edge of the river and waited behind a tree trunk. I unwrapped the scarf, which had been white, from my neck. Down the dried up river bed came a tank officer, plodding, head down, in the soft sand. With my hands held high above my head and my 'white' flag waving, I came out of hiding and approached him, aware that about six soldiers had spilled out of a jeep and were pointing their rifles at me. The poor man got the fright of his life when my shadow fell across his path. He looked up and exclaimed: 'Who the hell are you?' I told him, but he was unimpressed.

By this time the aforesaid soldiers from the jeep had slid down the hillside on the opposite bank and were in time to hear me explaining that I was an RAF pilot who had evaded the enemy. With one accord the soldiers called on the name of the Lord, shook me by the hand, shook each other by the hand and informed me that it would be their pleasure to take me back to Divisional Headquarters which was some miles down the line. Their self-congratulations were to celebrate the fact that they had won some kind of sweep which was being run – the winner being those who 'saved' a pilot who had been shot down.

The soldiers were of the Gordon Highlanders. We began something of a royal progress back down the road which I had recced seven days before. We were travelling against the tide of an army on the advance and everyone wanted to know what had happened and who I was. We never stopped but cigarettes were pressed upon me. I could not have been more moved by the obvious pleasure they got from my escape. These were men who would be going into battle the next day. Some of them would not survive to see the hills of home again and yet they rejoiced in my good fortune. At one Battalion HQ, tea was being brewed. I was given a mug and a medical officer poured some spirits into it. "'Drink up' he said. I did as I was bidden and almost immediately was violently sick. I was embarrassed and a bit concerned about myself. The medical officer re-assured me. 'I gave you the spirits to make you sick,' he said, 'After a week without food and only rather doubtful water, your stomach is the better of a good clear out. You'll be fine now.' Although I felt as weak as a kitten, the man was right. As we proceeded on our way I began to feel better. My escort brought me in the gloaming into the Headquarters of the British Second Division, to be greeted by an old friend Mike Hubble, who was acting as Liaison Officer. I had a hip bath and was given a change of clothing, then I ate with the Headquarters Staff. I was in a very highly strung state and could not stop talking. The Divisional Commander took me aside. 'We will get a full report from you tomorrow, but have you any idea regarding the Japanese troops you saw?' I told him that they seemed to me to be bigger that the general run of Japanese. 'I think they must be the Japanese Guards'.

'No, no!' said the General, 'we know where they are. They are not in this area.' The General then challenged me to a game of dice. As we played the tensions drained away and I felt completely exhausted. I staggered to the tent which had been prepared for me and with a more fervent prayer of thanks than I had ever offered before, I slipped under the mosquito net and fell into a deep sleep. When I awoke three mugs of tea stood on the table at my bedside. All were cold. An orderly looked in.

'What time is it?' I asked.

'Och,' he said, 'it's just about half past ten.'

'But I promised to see the General before he left for the front line,' I said.

'Aye, that's right, but the General said that you were not to be disturbed. He left about an hour ago. You've got to see the IO, when you're ready'.

I drank yet another mug of tea and took a slice of bread and jam before going to see the Intelligence Officer who gave me a bit of paper and told me to make out a full report. Having finished the task, I went back to the charpoy and had more sleep. At teatime I sloped down to the Headquarters again and was rather surprised to find the General back. He was in good order. 'We had a bit of a battle today,' he said, 'the Gordon Highlanders saw them off.' At this he handed me a set of Japanese identity tags. 'Keep them' he said, 'and when you tell your children about them you can also tell them that they proved you were right and the General was wrong.'

The identity tags had come from a soldier of the Japanese Guards.

And that was the Great Escape as far as I was concerned. Next day I was flown out of the front line in an Auster Army Air Corps machine, and on from Kalewa in an American Dakota. I was put down on the strip at Tamu from which I had left some ten days before. I had come home and found myself something of a celebrity and an excuse for a very liquid lunch. There was a lot of ribaldry and noise, when I was told that there was someone at the mess door who very much wanted to see me. It was George Kew and some of the ground crew.

'We just wanted to make sure you were real,' said George as we all shook hands.

'Oh I'm real enough,' I said, 'how did the party go on Christmas Eve?'

'It's tomorrow night,' said George, 'we knew you'd be back, so we just put it off till you appeared.'

I could have wept then, but managed to see them off with the promise that I would come down to the dispersal point later in the afternoon.

What with the parties and the celebrations I must have been in a frail state when I was flown down to Calcutta for a medical examination. Fl/Lt D. A. B. McPherson took me down in a Harvard and after I had been found A1 at the RAF Medical Centre, he and I repaired to Firpo's, one of the favourite watering holes on Chowringee. As usual it was full of young officers, some of them lucky enough to have female companions. We found to our surprise that we were quite thirsty and downed a few John Collins. We were aware, however, that we were being looked at with disfavour by some of the well-dressed clientele. It was only then that I realised that we must have looked somewhat out of place dressed as we were in our crumpled jungle green overalls and marching boots. McPherson began to simmer. He had had an escape of his own. He had flown into a hillside and the impact of his face on the gunsight had re-arranged some of his features. The Nagas however had succoured him and, against all the odds, had carried him back to the British lines. He had made a wonderful recovery but his social graces had not been improved by the experience. Now in Firpos I could see that we were on the point of explosion. Twisting his battered face into a horrible grimace he observed that if any gabardine-clad swine wanted a fight, he could have it. I defused the situation by leading him to the dining room where he allowed himself to be cooled down by the famous Firpo's ice cream y chocolat sauce.

When we got back to Tamu later in the day I reported that the medical examination had gone OK and wondered if there might be some suggestion of 'survivor's leave'. If Henry had heard of such a thing he wasn't saying. Instead he suggested that I'd better see if I could still fly an aeroplane, so on the first day of the New Year I did an Air Test, which was really a pilot test. Nothing had changed and I was back on operations on the second of January. For the fortunate, life went on, and with the army breaking out on to the Schebo plain, the RAF were busy keeping up with them. In two months the Squadron had three moves; to Kalemyo, on to Yeu and to Sadaung near Schebo.

While victory was now assured there was much fighting and grievous losses to be endured. Not to be outdone by the 'B' Flight Commander, 'Bob' Johnstone of 'A' Flight was shot down and was twenty-two days missing before turning up. The members of 'A' Flight pointed out that their Flight Commander had put the 'B' Flight Commander in the shade. My own lot gallantly defended their position by observing that it always took 'A' Flight a good deal longer to do anything! Amidst it all we rejoiced for Bob. Sadly, others were not so fortunate. In one dread day in February three pilots went missing before breakfast. They had been engaged in a dawn patrol south of the Irrawaddy and in spite of all day searches no trace was found of them. It was thought that they must have been 'jumped' by a stray enemy fighter. Among those lost on this occasion was Flight Lieutenant Ralph Hunter, our best pilot, a Canadian with whom I had become very friendly. He was somewhat older than the average but was a tower of strength to everyone. He was a douce man who used to smile at some of the excesses of his younger brethren. He loved flying and was quite brilliant in the air and his loss, so near the end of his tour, was a real blow to everyone.

The end had come for me. After a visit by the AOC to the Squadron, during which he had expressed some surprise that an 'evader' such as myself was still on operations, a signal was received to the effect that I was to cease operations and report to Headquarters in Calcutta. When the CO and the Adjutant showed me the signal I could hardly believe it. On the one hand there was a sense of utter relief – I had survived! On the other hand how could I exist away from the Squadron which had come to mean so much to me?

One thing made the parting easier. Henry too had been promoted and was about to leave. He and I had been together a long time and he had been a good friend. With the help of the Flight Commanders, he had moulded the Squadron into a happy and effective unit and had never failed to fight the Squadron's corner with the higher echelons. We sat in the orderly room and reminisced.

'You know Mac, you and I should have been dead six months ago according to the statistics.'

'I'm glad you waited until now to tell me, Henry,' I replied. 'It just shows you that there are lies and there are statistics.' A few hours later I was to regret the facetious remark.

I was having a bath when I heard Henry calling me. I indicated where I was and he came into my hut in a high state of excitement. 'Get dressed Mac,' he said, 'we're flying!'

'Very funny!' I observed, and called for more hot water.

'I'm serious,' went on Henry and, chillingly, I realised that it was not a joke. I was, however, quite unamused and also quite emphatic. 'Well, Henry, *you* may be flying but *I* am not. You saw the signal today. I am now off operations. I am not flying!'

'You are still in the bloody Air Force' said Henry, 'and if I say you are flying, you are bloody well flying.'

I couldn't believe my ears.

'But why?' I said. 'There are plenty pilots. What's the big deal?' By this time I was dressed and Henry took me aside.

'The big deal is that the army has had information that many of the Jap intelligence staff are having a top level meeting in a village north of Mandalay. They want a strike on that village tonight and

I've been ordered to take the four best night flying pilots to make that strike. You are still with the Squadron and you are one of the four best night flying pilots.' There was a pause. 'I'm sorry' he said.

So it was that I found myself with Henry, Earl Ross and Ian Gibson, making our way down to the airstrip. I could see it all. The one too many.

We got off safely with the strict instructions that if our radio was to fail we were to return to base. I was no sooner in the air than my transmitter went off the air. I could go back. I should go back. A foolish fear that someone might think I had chickened out kept me going, so I stayed in touch with the other three by keeping a watch on the exhaust flames. When we got to the target area I heard Henry giving the order to strafe and I watched the three go in with their incendiary cannon shells. Giving them time to get clear I then went in and pulling away, was astonished to see the village ablaze. Henry came on the RT, calling upon the name of the Lord and shouting 'Are you still with us Mac?' I could not give any reply. However, we repeated the strafing and, finding my cannons empty, I made tracks for home, landing some time before the others. By this time Henry had convinced himself that by great mischance I had 'piled in' to the target and was more than relieved to find me hale and hearty. It was quite a good note to finish on, however, for all the information we got concerning the strike indicated that we had more than upset a lot of the Japanese army's plans by our visitation of their intelligence.

And that was that. I found it very difficult to say farewell to my friends on the Squadron, for they had all shown me the greatest kindness and friendship. Their comradeship had been beyond anything I deserved and their loyalty beyond any kind of price. After my experience with 28 Squadron my view of life would never be the same again, for I had been privileged to know many who, although they had come from completely different backgrounds and sometimes with different beliefs, were still willing to lay down their lives on my behalf.

It was a humbling thought.

The rest of my time in India was brief. I spent a few weeks with 'E' Group, based in Calcutta, and met the bravest of men and women, those with whom you took dinner of an evening not knowing whether they would be with you at breakfast the next day. When they were missing you knew that they had probably parachuted into Burma during the night and were now hundreds of miles behind the enemy lines setting up pockets of resistance among the native population. I toured the front line squadrons giving good advice on escaping. None of the pilots thought they would ever need it!

At last it was back to Bombay where I awaited a berth on a troopship heading for the UK. Eventually I boarded the *Orion*. As she slipped her moorings and we watched the dramatic skyline of Bombay falling further away, I thought of how much had happened to me and how fortunate I had been. I put my hand in my pocket and drew out a rupee note. I had entered India with nothing in my pocket. After three years I was leaving with the same amount, but I had learned a lot and now I was going home.

We came into Liverpool and were sent directly on leave from the ship. In Glasgow I awaited the afternoon bus for Campbeltown and went to have lunch in the Grosvenor. Sitting in the lounge bar there, I was 'adopted' by a party of businessmen in for their pre-prandial drink. On learning that I had just returned from the East, they were more than hospitable and insisted on accompanying me to the bus at Wellington Street, where they poured me on to it. I slept most of the way to Campbeltown. There, at the Post Office awaiting my arrival, was my father, the Padre. He looked little different from how he had looked three years before, in spite of all that he and my mother had suffered. He hadn't changed much either. Having embraced and kissed his prodigal son he asked, 'Is that the best jacket you've got?' I realised that the battledress top which had been through many vicissitudes and many climatic changes was hardly looking its best! And so home to Southend and to my mother who tried so hard to hide the fact that part of her mind was with the son who would not return. Rona and John greeted me as if I'd never been away and Maimie, having grown even smaller, addressed me and the Almighty in affectionate and gaelic terms.

As far as I was concerned, that was the war over. To be sure I spent an artificial year working in the Air Ministry with the Public Relations branch where I had some good fun, met some interesting people and got no satisfaction from the work I was doing. During the year I met the beloved Isobel, and we planned to marry. When the crocuses came out in the parks to be followed by the daffodils, I knew that the time had come to return to civilian life. In the demob centre I got my civilian suit, my shoes, socks, shirt and tie and soft hat. I received my final warrant which would take me home. I walked out of the building and into the early summer air of London. Instead of taking the customary Tube train back to my billet I walked along the Embankment and, finding a bench, sat down and wondered at what had happened to me during the five years since I joined the University Air Squadron in Edinburgh.

While there had been many outstanding events and extra-ordinary happenings, it was always to people that I returned in my thoughts: I had just seen Henry – now a Wing Commander – back in the Air Ministry. We had been good pals. We had established a great rapport early on in our association and, in spite of all the differences, in background, in age and in rank, had always been the best of friends. Boris Buckland, Ian Gibson and I had been together through training, through operational training and on the Squadron. We relied on each other's friendship and support through good days and bad. Boris with his speech impediment became something of a mascot on the Squadron. Unfortunately his health did not stand up to the rigours of the climate in the East. Again and again he succumbed to malaria and eventually had to be invalided home. His way-going was a blow to Ian and myself. Ian was a calm soul. While the rest of us sweated as we awaited our operational briefings, 'Gibbie' could be found reading some botanical book, quite unconcerned that he might be facing death in the next few hours. He had volunteered to go with one of the Chindit columns as their Air Liaison Officer, had got himself wounded and was returned to the Squadron as good as new while we were at Dalbumgargh. He was still reading his botanical books – flying was an extra. Then there were the ground crews; George Kew from London, the classic cockney of the quick wit and affectionate nature. He had been my rigger most of the time; another Londoner, Charlie Heasman – good old Charlie – a butcher to trade but now an engine fitter; Sergeant Iles of the serious countenance – a good footballer; Corporal Champion with the 'cavalry' moustache – more of a gent than many officers; Dickie Bowser, armourer sergeant – a hell raiser of the first order; Admiral Matthews, the ALO from Bolton – singing in his deep brown voice the latest Miranda 'hit' *My Resistance is Low*; the adjutant, Eric Adams, who was like a father to us all, could drink gin to a band playing, and was always on hand to encourage us; among the pilots, the great Australian womaniser, Harold Glass, envied by us all; Ginger Wragg, Norrie Deacon, Dickie Baker; the brightest of all, Earl

Ross, the chuckling Canadian. Other great 'colonials' like Bob Johnston, Arch Guymer, D. A. B. McPherson, Jack Muff, Hank Macadams.

As I sat there alone by the Thames I was suddenly aware that my eyes were filled with tears as I remembered those who had been part of my life and could no longer be part of it; the gentle New Zealander Reed, Merret, Cade, Aussie Gray, Emmet and others, but, perhaps more especially, Ralph Hunter and wee Farquharson. None of them could ever be forgotten. What kind of a world had they fought for and died for? The war had been such a grim time for so many. Could it possibly have been worth it all? For me, of course, it had been a great learning experience and had brought me into association with some wonderful people.

Stiffly I stood up from the bench. This would never do. The worst thing is to live in the past and the future for me was not to be by the banks of the Thames, the hills of home were calling. I would take the night train to the North and perhaps tomorrow I would don the ridiculous trilby hat and plan for a future without war.

PART THREE

The Ministry

The Word was with God at the beginning and through him all things came to be; no single thing was created without him. All that came to be was alive with his life, and that life was the light of men. The light shines on in the dark, and the darkness has never mastered it . . .

Jesus said: 'I am the light of the world. No follower of mine shall wander in the dark; he shall have the light of life.'

(*St John's Gospel*)

CHAPTER TWELVE

Marriage and University in the Grey City

It was a pleasant summer and in the Southend of Kintyre life began to return to some kind of normality in the Manse. Angus was back home and striving hard to regain the ground lost in the war. Professionally he had suffered most and re-establishing his name as an author would be no easy task; Willie continued in his profession and was getting steady promotion; Rona was teaching in the Grammar School at Campbeltown, her singing was attracting notice and her presence at home was a special joy and support to her mother; John was doing very well at school and was preparing for the Highers which would get him into medicine when he left school.

What would I do?

There was no great spiritual visitation, but there was the birth of the feeling that perhaps I should follow my father's footsteps in the ministry. Isobel was all for it as she too had strong church connections. The thought was developed with the powers that be at university. Under the direction of my father and Isobel's brother, the Reverend Johnston McKay. I was accepted as a candidate and the authorities, when informed of my intended marriage, suggested that I pursue my studies in St Andrews where accommodation for married couples might be easier. My father tried to persuade me that I should not attempt the degree course. Kindly he argued that I had already learned more than any MA course could provide, but I had the feeling that he thought I might fail and would be disheartened. However, the decision was made that I should enter the Arts faculty at St Andrews.

Isobel and I were married by the two reverend gentlemen closest to us, in Stevenson Memorial Church in Glasgow. I managed to drop the ring but with reactions sharpened by fear I caught it before it reached the floor. Four weeks later we left for St Andrews and for our lodgings in Kinessburn Road. The first fortnight was one of the warmest Octobers on record – a good omen. While we were happy in our lodgings, we longed for more privacy. We were fortunate to get a top flat with a Mrs Mansell, who, although stern of countenance and somewhat brusque in manner, proved to be a good friend. We could have the flat as long as we had no children!

The studies began. I can admit now of course that I misused the University, taking little part in any corporate life and using the classes merely as a means to an end, but the golf was good and cheap! Happily Isobel managed the finances – five pounds a week – and we were succoured by our minister the Reverend W. E. K. Rankin and his wife Irma. They were kindness itself.

Halfway through the first session we knew that our first child was on the way. We told Mrs Mansell that we would have to be looking for another place. She said nothing. I struggled with the Anglo Saxon and the Moral Philosophy and at the end of the Session I passed English and History with something to spare, but did not pass the Moral Philosophy. Isobel was incandescent. The professors and examiners were either fools or knaves and probably both, but having been used to somewhat ordinary results I thought that two passes out of three was quite good. The summer days came and with the birth approaching, we began making efforts to find new accommodation. At this point Jessie, our Mrs Mansell, got quite broody herself and told us that she too was looking forward to the baby coming and we would just stay. This was an immense relief and in August Angus duly arrived and was brought back in triumph to the delight of all. In September, I satisfied the examiners in Moral Philosophy – much to my own surprise!

The second Session was without much incident. Our lives were very much dominated by the baby who was an excellent child but did not see any reason why he should sleep. In total weariness I sought a consultation with a paediatrician to find out if there was any good reason for Angus's wakefulness. As she took the £5 fee from me she laughed and said, 'It's just your hard luck!' As the Finals were approaching, Isobel took the child away to her parents so that I could get peace and quiet to study. In the awful peace of the empty flat I found I couldn't study at all. In spite of everything I made it, and was duly capped Master of Arts. We were very lucky to be able to celebrate the occasion with both sets of grandparents and other friends. Amongst these was a couple, Mr and Mrs James Donaldson, who had befriended us. Without children themselves they soon became Uncle Jim and Auntie Don to Angus, and their kindness was immense.

The summer days were fine but we had a worry. Our second child was conceived and we felt that we could not impose further on Mrs Mansell's goodwill. We eventually found a hotel cottage which looked very picturesque in the sunshine, with roses round the door. Although it was a few miles outside St Andrews we took the let and moved into it in September. Sad to say this was one of our big mistakes, for not only was our landlord some kind of 'nut case', the cottage was very damp. Isobel was not very well and Angus did not sleep much, nevertheless my training for the ministry began on time at St Mary's.

Bigger worries were around the corner. Isobel took very ill and was rushed to Robroyston Hospital in Glasgow where she was delivered of premature twins, one of whom was stillborn. The other 'scrap' of some two and a half pounds had a very tenuous hold on life. Isobel herself showed great powers of recovery and was able to leave hospital in a few days, but wee Kenny struggled to live. He was among the first babies to be treated by the new drug streptomycin. Once or twice the hospital thought they had lost him and told us to expect the worst, but Kenny battled on and when he had reached a decent weight we got him back to St Andrews. He never cried, was washed in olive oil, conserved his strength and grew a little healthier day by day. Poor wee Angus must have been bemused by all that was happening around him. He had got to his feet after ten months and was soon talking, but still we were stuck in the cottage with running water in every room – down the walls.

It was not the ideal place for a tender baby and to make matters worse there was coal rationing. Our landlord had decreed that he would get the coal ration for all his houses and give each of us our share. He reneged on this and for a while we had to transport coal from the rail depot in the baby's pram. We must have looked the proverbial refugees. The crisis came one Thursday afternoon when I returned from college to find Isobel sitting with the delicate baby over a one-bar electric fire, while Angus's nose was running with the cold. In a fury I stalked over to the hotel where I found our landlord behind his bar, half drunk and in abusive mood. I demanded coal. He sneered and observed that it was time people like myself remembered that the war was over and that we did not give orders any more. That was his big mistake for the day. Being

117

reminded of the fine men I had known who had died, I took a great dislike to the clown behind the bar, vaulted over and caught him by the throat, told him that I had been trained to kill better men than him with my bare hands (which was a lie) and that he'd better open the coal shed door before it all happened. Fortunately he succumbed immediately. We got our coal and just to underline the point I made him carry the pails to the cottage. I might have been triumphant but I was also shaken by the force of my own temper. What would have happened if he *had* put up any resistance? Of course we could not stay there much longer and in a week or two our luck changed quite dramatically. We were able to get the let of a larger house in St Andrews. It was a very pleasant house with far too big a rent, however Isobel took in two student sleepers and we managed. What a relief it was to be settled again in a good house. Life began to look rosier and with the summer coming on wee Kenny lay out in his pram and got stronger. It is difficult to believe that the studies in Old Testament, Divinity, New Testament and Systematic Theology went on while all these alarms were happening. That they did was due to great support from a growing number of friends.

The following summer was a sad and yet decisive time. I had been appointed student assistant with the minister of Aberfoyle, where my duties were to care for the outlying portion of the parish at Kinlochard. We arrived by train at Aberfoyle and made our way to the house where we were to lodge for the summer. Our landlady was a Mrs Wood who greeted us warmly and, as she gave us a welcoming cup of tea, asked if I had met the minister, Mr Strachan. I told her that I had yet to meet my boss. 'Och, you'll like him,' she said, 'he's just like yourself – plain as porridge!' We felt that this frankness augured well for the future and so it proved. It was a wonderful summer. The sun shone day by day and cycling up to visit the people and to take the service at the school on Sundays for thirteen weeks, I never wore a raincoat. Lying out in his pram in the sunshine, wee Kenny prospered, as did his grandmother McKay who had been unwell and had come to recuperate in the Highland air. Angus played happily in the garden which ran down to the railway yard where Peter Lambie, the engine driver, blew his whistle and waved to him as he passed. It was a lovely time and with the warm reception I received in all the houses I visited, I was confirmed in my desire to be a parish minister. Mr and Mrs Strachan were very kind – the minister would come on a Monday morning and, chainsmoking Woodbine cigarettes, would keep us all amused with his dry wit. Mrs Murray did her best to upset Angus's digestive system by feeding him 'wee fried tatties' in her kitchen and by taking him for walks in the evening along the railway line where bramble berries were growing in profusion.

The people around Lochard were very supportive and many came Sunday by Sunday to the service. A highlight was our harvest thanksgiving service when almost everybody arrived. One of the prettiest sights was a little cart drawn by a tiny Shetland pony with the cart overflowing with flowers and vegetables. Two of 'my' parishioners never made it to church. One was the old gentleman who kept guard on the Glasgow water supply which came through the glen from Loch Katrine. In his kitchen was a row of brass bells which would give warning of any fault along the supply pipes, so he could never stray further than the sound of the bells. The other backslider was an old lady who lived next door to the school. When, in the week before I left, I appealed to her to make my joy complete by being at the service, she told me that she couldn't.

'Why?' I cried.

'Because,' she said, 'when the minister comes up in the winter to take a service, I don't go, and I would hate to hurt his feelings by going when you're here.' I thought it was a most Christian reason for not going to church!

We loved being at Aberfoyle, but our lives were darkened in the knowledge that Rona was dying. In 1947 she had missed the National Mod because of an emergency operation. Although the growth which was removed from her back was cancerous, she made a remarkable recovery, resumed her life as if nothing had happened, and in 1948 won the Gold Medal, moving the adjudicator, Sir Hugh Roberton, to observe 'We have heard a girl with a golden voice.' For a few months she had enjoyed a round of engagements, but by Christmas time she lost her most precious possession – her voice. The disease had returned and by the summer it was obvious that she would not recover. Rona met the inevitable with stoicism and courage. While her body wasted she kept her golden hair to the end. When she died her father was broken for many days before beginning to recover, while her mother wept silently and kept the family home going with dignity. It was the opinion of many that although she lived for some fifteen years after, she never recovered from the loss of the daughter who was her friend and support.

At the end of September we left Aberfoyle. It was a place of good

119

memories and we had made many friends. Mr Strachan had assured me that in the ministry we were dealing in a very practical way with weak and wayward humanity, but there was little good in railing against them. Sometimes one had to be very practical. He instanced this truth on the evening when he invited me to share in a marriage ceremony in the Manse. When the bridegroom arrived, it seemed that he and his best man had been celebrating and were somewhat the worse of the wear. Without hesitation the minister took the two clowns and me into the garden.

'We'll have to sober you up,' he said to the bridegroom, setting out at a brisk walking pace, 'and if you want to be sick, be sick in the bushes.' An hour or so later, Mrs Strachan having given comfort and tea to the waiting bride, the marriage ceremony took place. When I view with nausea some of my unco guid brethren who balk at marrying couples who do not measure up to their standards of righteousness, I think of my bishop Strachan who viewed the whole of life with a somewhat jaundiced eye, but who took life and people as they are, and was always charitable in his judgements. I believe that he was more righteous than they and, more nearly, ministered in the spirit of Christ.

It was back to St Andrews and all of us better in health than when we had left. I also felt better equipped and more experienced. The final year at St Mary's passed without too many alarms and in March the Presbytery of St Andrews duly licensed me to preach the Gospel.

Now it was really crunch time. Who would want me as their minister? The short answer seemed to be 'no one'. I applied for all vacant churches, but very few even acknowledged my application. One morning I was sitting in our rooms at Abbotsford Place when the phone rang. It was one William Ross, who announced that he was the Session Clerk in Kenmore and asked if I could preach there on the following Sunday. I said that I could but then asked the question, 'Are you a vacant charge?'

'Yes', came the reply, which put paid to my preaching, for it was the rule that newly licensed ministers could not supply the pulpit of vacant charges. Mr Ross was devastated as he had tried so many and had failed to get someone to supply Kenmore. I suggested that if he could get the Interim Moderator to preach in Kenmore then I could come to supply his parish. That is what happened and on the Saturday I set off to preach at the church at Weem, the charge of the Reverend Ian McLellan. The said Ian had persuaded the vacancy committee to worship that morning in Weem church, and thus it was that I was asked to preach in the vacancy and have always maintained the empty boast that I was minister of a charge that I had not applied for.

Two or three weeks after being at Weem I was asked to preach at Kenmore. From the moment that I was met at Aberfeldy by Peter McRae who took me in his taxi to Letterellan, the home of the Misses Parker Ness, I knew that it was here I wanted to minister. I returned to St Andrews and to the family, full of hope. We packed up and brother Angus came and took us to Southend there to await the verdict of Kenmore. Eventually it came and the date of my induction was fixed for 10th July. After all the ups and downs of the student period we had a settled home to go to. And what a place – the Manse of Kenmore.

CHAPTER THIRTEEN

Kenmore – A charge to Keep

The weeks before we arrived in Kenmore were spent in a logistic nightmare of arranging for our furniture to be transported from a warehouse in Glasgow; curtains to be made and carpets to be measured. Auntie Don pitched in with an offer to make curtains, everybody wanted to help and there was a great deal of toing and froing. Both sets of parents had been more than supportive but we did not wish to impose upon their hospitality longer than necessary. At last a date was given for our removal to Kenmore but at the last minute there was word that the Manse would not be ready for us until after the induction. In the meantime we would be accommodated in Kenmore Hotel. The trek began from Southend; by boat from Campbeltown; to base camp at the other grandparents in Glasgow; from there by train to Aberfeldy via Perth.

It was simple and made easier by the help and kindness of others, but nothing is easy with two little folk in tow. Angus was just three and Kenny not quite two. With cases and prams and the dozen other things we knew we would need, our greatest requirement was the proverbial two pairs of hands. Add the natural anxiety regarding what lay ahead, and it was a very good thing for us that we arrived in Aberfeldy on a sunny day, to be met by an understanding taxi driver and given a warm welcome by Miss Rae the manageress in Kenmore Hotel. Soon we were ensconced in a room in the annexe of the hotel and the boys were 'adopted' by the two Glasgow girls who served in the Dining Room. Things began to look less daunting.

In the evening we would get Angus and Kenny ready for their beds and when we thought all was well Isobel and I would sneak over to the hotel for a quiet dinner. Came the evening, of course, when Angus did not sleep, wakened Kenny, and an intimation was brought to the dining room that two young men in nightgowns were running about on the lawn of the annexe. We were red faced but the incident did much to break the ice with the local people. Many of them were highly amused at our embarrassment and expressed some pleasure that the new minister's children had a streak of mischief in them. I suppose there were those who sniffed and hoped that this was not evidence of badly behaved children and foolish parents, but such sentiments were hidden from us. Each day we went to the Manse to see how things were progressing. At last the workmen were finished and Ruby, the beadle's wife and Peggy, her sister-in-law, scrubbed the Manse from stem to stern. The furniture arrived from Glasgow and the unpacking began. Jean, who with her husband John lived in the bungalow at the end of the Manse drive, brought tea along when she knew we were moving – good neighbours they proved to be from the very start. We sat on the packing cases in the Drawing Room drinking the most acceptable tea, while the boys staggered around their new abode exploring the many rooms and stairs.

'Well,' said Isobel, 'here we are!'

'I hope you like it,' I replied, 'because I don't think we are going to be leaving for a long time.' It was the one prophetic utterance of my ministry which was to have validity.

The ordination and induction service was a solemn occasion and I tried hard to concentrate on all that it meant to me. Like a wedding however, I believe that everyone is so keyed up that the true solemnity and relevance can be lost on the main players. The solemnity was certainly lost on my brother Angus who observed afterwards that the 'laying on of hands' of the Presbytery was like a rugby scrum. He had been terrified that the scrum would collapse on top of me! However, when the service was over I was finally and truly committed to the ministry of the Church of Scotland in the Parish of Kenmore. I hoped it would all turn out well but I was a little apprehensive. The evening 'social' doubtless was like all other of the same genre where ministers, including my father and brother-in-law, spoke. My father warned the congregation that I had a very quick temper but was really quite kindly at heart. Mrs Lamont, the oldest member, helped me into the robe which was the congregations' gift to me, Alma and Jimmy sang, the speeches went on and, at last, it was all over and we shook hands with the people who were there.

It was a real pleasure to meet again the Misses Parker Ness who had been so kind to me when I had come to preach for Kenmore. They welcomed me back and were delighted to meet Isobel, assuring her of the hospitality of their home any time she wished to call. The elder sister, Helen, was a handsome woman with tremendous style in dress and carriage, the younger sister Paquita, on the other hand, had been a victim of congenital paralysis and supported her frail and twisted little body on two elbow crutches. Although her body was weak she had the heart of a lion and a mind as sharp as a needle. Possibly because they had been the first to befriend us, these two ladies took a proprietary interest in all our doings from then on and were unfailing and generous in their support and kindness.

Another whose welcome was without stint was an old lady with snow white hair, a Mrs Menzies, who told us that she lived in the village and that we were to feel free to drop in at any time. Little did we know that evening of our induction what a haven her house was to become or how many times we would 'drop in' for the proverbial cup of tea which would turn out to be a feast of sandwiches and cakes – not to mention the apple tarts. Hers was one of the first houses which I visited because she had told me that she had her mother living with her. The old lady was well into her nineties and the day I called, Mrs Menzies had two of her sisters with her, all in their sixties. Having been introduced to us, the mother attacked her daughters for taking their seats. 'Have you lassies nae manners – sitting down before the minister has taken his chair!' We all laughed, except the old lady. She was deadly earnest.

We had been very fortunate having so many friends and relatives to share our great day with us. We had both sets of parents, Angus and Jean and Johnston, but when they left we knew that we were on our own and that we had better get on with it.

When we moved into the Manse there was so much to be done that I have to confess that I did not sit down and consider what style of ministry I would carry on in Kenmore Parish. I had however a good idea of the kind of minister I wanted to be and I also knew the style of Gospel which I wanted to convey to the people in the parish. Above all I wanted to be the parish minister. I knew that I was fortunate in that I had come to a parish which had but one church. I knew that there would be people of different denominations and that there was a reasonably strong episcopal congregation in Aberfeldy; that in fact there were no less than four churches there, as well as the two Church of Scotland charges. Whether this plethora of religious groups made Aberfeldy a holier place is not for me to say. Of this, though, I was sure; no matter of what denomination or none, I would care for every soul within the Parish bounds. To demonstrate this my first priority would be to visit every home.

It was a bit of a shock to discover that many of the people whom I visited were not at all like the people I had known in the Southend of Kintyre. They had a reserve about them and did not wear their hearts on their sleeves. They were pleased enough to see the new minister but they would wait and see what kind of man he proved to be. I sometimes wondered if this reserve arose from the fact that for generations they had lived on the borders of the Highlands, and their forebears had never been quite sure whether they were going to be invaded from the north or the south. In these circumstances one kept one's own council and undoubtedly many were good at that. They also had had experience of living under the feudalistic government of the Castle. Again it was sometimes politic to keep one's opinions to oneself. Many were good at that, too.

I discovered early on that the Parish was not as united as I thought. Having learned that the two churches, Parish and United Free, had been united under Dr Gillies in 1931, I took it that all residual bitterness had been dissipated. I was soon disabused.

I was visiting a family of elderly sisters who, with their brother, had retired from farming and were resident in one of the village houses. They were not communicative. I prattled on about this and that without any great response. I told them that I had been reading a scrap book which had been left by Dr Gillies in which there had been an account of the service when the two churches had been united. The temperature in the little living room dropped quite a few degrees and I began to feel that I had said the wrong thing. The eldest of the sisters at last spoke through pursed lips. 'There never was a union in Kenmore – and never will be!' Encouraged, another sister continued 'And none of us will ever darken the door of Kenmore Kirk!' End of story! I felt utterly deflated and searched for some reasonable response. I told them that I was sorry that they felt that way and hoped they would still think of me as their minister. We shook hands solemnly and I left wondering about the kind of God who could be worshipped in a UF church but not in another. They and I were soon to discover that 'never' can be a long or a very short time. In the nature of things one of the old ladies died and the remaining members of the family seemed to find my care for them helpful. When I visited them a few days after the funeral they graciously thanked me. I told them of the service I was starting in the school every second Sunday afternoon. Nothing was said but the following Sunday I was overjoyed to see two of them making their way up the road to the school. Their black skirts and jackets were of a bygone age and their religious observance was serious. Sunday was no laughing matter but I felt a great affection for them, the first to be won back into the fold.

I was soon to learn that there were others still bitter about the union. One old lady of ninety-five when offered com-munion in her own home wondered if she could take the elements from an established church minister. I was really quite shocked at this and, possibly foolishly, told her I was shocked. Perhaps she was more gracious than I, for I received a letter some days later asking me to bring her the sacrament. Another of the 'narrower' ex-members of the Free Church was in fact a very good attender at Church, but always assured me that she had never agreed to the union and disapproved of my predecessor who had brought it about. She excused me from any blame for the state of affairs but thought I would do better if I approached the conversion of the parish with more seriousness. She told me, 'It's not for a man of the cloth to be chasing a wee white ball round the golf course or hitting a bunch of feathers on the badminton court.' But she was originally from Argyll and we got on just fine!

Among the invalids whom I visited in the early days was a young woman in her twenties, who had a heart defect. It was clear that she was not long for this world and I was in and out of the house quite a lot in the first few weeks. Her mother, a widow, was a most cheerful soul and was gifted with many malapropisms. She prattled on about the 'university' of her wedding – reminded her son to take his 'ulcer' in case it would rain – signed the notices for an coman ghaileach as the 'honourable' secretary; and was always ready for a laugh. She was also near to tears much of the time as her daughter's condition became worse. I looked in early one afternoon and the girl's condition had not changed much, but all afternoon as I visited others I knew that I would have to return before going home. I came into the house and into the bedroom just as Violet slipped from life to a brighter day. It was the first time I had been at a death in the parish and for a moment I found myself completely at a loss, but the mother, though devastated, came to my aid. She took my hand and said, 'You were sent to be with us.' I think we both wept a little but the Good Spirit then took over as we thanked Him for the life which had ended.

Violet's funeral was thus the first that I had to conduct. As I made my way over to her home to conduct the service, as was the custom then, at the door of the home I felt an awesome inadequacy. In the face of this family's grief how could I transmit to them the words of comfort from the Gospel in a way which would bring peace to their hearts. Inwardly I prayed for guidance and strength. The sun shone down upon us, the neighbours and relations and friends gathered to pay their respects. Everything was done with simplicity and, I hope, with dignity. The little undertaker – Willie Moyes – was kindly and kept me right and Mr Fraser, who was a close neighbour, supported me throughout the service. We walked over the bridge behind the cortege and laid Violet to rest in her father's grave. There were some tears and solemn handshakes as it was a community in mourning, each one lending support to the other. There was something of a healing in that, and I was glad to be a part of it. It gave a strength to me too.

So the first few months passed and we began to settle in to the job. People from inside and outside the parish called at the Manse to express their welcome to us. Mrs Hutchison from Bolfracks came with her husband Jock. Their son Bobby had been killed while with the Black Watch, fighting at Gerbini in Sicily in the same action in which my own brother had died. Such coincidence created something of a bond. It turned out too that there were Hutchison grandchildren of the same age as our two little boys and parties were planned for the future. The attendances at church and school services continued to be encouraging and I had quite a few baptisms, some having been held back until I had been inducted. Sadly I had quite a few funerals to conduct as well, prompting one of my irreverent brothers to remark that he could understand parents delaying the baptisms until I arrived but he could not believe that there were those who delayed their death until I was available to bury them!

To begin with I travelled round the parish on my bicycle as I had no car and there was certainly little chance of affording one. On being inducted to the charge I found that the stipend was £450 per annum, with a Manse – not that I would receive £450. Part of the emoluments came from a let of the Glebe where the rent was £12, but £3 of that was in kind – namely the rabbits which I might take off the Glebe – plus two cart loads of farmyard manure which would be delivered annually. I have often wondered if I am the only living person who has been partly paid in farmyard manure. Kindly family and friends remarked that it was all very suitable. However, with a stipend of such proportions I was not in any position to have a car. Cycling around the parish was no bad thing, for as well as visiting people at home, one often had contacts on the road. In days to come, when the car became an absolute essential, I was often aware that I spent too much of my time cocooned inside the vehicle without having the chance encounters which were so valuable in my early days.

Two such encounters brought me into contact with two of the local worthies. Cycling along the south road below the Manse I came on an ancient who had fallen out with his bicycle and was kicking it. He was also addressing it in very unseemly terms. I got off my machine and enquired if I could help. I recognised my fellow traveller as one who gloried in the nickname 'the prairie wolf' and who had been renowned as a poacher of rabbits off the Manse Glebe. My offer of assistance was greeted with several expletives, but when I turned the cycle on to its saddle and got the chain back on, gave it a whirl and found it was still working, the old boy fell silent before enquiring 'Are you the new man up the hill there?' 'Indeed I am', I replied, and put out my hand in greeting. He jumped on his bike and left me at speed, as if pursued by the hounds of hell. He, for one, was taking no chances with the new minister.

Another 'character' was Jimmy, a man well into his nineties whose friends told me early on was one of the best advertisements for riotous living. Certainly even at his great age he managed to cycle the two miles from his home to 'Archie's' bar at Kenmore Hotel most evenings of the week. On arriving at his destination one noticed that he always took the precaution of turning his bicycle to face in the direction of home before resting it on the paling fence near to the pub. One evening, coming through the village, I came upon Jimmy leaving the hostelry. He obviously felt that this was not the time to engage me in conversation and he jumped on to his bicycle. I wondered at the agility of the man. However, there was no forward motion and I had time to enquire if all was well. He muttered that there was something wrong with his left pedal but there was nothing wrong with any of the pedals. In his haste to make a quick getaway Jimmy had flung his leg not only over his bike, but also over the paling fence! It took a certain amount of manoeuvring to get him unravelled, but eventually he left with a very straight back but on a rather erratic course. I made my own way home pondering on the straight and narrow way.

One of the greatest 'characters' in the parish was Sandy Butters. Although he was no churchgoer I was not long until I made his acquaintance, first because he was the roadman between Kenmore and Fearnan and secondly because his voice carried across the loch to the Manse garden. It was quite extraordinary how one could hear every word bouncing across the water on a calm summer's day. Sandy's vocabulary was very interesting to the children. He had a remarkably strong voice and this strength was reflected in almost every part of him. I got to know Sandy well because of a tragedy which struck his family shortly after I came to the parish. Sandy became the champion of the new minister and having been to church once – and that at a funeral – became an expert on ministers in general.

One Sunday morning Sandy was sitting on the seat in front of his house, contentedly puffing on his pipe, at peace with the world but not for long. He was approached by two missionaries of a fringe sect who thought that they might find some fertile ground among the non church attenders.

'We see you are not at church,' said one.

'No!' said Sandy non-committally.

'Perhaps the minister doesn't understand your needs. We are here to help.'

Sandy rose in wrath and wielding his stick and calling his collie dog to his aid, he chased the poor souls down the road.

'Get the . . . . . . oot o' here – Ah've got a . . . . . . minister o' ma ain.'

When I heard of this, and secretly rather pleased with Sandy's robust approach, I was reminded of Katy in Southend whom I visited shortly after coming back from service in the Far East. It was a pleasure and a privilege to call on the old lady who had been so kind to us all as children. Katy had kept house for her brother the shoemaker, whom we all knew as 'the stitcher', but now she was alone and approaching ninety years of age. She was bright and so pleased to see me and soon the tea was set out and we settled down to chat. She had just sat down when there was a loud knock on the door. Impatiently she went to answer it to find there two very sincere young people, members of an evangelical team who had been visiting the parish. Without preamble they announced their message:

'Believe in the Lord Jesus Christ and Thou shalt be saved.'

Katy did not waste any time either.

'Ah kent that afore ye were born' she said, and shut the door quite firmly before resuming our 'crack' by the fireside.

When I am downcast at some of the namby-pamby saccharine sweet platitudes which pass for Christian witness, I pause to bless the memory of Sandy and Katy.

Sandy had been a soldier in the Black Watch during the First World War. Rumour had it that he had been promoted many times in battle because of his courage and leadership, only to be demoted a similar number of times because of his extramural activities away from the battlefield. Sandy and I would sit on either side of the kitchen range recalling the days of conflict and trying to emulate each other in our tales of 'derring do'. Sometimes Sandy would get irritated at my interjections. 'I'm no' talking aboot your war – Ah'm talkin' aboot the big war.' Thus the Second World War was consigned to history as a minor engagement.

Certainly Sandy enjoyed his drink and on one famous occasion during the 'big' war, having been wounded, Sandy was sent home on leave. The troop train arrived at the station in Perth, where the second VAD had a reception post to give comfort and assistance. Sandy came off the train giving a good impression of a rather tattered Christmas tree, trailing rifle and kit and with a bandage round his head. He was approached by a very genteel lady, well known in the district, who recognised Sandy.

'Welcome home, Private Butters! Are you looking for the second VAD?'

'No, Ma'am!' replied Sandy, 'I'm looking for the first . . . . . . PUB.'

Sandy's greatest story, however, concerned the dread conflict in the trenches. He had been born in the village of Camserney, a hamlet of some ten houses to the west of Aberfeldy. Only the most detailed maps recognise its existence.

'Ye ken,' Sandy would begin, 'when we were in the trenches for a while, ye got tae ken who was on the ither side o' the wire, and the Germans wid ken who we were. When we wid go ower the top ye wid hear the Germans shoutin' at each ither. "Get yer heids doon ye . . . . . . Here come Butters frae Camserney".' I often wondered how it sounded in German!

Sandy won the Military Medal and doubtless deserved more than one. When the war was over he married Lucy and tried to settle down to the less exciting life of keeping the roads tidy. He had great strength and was ever ready to use it in a good cause, as on the day the lady came along past Sandy in her brand new Morris Minor. Then as now, many of our tourist friends allow their eyes to be drawn to the beauty which is around them and away from the road which is in front of them. The lady in question found herself sliding into the roadside ditch which was rather deeper than usual because Sandy had just cleaned it. She struggled out of her car in a great state.

'My new car!' she cried, 'what will I do?' By this time Sandy was striding towards her and he tried to reassure her.

'Dinna fash yersel, wumman. Ah'll soon get ye oot.'

Suiting action to the word he took hold of the little car's back bumper and with much groaning and grunting, and calling on the Name of the Lord, he lifted it out of the ditch and practically threw it back on the road. While all this had been going on the car's owner was twittering away.

'Watch the paint. Remember it's a new car.'

When in triumph Sandy turned to her: 'There ye are, missus,' her only word of gratitude was indeed a complaint:

'Look what you've done! You've scratched it!'

Sandy was speechless, which in itself was something unique. He was not, however, powerless, and grasping the bumper again he returned the Morris Minor to the ditch before picking up his shovel and striding with an air of injured dignity, to the West.

But the big strong Sandy had a soft heart. One day watching him 'edge' the roadside with his spade and wondering at the neatness of his work, I was astonished to see him forsake his straight line to go round a primrose plant which was growing on the verge.

'That has spoiled your line Sandy,' I suggested.

'Ach man!' he replied, 'Ah widna like to hurt the pretty wee flow'r'.

Deep down in Sandy, who could strike terror into the heart of the enemy with his fierceness in battle, was the kindly soul not dissimilar to that of the poet who related to the 'wee modest crimson tipped flow'r'. Circumstances dictated that Burns had to crush his daisy beneath 'The furrows weight,' but Sandy could spare his primrose on the lochside road.

When, like all good soldiers, Sandy eventually faded away, I missed my brother in arms.

CHAPTER FOURTEEN

The Manse, Kirk Session and Local Worthies

While I was trying to establish a ministry in the Parish, Isobel was busy trying to establish a home for us all at the Manse. The house had been built as a Manse during the 1770s to replace the old Manse at Inchadney. It was a gracious Georgian house, firmly built, some of the outer walls being more than a metre in thickness, and had been added to during the nineteenth century. When we came to Kenmore the Manse consisted of three public rooms, five bedrooms and three attic rooms which could also be used as bedrooms. It had a kitchen and pantry with a large utility room, and one smallish bathroom. The front garden consisted of lawns and an orchard while there was a large walled garden to the rear. After the years of living in rented accommodation and other people's houses it was as if we had come to a heavenly place. We loved it and we looked from our front door at the magnificent view in all directions; to the west the loch running up to Ben Lawers; to the east the bump of Faragon above Pitlochry; in front of us the village of Kenmore with the church dominating the scene, and we could not believe our good fortune.

To assist in the day-to-day housekeeping we had engaged the beadle's wife, Mrs McGregor, to come some mornings during the week. As well as being a cheerful character, Ruby was also a mine of information and nothing happened in the district but she would report at great length. Deaths were reported with due solemnity, forthcoming marriages with ribald cheerfulness and impending births with what seemed prophetic intuition. The wee boys loved 'Gregor' as they came to call her and followed her through the house. She was never short or impatient and carried on non-stop conversations with them.

Furnishing a Manse of these proportions always poses a problem for any new minister, but we had been fortunate in being able to purchase much of what we would need from a maiden lady in

Glasgow who was moving from a house to a flat and wanted 'a good home' for the bigger items which would not suit her new place. In the event we were able to obtain almost all we needed to start with, at a very reasonable price. During the flitting, however, we discovered that the stair at the Manse had not been built to take large items and much of the bedroom furniture had to be taken in through the bedroom windows. To assist in this operation we had been advised to approach a 'handy man' in the village by the name of George. This I did and made the acquaintance of an extraordinary man. George was from Glasgow, had come on holiday to Kenmore some fourteen years previously and had just settled down with his wife and daughter. He was the nicest of men, a small roundish man, always dressed in brown, never drank strong drink, never swore, and would tackle any job. He took out the windows where necessary and restored them, mended the broken panes of glass, laid the carpets, fixed the floorboards and while doing this kept up a constant narrative concerning the things which had happened in his life. 'Boys o' Boys' he would begin before launching into a tale of wonder, for George was a Walter Mitty character who had come to believe his fantasies. I always think of George as the forerunner of the talking book. Certainly he was a most entertaining character as he hammered away on the stair. As a taste of his special brand of entertainment I give two examples:

'Boys o' Boys – there Ah was on Alexandra Parade in Glasgow, trying to start ma motor bike. She widna start and so Ah thought Ah wid try a runnin' start. Ah put her in gear and ran as fast as Ah could doon the street. When I let oot the clutch, she fired, but then Ah discovered that the accelerator was too far open, that the machine was gaun so fast Ah couldna' jump on. Ah had to run wi' it till it ran oot o' petrol. It didna stop until we were within three miles o' Stirling. By this time Ah had nae soles on ma shoes.'

There was no doubt that this tale impressed the listeners. Encouraged, George would go on:

'Boys o' boys! Anither time Ah wis workin' on the King George the Fifth bridge. Ah was usin' a hollow ground axe. Oot o' the corner o' ma eye Ah saw a steamer comin' up the river. Ah took ma eye aff whit Ah wis daein and the next thing Ah kent Ah had struck aff three o' ma fingers. Ah juist caught them afore they fell in the water. Ah went doon tae the first aid post but the chap there telt me that Ah wid be better tae go tae a doctor. Ah went tae Dr Paul who pit the fingers back on and bandaged up ma haun'. He tellt me tae tak' the rest o' the day aff. That night Ah couldna' sleep for the pain and in the middle o' the night Ah went back tae Dr Paul. He took me intae his surgery and Ah tellt him that Ah couldna' sleep fur the pain. He unbandaged the haun' and then he said "Well, George, no wonder you had pain – I've been a complete fool. I put on the fingers the wrong way round!" Wi' that he put them on right and bandaged the haun' up again. It was some relief Ah can tell you.' Then prodding his fingers with a nail, George would conclude, 'That's why Ah've got nae feeling in thae fingers.'

One was left quite speechless. Who needed micro-surgery with people like Dr Paul about! George kept the wolf from the door by doing odd jobs for everyone around the parish and by buying and selling. He was a kenspeckle figure at all the auctions within a radius of forty miles and his great boast was that he never paid more than 'Three half-croons' for anything. His workshop was a veritable Aladdin's cave where he entertained everyone in the village who wanted anything from a needle to an anchor – and who had time also to listen to a story or two. It was not a place to visit if you had a time to keep.

On one famous occasion we were having a fete in the Manse gardens. A lady in the congregation offered to read teacups as a side show, but requested a suitable cubicle in which to do her stuff. I put our problem to George who appeared at the Manse the evening before the fete, bearing a collapsible object which when erected turned out to be a movable confessional. It couldn't have been better for the job! We had no bolts of lightning the next day, but I felt sometimes that my predecessors must have been turning in their graves!

George was a devoted husband and father and as long as wife and daughter were looked after, he cheerfully accepted whatever life had in store. We enjoyed his company for some years until, after many operations, he eventually left us. The accounts of the operations might have worried the British Medical Association as they were so graphic that one was bound to wonder if George ever had an anaesthetic. When I laid George to rest beside his beloved wife, I was sure that the Almighty would be getting accounts of some doings on earth which He had missed.

But we missed George!

It didn't take long for us to get settled into the Manse. Suddenly we became very popular with friends and relations who found the Manse at Kenmore a most desirable stopping place. We were delighted to have them and especially pleased that we were now in a position to return some of the hospitality which we had enjoyed from our parents. They came quite regularly. My father assisted me at my first Communion in the Church, Maimie came for a few days and enjoyed the style of the place. Some of the parishioners took it upon themselves to introduce us to the 'society' of central Perthshire, and while their efforts were kindly meant, we sometimes felt that two very important factors were being ignored. The first was that we had two young children who required looking after every time we were both absent from home and secondly that while we might enjoy the company of most of the people who frequented the cocktail parties, it was really the parishioners who had the first call on our time.

The question of priorities started to arise. The work of a minister in a rural parish in the 1950s depended very much on the individual. It was possible for the minister to retire into his study and pursue his studies there for the benefit of himself and the church at large. It was possible for him to devote much of his time looking after the great garden to which he had fallen heir. He could also involve himself in every organisation in the parish where the members would be only too keen to appoint him chairman, or secretary, or treasurer – perhaps all three. It was possible for him to have a one to one relationship with everyone in the parish by visitation and by showing a desire to be involved with them in all aspects of their lives, at the same time providing services and organisations for the proclamation of the Gospel. For good or ill, and because of my temperament and inclinations, I chose the latter course hoping that there would still be some time for the secular organisations and the studies, not to mention the garden.

When I arrived at Kenmore there was a Kirk Session of four elders; Messrs Alex. C. Fraser, Bill Ross, Peter Spence and Duncan McNiven. Alex was the local plumber and senior elder. He felt that he had been instrumental in bringing me to Kenmore and was very much the boss as far as the Session was concerned. It didn't take me long to realise that he was a very strong character who liked to get his own way. Alex had been a sergeant in the Home Guard and I was not surprised that he was known in the parish as General de Gaulle, after the French wartime leader, who also liked his own way. Bill Ross on the other hand, was a man of peace. He was the head forester on the Drummond Hill Forest and was a well educated and gentle man. Peter was a man of few words who had toiled at the wood most of his days, while Duncan was a retired gamekeeper, stalker and ghillie who had the native charm of his Highland kind. He too was a man of few words who confided in me early on: 'You'll never hear me speak in the Kirk Session, but if it ever comes to a vote I'll vote with you.' This was a man to cherish.

All four had one thing in common – they were all freemasons and it was something of a disappointment to them that I was not. It was put to me that I would have a far greater influence on the men in the parish if I became a mason and it was shown to me that the freemasons did much philanthropic work. I was often tempted to take the easy way out by joining, and then, like my father, taking little or nothing to do with the lodge, but the secrecy bit stuck in my throat. As parish minister I felt that I would have to treat everyone on an equal footing, whereas in the masons I would be sharing part of my life with some but not with others. I felt that I had spent a lot of my life striving after a more open society and while I recognised the sincerity of the keen masons, I couldn't go along with them. Eventually I made it clear that I would not be joining. Much to my relief my decision was accepted without any kind of rancour.

It was not long however before I realised that my predecessor, in the latter years of his ministry when the parish was ticking over, had found that the four elders were sufficient for his purpose. They distributed the communion cards, served at communion and attended infrequent Session meetings where they were expected to homologate what Dr Gillies had decided. Now, however, there would have to be changes. Alex Fraser with a twinkle in his eye would remark that he was all for committees of one – he being the one! Having the same kind of inclination myself I should have seen that it would not be long until Alex and I came to a confrontation. It came over the installation of electric light in Kenmore Church. At a Session meeting we both got heated, Alex offered to resign and I accepted his resignation with righteous indignation. As soon as the meeting was over of course I regretted what had happened and wondered why I had allowed it to happen. The rest of the Session were upset and I've no doubt the entire parish was in a high state of excitement when they heard of the falling out. I was not happy and when I heard that Alex too was in a depressed state I went to see him. I found him very ready to bury any hatchet. From that moment on I could not have asked for a more supportive or helpful elder. To be sure he could not help but be abrasive on occasions, but we never had another row – we had both learned a lesson.

I was sure, however, that for the ministry I had undertaken, we would require a stronger Session, and we started to search for new elders. In the event I was instructed to approach three men. After due consultation with them two agreed to serve while the third asked to be excused – for personal reasons which were never revealed – although the gentleman involved could not have been a more loyal member and attender of the church or a better supporter of the minister. The two who agreed to be elders were Mr Alistair Duncan Miller of Remony and Mr Callum McDiarmid of Fearnan. These two individuals could not have been more unlike in so many ways; the one the young laird with a degree in civil engineering deeply involved in politics both national and local, the other a member of an old and respected Tayside family thirled to the land and with a profound knowledge of it and respect for it. Two very different individuals, but if all my decisions had been as successful as these appointments I could have had no regrets, for they were to serve the Church and community with great distinction for many years.

It was the beginning of great good fortune as far as I was concerned, for over the ensuing years we were truly blessed in the calibre of the men and women who made up the Session. Some were appointed from the local congregation, some we fell heir to from other parishes, but all had their own distinctive wisdom and charm. As in all spheres there were outstanding characters; Alex Law, the blacksmith, who became our fabric convenor; Robert Jamieson, a keen Methodist, who retired to the lochside and eventually became our Session Clerk. He was a rabid socialist and pacifist and he and I agreed on nothing but we were the best of friends; Lt. Col. Neil Blair who had commanded the Black Watch in Sicily before being grievously wounded. He too became Session Clerk and ordered affairs with true military precision and a great sense of humour. Our first lady elder was the youthful Morven McCallum who had been teaching in the Sunday School. Over the years, with the natural wastage, we renewed and built up a marvellous team.

We were very sad to lose Bill Ross after a few years. Bill was struck down with a brain tumour and it was not long before we knew that there would be no recovery. It was my first experience in the parish of ministering to the terminally ill and their close relatives and I found it a great burden. I could not bring myself to mouth the easy clichés about it all being God's will as I had grave doubts about it being other than a fateful chance in one's physical make up. I tried to comfort them by holding out to them the promise of the Gospel and above all I tried to assure them of the reality of God's Presence with them. Perhaps the best way of doing this is just to be there sharing their trial, sometimes saying little but ready always to listen. I always thought that weeping with those who weep was an essential part of the ministry of our Lord.

The Kirk at Kenmore is a beautiful little church which has a dignity and a warmth about it. It lacks two things however – a Session house and a W.C. Because we had no place for the elders to meet I always encouraged those not on door duty to meet in the vestry. While sometimes I could have done with some peace and quiet before the service, the custom of having the elders around me gave a great feeling of strength and fellowship. I hoped that they shared with me the preparation for the service of God. Listening to their conversations I must admit that the preparation seemed to be along very strange lines. Much banter concerning the football results, many observations regarding the weather or the state of the gardens, the harvest and the lambing. Local news was discussed and I acquired a lot of useful information regarding many local problems. It was during one of these Sessions that I picked up a phrase often used by Callum. Being a devout man, Callum would have been horrified to have been accused of gossiping. To prevent such a charge being made and as a disclaimer of responsibility for what he was about to report he would preface his remarks, 'Ah'm no' saying, but they're saying . . . . . .'

There were highlights of course. Shoeing a horse in his smiddy, Alex Law had the misfortune to be bitten on the top of his bald head by an ill-tempered beast. It must have been very sore but was a superficial wound. Much to our surprise Alex arrived in church the following Sunday with his head bandaged, and in the vestry, as well as sincere enquiries as to his wellbeing, there were teasing remarks regarding Sikhs not being allowed on the Session. Into this somewhat unruly company came the dignified Alistair who expressed rather serious regret over Alex's accident. In his broad Brechin accent Alex responded 'Aye man it's just as weel it wisna the ither end or Ah widna be able to sit doon!' With that the Beadle arrived to show me into the Church where I was expected to conduct public worship with a reasonably straight face.

If any success attended the ministration of the church over the forty years I was there, much credit is due to the men and women of the Kirk Session. This body evolved from the small but loyal Session which I had inherited, to become a body of men and women which reflected the various strata of the parish life. As time went by we were able to introduce more younger people and the mix seemed to be just about right. We had disagreements of course but never a cross word, and a great deal of rich friendship and companionship. Isobel played her part in this too. Each year at the annual business meeting of the Session, always held in the Manse, she provided supper for the elders when we had finished the business. The sausage rolls and potato scones became a byword, so much so that on the final occasion when the elders were leaving, the normally reticent Ian said to Isobel, 'It doesn't matter who comes to take the minister's place, you'll have to come back and do the purvey!'

The early years in Kenmore were brightened further by the arrival of our third son, Cameron. While we were delighted with the gift of this wee boy, some of the female parishioners expressed their disappointment that we had not been blessed with a girl. But Cameron was received as one of their own and it was amusing to note that while the two older boys were accepted as part of the Manse family, they were never looked upon as 'natives' in the same way as Cameron and Jean. We had some indication too that we were being accepted. I was amused and gratified that some of the younger members of the church felt able to address a congratulatory message at the time of Cameron's birth to – The Reverend Father, at the Manse of Kenmore.

CHAPTER FIFTEEN

The Presbytery Clerk at Work

While the work in the Parish went on, it was not long before I got involved in the work of the Presbytery. We belonged to the Presbytery of Dunkeld, and it was, of course, my duty to play my full part in the work of the court. I was pleased to make the acquaintance of my colleagues in the other parishes and with the parish elders. My own elder in Presbytery was Alex C. Fraser. The Presbytery brought me into closer contact with Ian McLellan, the minister of Weem and later of Dull and Weem. He was the Presbytery Clerk. He was a little round man who had lost an arm at the Somme on St Patrick's Day in 1917, and was a cheerful Highlander full of Gaelic and good humour. He had a kind heart and a deep understanding of the human situation. This little hero with one arm kept the large garden at Weem Manse in neater condition than many ministers keep theirs with all their limbs. He could also use a .22 rifle to great effect and gave short shrift to any rabbit that was foolish enough to invade the said garden. I was very grateful to him that he took his fellow West Coaster under his wing.

I had come to Kenmore a week after John Gow had been inducted to Dunkeld Cathedral. He and I as new boys were introduced together at our first meeting with Dunkeld Presbytery. John had many sterling qualities – he too was a brave man and this had been recognised by the award of a Military Cross. He had a droll and dry sense of humour which was very appealing. On one occasion when he and I were travelling to a very solemn appointment which neither of us was looking forward to, he announced with great seriousness that he was thinking of leaving both his wife and the ministry. Having seen his wife and himself together in seeming domestic bliss I was shocked and searched for words.

'What's gone wrong?' I asked.

'Well!' he said, 'Things came to a head today. She has always nagged me about my laziness. Today she went on and on about it until I could stand it no longer and I said to her, "I'm fed up with all your nagging. I wish I was dead and in my coffin."'

'How awful!' I murmured.

'You'll never believe what she said Kenneth.'

'No?'

'That would suit you fine – lying on your back all day doing nothing.'

I shot a glance at my travelling companion and saw the twinkle in his eye. The appointment to which we were going did not seem so daunting. John was a man of great worth and common sense and it was a great loss when his outstanding ministry was brought to an end by his untimely death.

Donald Cameron at Blair Atholl was another good companion to whom I was immediately drawn. A man from North Argyll, he had all the kindness and attractiveness of the country-man from the West. He too was a great believer in the ministry for all the souls in the parish. Donald took people as he found them and was a great support to all who were in trouble, especially those who had had to struggle through life. He found the idiosyncracies of some of his colleagues in the ministry highly amusing.

Ministers came and went. In Aberfeldy there had been two elderly men, the rather severe Mr Mitchell in the St Andrews Church and Mr Smillie in the Breadalbane Church. Both were kindly disposed to their young neighbour, but when they retired the question of a Union in the town was raised. Needless to say the community was immediately split into warring factions and it was obvious that while agreement to the Union might be accepted in principle, the decision on which church should be retained would not be easily resolved.

It was my first experience in the field of church union. Eventually much to everyone's delight all was resolved by the unanimous agreement of the joint congregations that they would leave a decision on the churches to a panel of arbiters. Each side was convinced that 'their' church would be chosen – it was this confidence that made them so ready to accept outside arbiters. Sadly only one set could be right and when the decision of the arbiters was announced there was an outcry from the members of the congregation whose church had been rejected. It was not a happy time and there were a number of unpleasant meetings before a solution was found. The whole thing reflected little credit upon anyone. The solution meant the virtual overturning of the arbiters' decision and, while if affected me not at all, I was concerned that church members could overturn a decision taken in good faith and set aside previous decisions so readily.

The trials of Aberfeldy, however, were as nothing compared with those which were about to beset Pitlochry. As misfortune would have it I was Moderator of the Presbytery when the trouble arose. We had mutterings from some office-bearers in Moulin and Pitlochry West that all was not well within the congregations. They wished the Presbytery to question the minister whom they blamed for the trouble. As always the Presbytery appointed a committee with the Moderator as Convener, to investigate the same. It was soon apparent that the trouble had arisen when a very generous donor had given a gift and had not received all the thanks which he thought he was due. All this confirmed me in the view that while the church is in little danger from its enemies, it is always under threat from its so called supporters. Sides had been taken and faults and flaws in the minister which he shared with most of his colleagues and which, before, had been ignored, began to loom large in the minds of the ill disposed, who, for reasons of their own, found it politic to support the donor of the gift. They wanted their minister put down the road. It was all very unpleasant and depressing to find that men and women within the Christian Church could be so uncharitable.

Poor Ian McLellan as Clerk to the Presbytery got more and more nervous over the whole issue. He and I went to Edinburgh to consult the Procurator. It became obvious that Ian was feeling the strain and when my year as Moderator was over he asked if I would be willing to relieve him of the Clerkship, as he was spending sleepless nights worrying about Pitlochry. I was very vexed for the good wee man. In his youth he had faced the foe with courage and it seemed to me a shame that at the end of his days he should be worrying his head over people who had forgotten the true mission of the Church. The Presbytery duly appointed me Clerk, and as so often happens, after all the sound and fury the unfortunate minister received a call to another charge. Peace descended on Moulin and Pitlochry West. After a long association with the Pitlochry congregations I can now write that I have received great kindness from many people there. It took me many years however to get over the shock sustained in the gateway to the Highlands at the time of the troubles. While I always knew that there could be a lot of heat generated when differences arose in the church, I was not prepared for the viciousness displayed or the desire to wound which was shown by a few. I still believe that such attitudes have no place in the Church.

Although the beginning of my Clerkship was spoiled in many ways by the Pitlochry experience, I was young enough and perhaps arrogant enough to handle the pressures and still get on with the day to day work, not only of the Parish but of the Presbytery. In this I was assisted by many friends. Ian McLellan, renewed by getting rid of his responsibilities was a tremendous support and the vast majority of members were very kindly, and I soon settled into the job. My father was pleased that I had followed in his footsteps and bought me a typewriter. We were amused at this, thinking that he might have bought himself one as his handwritten minutes of the Presbytery of Kintyre are likely to frustrate future decipherers.

Most of the Presbytery work was routine. Ministers came and went and demissions and inductions brought their own difficulties. As time went on demissions always meant some kind of readjustment as each proposed union or linking was resisted with the greatest passion. Interminable meetings were held with the same old arguments sincerely put forward. If the Presbytery's proposals were followed Christianity would come to an end. One very devout old elder suggested that if the service in his church was moved from 12 noon to 11.30 a.m. we might as well close the doors of the church. Not being able to curb an incipient facetiousness, I asked if he was suggesting that God was not at home at 11.30 a.m. He was not amused and I was sorry that I had been so glib, but it brought matters to a head and we went on our homeward way.

I greatly enjoyed being Presbytery Clerk and got the feeling that in some small way I was giving something to the life of the church not only in my own parish but in the wider field. I like to think that I had a good relationship with all the members – I certainly had a great affection for most of them and always felt it my duty to be supportive of the ministers. Ministers, especially in our day when their position has suffered erosion like all positions of authority in our society, can be very vulnerable in their relationships with so many different kinds of individuals in their charges. They need a lot of support and I always saw that they got it from the Presbytery Clerk. Needless to say there were many who did not need my support and others who needed more divine intervention.

The longest serving minister in the Presbytery was the minister of Little Dunkeld, the Reverend T. Rodger Gillies. He was a native

of Glassary in Mid Argyll, had been a marksman during the First
World War, had been a boxer of some renown at university and a
'character' of the first order. He was not much more than five feet
in height and informed me early on that he was known as Patsy
Gallacher by his congregation. This because though small, he had
a good kick in him! He was a maverick who enjoyed shocking the
establishment both in his personal behaviour and in his theological
statements. He also kept the Presbytery Clerk out of his bed on
many occasions by ringing him at 11 p.m. and then talking on the
telephone for more than an hour. He was also a very kind and
generous man whose sense of humour was not always appreciated
by those of a more staid temperament.

On occasion he would delight in springing a 'hare' which, he
would hope, the Presbytery would pursue. Such was the 'half-horse'.
He introduced the 'half-horse' at the end of a particularly long and
tedious meeting and I was anything but pleased with him. I knew
however that the worst thing to do was to resist the little man.
Thus we heard that some benefactor in the dim and distant past
had donated to the Parish of Dunkeld a sum of money which would
provide a horse to take the minister to the more remote regions of
his parish. Because of various schisms, splits and readjustments
over the years the benefaction had been lost in the great financial
purgatory which is the General Treasurers Department at 121
George Street. By some 'cantrip slight' Gillies had got knowledge
of it and since the Parish of Dunkeld was now divided between the
Cathedral charge and the charge of Little Dunkeld, he claimed a
'half-horse'. The Presbytery was amused and some even laughed in
a condescending manner, but they had reckoned without the good
kick in the wee man. Unfortunately the Presbytery Clerk was the
man in the middle, writing innumerable letters to Mr Colledge
the General Treasurer, who fortunately took a liking to Mr Gillies
and was amused enough by the whole affair not to mind the interminable correspondence. Much to everyone's surprise the 'horse'
money was discovered and Little Dunkeld was credited with the
'half-horse'. We wondered what he would dream up next but fortunately Mr Gillies decided to get married again and had enough
to keep him occupied without starting any further 'hares' or 'horses'.

It was always a very pleasant occasion when a new minister was
inducted to a charge. As Presbytery Clerk I liked to see these services
carried through with proper dignity and sense of occasion, so that
the new minister might feel that he or she had been given a good

start and that the congregation might feel that they too were being given a new start within the context of the wider church. Most inductions passed off without any kind of problem but sometimes dangers lay along the smoothest path. It was the Presbytery's custom to have the newest minister in the Presbytery conduct the first part of the service and preach a sermon. On one occasion I was nervous for, unlike the other members of the Presbytery, I knew that there was a question mark over the sobriety of our latest addition. There were fairly well-documented rumours that now and again he strengthened himself with a dram or two. Being aware of this I had taken the precaution of having a sermon with me and as the hour approached it became more and more likely that I would require to use it. With two minutes to go I got the Presbytery into position for the procession into the Church and was about to tell the Moderator of the change of plan when the door of the meeting room opened and our would-be preacher appeared. He was in excellent fettle and full of the joys. I took him aside and tried to gauge whether he was suitably in charge of himself – he was amazed that I could even question his competence and we all proceeded solemnly, and on my part nervously, to the service. I have had the privilege of hearing many great preachers, but I have to relate that I have never heard a more moving sermon preached, nor have I heard more beautifully phrased prayers given than I heard that day. As far as I could tell the preacher used no notes of any kind. After it was all over and the Presbytery meeting had been closed and the members had dispersed, John Wright, Minister at Moulin, and I were left alone.

'You know, Kenneth,' John said, 'it's not a fair world. You and I could have prepared for weeks, been stone cold sober, and we could never have preached and prayed like that man.' I could only agree and was mightily relieved that all had gone well. I could not help being anxious however, for I was experienced enough to know that no minister can misuse alcohol without eventually causing sadness to himself and to others and grief to the church at large.

In some ways I was sorry that my time as Presbytery Clerk coincided with the fall in the number of ministers needed in the rural areas. On the other hand it had to happen, and while it was always sad to see devoted people being forced to give up their own church or their own minister, it was worth reminding them that Scotland had been over-churched and over-ministered since the disruption and the other schisms which had split the church. Much of the so called 'health' of the church when, according to received wisdom the churches were full and the roads black with people going to church, was due to a competitive and confrontational type of congregationalism and the unChristian attitude that 'anything they can do, we can do better.'

No matter how anyone felt about the new situation, it had to come. The motor car made distances less of an impediment both for minister and parishioners; inflation caused a huge diminution in the value of parish endowments which made it more and more difficult for small congregations to meet the minister's stipend. Depopulation of the rural areas along with a scarcity of ministers caused further crisis and made readjustment not only necessary but desirable. It was with some dismay however that I saw the number of ministers in Dunkeld Presbytery reduced from over twenty to eleven, and by the mid-seventies it was clear that our Presbytery was too small to fulfil all its functions. After the regionalisation of local authorities the church followed suit with the amalgamation of many of the smaller Presbyteries. We were united with Meigle Presbytery. The Clerk of the latter was the Reverend J. Sibbald Clark, the minister of Alyth. He was a much more experienced man than I and I was more than willing that he should continue as Clerk to the united Presbytery. They were kind enough to appoint me as their Moderator for the first year.

Although I could never subscribe to Dr Kenneth Macleod's famous remark to my father: 'I love the brethren but I hate the Presbytery', much of the work was of a fairly dull and routine nature. There were however high points, such as the visits of the Moderators of the Church of Scotland. These visits gave the Presbytery Clerk a lot of extra work. The Business Committee would agree or disagree with an outline programme which would then be changed or approved by Presbytery and the Moderator's office. It was then the task of the Presbytery Clerk to make all the arrangements regarding accommodation, meals and transport. In the early days when Moderators were usually accommodated in Manses or other private houses this could become quite complicated. Latterly, when the Moderators expressed the wish to have hotel accommodation, it was in some ways easier for the Presbytery Clerk who, having got him booked in for the entire visit, knew where he could be contacted and could arrange briefings with him each morning without upsetting any host or hostess.

We were most fortunate in the Moderators who visited us. The stately and dignified Dr Whyte Anderson came from St Cuthbert's in Edinburgh. As I drove him up Glenlyon one wild and dark winter night, the car buffeted by squalls of wind and rain, I am sure he felt out of his element. Suddenly, as we made our way up the narrow roads in the long glen, he asked, 'Will we ever get there, Kenneth?' I reassured him and told him we had just passed the point where Adamnan had halted the plague. 'I'm not surprised it didn't go any further,' was his rather baleful reply. At last I delivered him into the warmth of Glenlyon Manse and the welcome of Mr and Mrs Taylor. He was restored and the following day having seen the beauty of the glen in the daylight, he was full of enthusiasm for it.

We had the calm and serene James S. Stewart who, with Mrs Stewart could not have been easier or more pleasant company. Always gracious and never ruffled, Dr Stewart impressed everyone every time he spoke or preached. I can still recall how he held the attention of hundreds of teenagers in the Pitlochry Theatre with a consummate ease and without any kind of gimmick.

We had the irascible and kindly George Reid who, having served with the Scots Guards, liked things to be done with military precision. Mrs Reid made a very good adjutant and made sure that all was done as it should be. While they were with us the Royal Garden Party took place and they accepted our invitation to convey them thither. Much energy was expended on making sure that all would go according to the timetable and I was duly pleased that I presented the Moderator and his lady at the entrance gate at the appropriate time. Having got there I proceeded to persuade the other guests to allow the Moderator free passage. Everyone was most cooperative and then disaster struck like lightning from a cloudless sky! Dr Reid could not find his tickets of entry. They were in fact back in the Kenmore Hotel! The guard on the gate was unmoved by my argument that no one but the Moderator could be dressed as he was. At last I found an official who knew both the Moderator and myself and we were allowed in. I was mightily relieved as Isobel and I abandoned them for the afternoon – 'Moderator barred from Royal Garden Party' did not become a headline but it had been a close call. On the final day of his visit Dr Reid was to preach at a service in my own Church. He'd had a heavy day and when he arrived at Kenmore Church he asked wearily what the praise list was. I went through it with him.

'And we finish with "The day thou gavest Lord is ended".'

'And not before time' was the tired Moderator's somewhat sour remark.

The last Moderator whose visit I administered was the Reverend Dr Shaw, whose break with tradition regarding Moderatorial dress encouraged people to wonder whether it was good for the image of the church that its ambassador should be dressed like Dick Turpin. Dr Shaw had a very relaxed attitude towards his position and this lack of formality did not go down well with some. He had, however, a great skill in communicating with people on a one to one basis. This was his strength and, playing to it, he gave a lot of pleasure to many people.

While involved with these visits I tried hard to support the Moderator, for it soon became clear to me that the Church expects too much from those whom they appoint as their Moderator for a year. While the Moderator has the Principal Clerk's office as back up for correspondence and arrangements, he has no such support when he is away from Edinburgh. If the Presbytery Clerk for example is either too busy with his own affairs or is not very good at the detailed planning required, the Moderator could find himself in very awkward situations. No Moderator should return to his base after a busy day and be expected to deal with correspondence and messages. The Church should provide the Moderator with a chaplain or an aide who would oversee all the arrangements, attend to day to day business and free the Moderator to give his whole attention to his role as temporary head of the Church. Above all such an aide would protect the Moderator's privacy. The provision of the Baird Flat has been of immense benefit when the Moderator has to be in Edinburgh, as there he and his wife and family can relax. It was an inspired idea of the late Colonel Baird who, as chairman of the Baird Trust, was the instigator of the plan to provide a residence in Edinburgh for the Moderator. It is my opinion that the Moderator would benefit further from the appointment of a personal aide who might also prevent the Moderator making off-the-cuff political pronouncements which in the past have often been unhelpful to the good estate of the Church. It is the duty of every Christian man and woman in a democracy to play a full part in the political life of the country and community. To do this, each individual has to decide which political party to support. It is, however, quite naive to believe that any one political party or ideology fits in with the teaching of Christ more than another. It is a matter of judgement and when those who in the public's perception speak in the name of the Church in a way which may please one party while offending another, such utterance is bound to cause offence to some. This can do nothing but cause division within the Church where members of all political parties and of none are to be found.

Over the years members in church courts and in the Assembly have got themselves all steamed up over many subjects of topical interest. As Presbytery Clerk I have attended more than my fair share of Assemblies and over a period of some forty years I have seen and heard many extraordinary things. I have heard the great and the good in the Assembly extol the virtues of Dr Hastings Banda, proudly claiming a connection between the good Doctor and the Church of his adoption. This was at the time when it was politically correct in the Church to support any revolutionary who was leading a revolt anywhere against British rule. It was interesting some years later to hear the similar great and good washing their hands of the same Dr Banda who, like many of his ilk, had replaced the 'wicked' British rule with government of a dictatorial variety which they jokingly called the 'one party' state. I have been in the Assembly when it voted to support the nuclear weapon and I've been there when it voted against having the same weapon. Those seeking a political stance for the Church in recent years have been of a pinkish hue as far as their policies have been concerned. This has led them into 'pacific' stances over the Falklands conflict and the Gulf War. Passionate speeches have been made on the evils of conflict. On the other hand when the peace dividend leads to the closing of defence establishments, the same pacifists play the 'nationalist' card and get very hot and bothered about Scotland losing so many jobs. Sadly, like their fellow pink panther many who would claim to speak for the Church, end up by falling flat on their faces. This might be quite amusing for some of us but it does not do the image of the Church any good at all. There have been occasions indeed when I have wondered if God had turned his face away from the Assembly altogether. My most awful memory of the Assembly is of the morning when, in the space of half an hour, it solemnly voted on two momentous issues. The first vote was on a motion amending the Loyal Reply to the Queen's message. Instead of referring to the heir to the throne as the Prince of Wales, he was to be given the title Duke of Rothesay. The second vote was to refer the question of the gender of God to the Panel on doctrine. Unbelievably the Assembly passed both motions and I began to feel alienated from the current thinking in the church of my fathers. The more one thinks about the futility of these motions the less does one need to wonder why the Church sometimes is not taken seriously.

One must always bear in mind that the church courts are made up of fallible and sinful human beings and individually or collectively they are not ever going to be the fount of all wisdom. It had been my opinion for some time, however, that we might save ourselves from our worst follies if we could concentrate on seeking the best ways by which the Gospel of Salvation might be winsomely proclaimed.

It was my privilege to attend my first Assembly in the company of my father and Dr Kenneth Macleod, one time minister of Gigha, poet and visionary. On the second afternoon there was a wearisome debate on some report and my father noted that his friend had wisely stayed away. A vote was called and Dr Kenneth appeared and duly voted. When the tellers were counting the vote he turned to me and said,

'What was that all about?'

'Don't tell me you voted without knowing what you were voting for!' I chided him.

'Oh I knew what I was doing,' he said. 'Do you see that bald headed man near to the Moderator's chair? He has never made a right decision in the Assembly any time he has been here, so I watched how he voted and then I voted the other way.'

I was rather taken aback at the time, but as the years passed I realised there was some merit in his reasoning and followed his example on more than one occasion.

CHAPTER SIXTEEN

Form of Ministry
and Church Activities

A s the summer of 1950 ended, I began to give serious thought
to the formation of some church organisations. Not unnaturally
the aged and tired Dr Gillies had allowed some of these to wither.
There was, however, a good going Sunday School and I had little
doubt that we could continue it quite successfully. It was with some
trepidation however that I sought members for a church choir and
called for candidates for a Bible Class.

I was fortunate that my coming to the parish coincided with an
upswing in the numbers of teenagers in the district. Some of these
very pleasant schoolgirls, along with a few men and women of more
mature age formed a choir which greatly improved the congregational singing, and with great courage we prepared for a special
Christmas Service. The postwar hydro electric schemes had made
possible the electrification of houses in the village and we had
installed electric light in the church, so for our Christmas service
we were able to introduce a decorated and lit Christmas tree. This
was innovation for Kenmore and I wondered how people would
react. From the start the Christmas service held on the Sunday
evening before Christmas became a very special occasion, with the
church filled to overflowing and a happy atmosphere prevailing. It
has to be said that many at the service were not to be seen in church
again until the following year, but we were happy to see them and
it gave them a feeling of belonging to the church. Mrs Wynne, one
of my favourite 'lapsed masses', spoke for them all. On leaving the
church she would shake my hand warmly and with a twinkle would
remark, 'That was lovely! You must have been feart the roof would
fall in wi' me being here.'

While the choir benefited from having so many nice looking
young girls in it, therein lay its weakness, for young girls get
married and move away. I had to accept the cyclical nature of rural
population patterns which affected all the organisations. For a few

151

years they would flourish because of an increase in this or that age group but suddenly the numbers would fall away and one had to be patient while awaiting another upturn. It was one of those things one had to live with. As far as the special Christmas services were concerned, while the adult choir sustained the first of these we gradually went over to services which were sustained by the children and young people. I wrote simple scripts around the nativity theme and introduced a little theatre into the services. These were truly parish affairs and everyone felt involved. They brought the minister and, I trust, others, a great deal of joy.

As I had little or no musical talent, much depended on the cooperation of the organists and anyone else that I could recruit. I was most fortunate that I had a very good relationship with all those who played the very simple but sweet pipe organ which gave music in Kenmore Church. It was a one manual instrument which in the early days was 'pumped' by Sandy the Beadle. We were utterly dependent on Sandy giving air to the organ – if he failed, the music collapsed with a pathetic sigh. Fortunately for most of the time Sandy was reliable but there were one or two occasions on a warm Sunday morning when Sandy was overcome by the soporific effect of the sermon. Then the voluntary for the up-taking of the offering was somewhat delayed while the organist brought Sandy out of his religious slumbers.

The organists themselves came in many shapes and sizes. My first was a young man, David Wishart, the son of a widow. He cycled the six miles from Aberfeldy every Sunday and to the choir practices during the week. He was a most attractive and well-mannered young man who, like so many of his age group, had to leave the district to forward his career. We missed him very much. He was followed by Miss Deas, a native of Fife, who had come to the Co-op in Aberfeldy as a book-keeper. She was a loyal servant of the church and played a limited repertoire with great accuracy. It caused great amusement when, after the chart-topping success of The Seekers, her final voluntary was invariably 'The carnival is over'. I often wondered if she was having me on. When she retired her place was taken by Miss McLaughlan who was more local, having been for some time the postmistress in Fortingall. On her retiral she came to live in the Kenmore Library building which made things easier for us all. For a time we had a Mrs Scollay, the wife of the Burgh Surveyor in Aberfeldy. She was a most kind and courteous lady with whom it was a joy to work. Finally I had Dr

Kerr Grieve. Dr Grieve was a consultant gynaecologist from Motherwell who had bought a house in Fearnan. For over twenty years he was the regular organist at Kenmore Church on most Sundays travelling to and from Motherwell in all kinds of weather. There were occasions when I had grave doubts regarding Dr Grieve's arithmetic, for often he played either a verse too many or one too few, but his playing was a joy to listen to. His voluntaries were a delight and he had an uncanny knack of being able to produce a voluntary which was fitting either to the theme of the service or to the season of the year. The minister and congregation at Kenmore could never repay Kerr Grieve for this completely unpaid contribution to our worship over these many years. We were more than grateful to those who 'stood in' when the regular organists were off for one reason or another: Mrs Sallie Opie, Mrs Margaret Oswald and my own wife often had to play at very short notice and did so with a good heart.

We started the Sunday School as soon as the summer holidays in 1950 were over, and I was gratified with the numbers who attended. For better or for worse I thought that 10.15 a.m. was the time to meet. This meant a good deal of hurry and scurry, not to say ministerial impatience in the Manse, especially when our boys were of an age to attend. I again recruited some of the teenage girls as teachers. Margaret Campbell loyally cycled down from Remony Sunday by Sunday, and the Mowbray family produced a succession of infant teachers in Margaret, Phyllis and Irene. They, with the Ramsay girls, Christine and Hughina, came from Balnaskeag and brought a flock of children with them. The children were the usual mix, from the shy little girls to the mischievous and rowdy older boys and we had no great problems with them. They were all of an honest disposition, but a mystery remains to this day. On the morning of the Harvest Thanksgiving, when the church was beautifully decorated and the chancel was groaning with fruit and flowers of all descriptions, the bunch of grapes which had been fat and plump when we left on the Saturday afternoon, had an awful lot of bare stalks and looked mighty thin when we arrived in the church on the Sunday morning!

The demographic cycle was very evident as the fifties moved on. When I arrived in the parish the Acharn School, which catered for the children on the south side of the loch from Kenmore to Callellochan, had only 17 pupils on the roll, but with the postwar baby boom the numbers increased steadily and by the sixties the

Acharn and Fearnan schools could not cope. A new school was opened in Kenmore to cater for all the children on both sides of the loch and when it opened in 1967 over 60 pupils enrolled. This rise in numbers was greatly to my advantage as I sought to start organisations which would meet some of the childrens' spiritual and social needs. The Sunday School grew, there were viable numbers in the Bible Class, and I was able to start a small company of the Boys' Brigade and a Youth Club.

Twelve boys enrolled in the B.B. and I had the assistance of my senior elder, Alex Fraser, whose keenness and energy belied his years. We met in the Holder Hall which was the meeting place of the parish. It had been donated by one Sir John Holder, a fact which was kept before us on a scroll above the platform. He had been a shooting tenant in Remony Lodge around the turn of the century. The hall was constructed of wood and corrugated iron and being of a good size it met most of the needs of the local organisations. It was very utilitarian with a rectangular floor space and a square wooden platform at the west end. Behind the platform partition were two smaller rooms to serve as kitchen and changing rooms, but while it served its purpose well over the years, it was obviously coming to the end of its days. The heating system which was coal fired could only be used for big occasions and was temperamental to say the least. With the wind in certain airts the boiler fire did not 'draw' very well and one usually had the alternative of a warm hall filled with smoke, or a smoke-free hall with an arctic temperature.

There being no decoration to speak of and no ornamentation at all, it suited my Boys' Brigade and Youth Club very well. We played some very hectic team games and it has to be said that on the odd occasion windows were broken. In the morning the minister could be seen chasing up some local joiner or glazier to get him to repair the damage before some of the more critical parishioners could see what had happened. The Youth Club met on a Friday evening and to begin with we played badminton and table tennis. It was a meeting place for the young people and was so successful that we had to extend the meeting times, the early part of the evening for the younger children while the older teenagers came for the final two hours. I found it most rewarding having this weekly relationship with some thirty to forty young people.

Having joined the local Golf Club and Badminton club, I had many opportunities of getting to know the people to whom I was ministering. Many of those whom I met on these occasions were not regular church attenders but this did not upset me unduly for I felt I was building up a relationship with them. I knew, and I think they knew, that the day would come when we would deal with each other on the more important matters of life and death. We all knew that the establishment of friendship would help when these times came. It did too. The days came for so many of them when there were many tears, but the fact that we had played and laughed together on the good days helped us all.

In reaching out to the community the Boys' Brigade, the Youth Club and the choir got very daring. As well as putting on annual services and displays we produced concerts, one of my brother's plays, *Minister's Monday*, and a pantomime – *Cinderella*. I am sure that they were all very amateurish but the public responded well. The Holder Hall was filled to overflowing and everyone enjoyed themselves, except perhaps the minister wracked by anxiety neurosis and on one occasion the realisation that he had committed the ultimate folly. The young people had been resisting the idea of performing at a concert but eventually agreed but only on the understanding that I personally would do a 'turn'. Foolishly I agreed, thinking that as the time approached they would forget my undertaking. Instead, the nearer we got to the date the greater their insistence became, until I knew that I would lose all their support if I failed to keep my side of the bargain. I was brought face to face with the fact that I was virtually without any performing talent – I had, however, learned to dance as a child and in desperation I hired a sailor's suit and gave some practice to the Sailor's Hornpipe. Needless to say this folly brought the house down. The calls for an encore were ignored for I felt that they were more to test my stamina than to commend my perform-ance. That was a 'one-off' performance not to be repeated!

Before the advent of television the Whist Drive was a regular entertainment in all the village halls. One learned very quickly that while the many were there for an evening's entertainment, a few were there for the prizes. If fortune brought you a partner of the latter variety it was politic to play the hand to the best of your ability lest a snide remark regarding your intelligence was to be your lot.

By the early sixties people had got fed up with the discomfort of the Holder Hall and there was talk of a replacement. The decision to have a school at Kenmore came at about this time and after a lot of negotiation and discussion it was agreed to put forward an imaginative scheme in which the school would incorporate a community centre with a hall which would serve both school and community. Great efforts went into raising the money to meet the Parish part of the bargain.

In many ways I missed the Holder Hall as there had been many splendid functions there. We had often given it a face lift when decorating it for Christmas parties and Sales of Work. Concerts of all varieties had been successful there and the local amateur dramatic club – the Acharn Players under the direction of Robert Jamieson – had entertained the whole community. The new Hall in the community centre was magnificent in comparison, well heated and beautifully decorated. It was restricting however to the childrens' more hectic activities. The hall had to be returned to its pristine condition after every let. However, with all its drawbacks, the Youth work continued and was a great joy to me in spite of the fact that every breakage or mark on the wall was blamed on the young. We were of course an easy target. It was almost worth it for the pure delight it gave us when we could prove that someone else was to blame.

Of all the church organisations the one which gave most to the immediate life of the congregation was undoubtedly the Woman's Guild. In the winter months following our arrival the Guild, which had been kept in being during the vacancy with Mrs Wilson, Portbane, as President, met in Portbane. Everyone was glad when it was decided to return the Guild meetings to the Manse and when it came to the election of office bearers, Mrs Wilson graciously stepped down and Isobel became President. Miss Helen Parker Ness was Secretary and Treasurer. The Guild met once a month and the logistics of the first Wednesday in the month put a strain on the family life, especially if a speaker had to be entertained. He or she, if without a car, had to be fetched from Aberfeldy where they had arrived by bus or train. Often they had to come the night before and be given hospitality. With two young boys and in a year or two three, it was not an easy task. On the day of the meeting all the chairs in the Manse had to be put into the drawing room and the ladies began arriving early, on foot or by car. When they were all on parade there was quite a pressure on the seating, and we still have a sofa the springs of which have never recovered from the weight of three large ladies squeezed into it. My own ministerial duties were limited to opening the meeting with prayer before removing myself and the children to allow the ladies to get on with their business. Problems arose when I had to be at another engagement, which meant poor Isobel had to cope with the meeting with the two boys clutching her skirts. Undoubtedly these women were the greatest support to the church and to the minister. Every year they willingly supplied all the 'goodies' for the parish children's party and in every second year they organised the Sale of Work which was one of the main fund raising efforts. In church attendance and in every other way the Guild members were of immense importance and it was not long until its very success made it necessary for us to have two meetings – one in the afternoon in the Manse and the other in Fearnan in the evening. When Lawers Parish came into the linkage in 1958, the numbers in the Guild became such that the Manse meeting was abandoned and the Guild moved to an evening meeting in one or other of the village halls. Naturally the Guild changed in personnel over the forty years, but throughout these years the Guild was a constant source of inspiration and support.

Until 1958, Ardeonaig on the south side of Loch Tay and Lawers on the north had both had their own minister, but when Mr Grieve and Mr Horne retired it was obvious that readjustment would take place. After lengthy negotiations it was agreed that the Ardtalnaig district should be detached from Ardeonaig and, with Lawers, be added to the charge of Kenmore. I was happy with this outcome, but although the numbers were small, providing regular services for Ardtalnaig and Lawers meant that I had to have an extra service on the Sunday afternoon. On one Sunday I took services in Kenmore, Acharn and Ardtalnaig and on alternate Sundays at Kenmore, Fearnan and Lawers. With a morning Sunday School and an evening Bible Class the Sundays became rather hectic.

I greatly enjoyed the new work but was soon to learn that a minister can only give of his best if he is physically, mentally and spiritually alert. So it was that when I started to have some influence over affairs I was always against a minister having more than two services on a Sunday on a regular basis. No matter how keen a minister is he will not be doing his best if he is wondering if he has enough time to get to his next service. It is not only he or she who suffers tiredness, one or other of the congregations will be 'short changed'.

In both Ardtalnaig and Lawers there were devout and loyal people who added strength to the Kenmore situation. John Crerar, the elder at Ardtalnaig, a retired farmer, always led a devoted if small band of worshippers in the schoolroom at Ardtalnaig. It was in that schoolroom that I gave a child the wrong name in baptism – the only time. The dear girl was to be named Janet Edith but was offered to the Lord as Judith. The parents were a splendid couple who easily forgave me. As the father said, I got the first letter and the last two right! It was in that small schoolroom that I was first aware of an outstanding voice in a young girl who, with her parents, had come to the service as visitors in the district. Her name was Mary Sandeman and at the door of the school I prophesied that one day she would be a mod medallist. She smiled that smile which has cheered so many. Even I could not have known what fame was before her.

Lawers maintained its separate status. The community was almost entirely made up of farming families who had been able to purchase their farms from the former landowner. While there were but some forty members I was a little surprised to find that there were two church buildings. The little mission church at Carie, the result of a congregational dispute early in the century, was still in use. One of my first moves was to rectify this ridiculous situation but before disposing of the Carie building we had a combined service of thanksgiving, including the baptism of the local laird's infant son. Carie did not boast any musical instrument and I tried to lead the praise as best I could. The result was only partially successful as I pitched the singings either too high or too low. So that I might not forget the occasion, I was amused to receive a gift from the laird. It was a silver tuning-fork!

Many of the families had been on the lochside for generations and were well set in their farming ways. They were thirled to the land and when anyone criticised their way of doing they could point out, with some reason, that they had survived through some bitter times while others had gone to the wall. They were well set in their church ideas as well. It had been difficult for them to give up their own minister but they welcomed me with kindness and hospitality. I was greatly helped by the friendship shown by the Session Clerk, the late Ian McDonald, whose early death left a great gap in the congregation, and by the late Miss McDiarmid, the Treasurer, who also went out of her way to smooth the path of transition.

Attendance at church was generally very good as was the financial support. The organist was Mrs Robertson who had been the school teacher in Lawers before marrying Alistair Robertson of Ben Lawers Hotel farm. She was a gentle soul who confessed to a limited repertoire on the little harmonium. We got through some of the better known psalms, paraphrases and hymns fairly frequently. We got on splendidly, even though we lifted our eyes to the hills rather more often than might have been necessary. The aforesaid harmonium eventually gave up when the proverbial church mouse chewed a hole in its bellows. We were greatly indebted to one of the local lairds who, herself an organist, presented us with a spanking new electric instrument. However, the church mouse was not finished with us yet. It ate the plastic covering on the circuits and silenced the organ again. When we renewed the circuitry we made sure there was no repetition by making the inside of the organ resemble a veritable rodent Alcatraz!

Lawers Church, a plain rectangular building, was built in 1833 when the previous church on the lochside had become derelict. This former church had had a close connection with the famous seer, The Lady of Lawers, who in the seventeenth century had made prophetic observations which at the time must have appeared impossible but which, through the years, have been fulfilled. One such referred to the decline of the Campbell family. At the time of the prophecy these Campbells of Breadalbane were stronger in central Scotland than the kings. But the Lady prophesied that the day would come when all that the Breadalbanes owned on Loch Tayside could be carried by a pony. The twentieth century was to see the prophecy come true and one of the last feus held by that family concerned the Manse at Lawers. It being redundant as far as the church was concerned we wished to sell the Manse. We were not able to do so until we had bought out that feu. In a small way we had been instrumental in bringing about the prophetic word of the Lady. The family which had owned everything from 'Kenmore to Benmore' were landless in Breadalbane.

The north side of Loch Tay had been densely populated. Pennant in his tour through Scotland reports in 1769 that there were 1786 souls on the North side. From the beginning of the nineteenth century and the enclosure of the farms the population had decreased dramatically and when I became minister of Lawers there were only twenty households. This fact was never quite digested by Peter Anderson who was my senior elder. At every session meeting he complained of the smallness of the congregations in church, reminding us that when he was a boy he had to sit on his father's knee because of the numbers present. I would point out that if every living soul in Lawers were to attend, the church would still be but a quarter full, but he would not be comforted. Dear old Peter! When I was visiting him on his deathbed he gave me a gold half-sovereign. I had never seen one before but it has remained a precious possession and one which reminds me of the old fellow – a faithful soul – for whom all the changes had become too great to under-stand. I like to think of him with the ten thousand thousand before the Throne – a decent congregation.

Visiting in rural congregations has its own dangers and challenges. With the deification of Lassie many think of collie dogs as being faithful and gentle beasts. Many are, but there are others. In one of the farmhouses there lived two brothers with their two sisters. Each had a collie dog. One by one the two sisters and one of the brothers died. The survivor lived on with the four dogs and my visits always began with an undignified shouting match carried on with a chorus of four wildly barking dogs. The minister: 'Get these dogs under control before I come into the kitchen'. Much shouting and barking within and then the cry 'Ye're alright, come in!' On entering the kitchen I would see the steely eyes of the dogs now cowering beneath the kitchen settle, gleaming with disfavour at the stranger. The old boy and I would have our chat and discussion. One day however we were getting on fine when suddenly one of the dogs shot like a bullet from his place and took hold of my shin bone. There was turmoil in the kitchen. Oaths were exchanged and it took a great deal of shouting and stick waving to restore order. When all was quiet again and it was obvious that no permanent damage had been done to my leg, the old boy observed: 'It was yer ain fault – ye were shaken your leg.' When I left I could not help wondering what the Panel on Doctrine would make of that.

The Lawers natives had a well developed sense of direction. While in Kintyre we went 'up' or 'down' the road; in Lawers one went 'East' or 'West'. At table, one had to have a mental compass ready when asked to 'pass east the scones'. My own confusion reached the ultimate on the day when I was asked in all serious-ness: 'Have you seen West going East?' I was quite sure that I had eventually gone 'round the bend' when someone was kind enough to explain that West was the driver of the grocer's van from Killin.

Lawers Parish in the past had been noted for two things. It had been the scene of two great religious revivals at the turn of the nineteenth century. It was further noted for the number of notably well-educated people it had produced. As well as one Member of Parliament and a Professor, nine ministers, eleven teachers and seven doctors were natives of the place. While I was minister Lawers was more noted perhaps for the quality of the sheep and cattle produced by its farmers but there is no doubt that the people to whom I ministered there were of sterling quality and kindly hospitality, some of whom would have made their mark in any of the professions if they had not decided to stick by the land they loved. I am glad they made that decision.

My mother's gracious humility had always prevented her being over ready with advice. However, wishing to save her son from at least some of the slings and arrows, she did advise me against putting myself up for election to any position within the parish. 'Never trust a ballot box!' she said to me. The distrust of the ballot box did not reflect any doubts she might have had regarding the democratic processes, but arose from her very personal experiences when my father had put himself up for election to the Argyll County Council. There had been one or two bruising contests and in the way of such things he won some and he lost some. My mother was never very sure whether his health and his ministry suffered more from his very public triumphalism in victory or from his just as public rage in defeat.

When the time came for me to play a part in local affairs I was conscious of the great merit in my mother's view. It seemed to me that a minister should take part fully in all aspects of the life of the parish but that he should avoid at all costs anything which might cause division within his charge. While in a perfect world elections should be fought keenly but without rancour, within a community where everyone knows what everybody else is saying and doing, it is difficult to avoid damaging divisions when sides are taken. I decided to follow my mother's advice. However I was asked to become the District Councillor for the parish and no one saw fit to oppose my nomination. Thus I became a member of the Highland District Council and as such worked very closely with Alistair Duncan Miller who was then the County Councillor. While we did not agree on everything and were in fact of different political persuasions, we pulled together very well for the benefit of the people we represented. New local authority houses were built in Kenmore, Acharn and Fearnan; street lighting beamed forth in the villages; the roads and the environs were improved. The meetings in the rather spartan conditions of the Ballinluig Hall were always courteous and while sometimes the arguments were put forward with vigour, there was never any ill-temper. I always found the great advantage of these meetings lay in the fact that the various officials from the departments were present. Most of them lived within the Highland area and were known socially to us. While matters of principle might be decided by the council, if one wanted some improvement made in roads or drainage etc., a word to Charlie, or Bill, or Tom after the meeting produced more immediate results than letter writing or pontificating. While I realise that the demise of the small authorities like the Highland District was inevitable, I feel that the impersonalisation of the Council work which has resulted in officials getting even further away from the daily needs and complaints of people, has been to the detriment of local government.

Of course things could get a little too parochial.

On one famous occasion I was contacted at lunchtime by one of my parishioners asking if I could ensure that the road be-tween Aberfeldy and Kenmore would be properly gritted before six o'clock. I did not feel that attendance to such detail came within my remit unless there was some compelling reason.

'What's the trouble?' I asked.

'Don't you know?' said the lady, 'that this is the night of Madame Stewart Stevenson's cocktail party? We must be able to get there.'

It was good to know that somebody had their priorities right!

Our efforts in the interests of our constituents sometimes had results which we could not envisage. With the tourist industry bur-geoning, it was necessary to have erected some Public Lavatories at the East end of the Loch. After much battling these were eventually built. One of the visitors benefiting from this facility was my dear father-in-law who had reached that certain age when the walk to the village and back to the Manse was rather long without relief.

'Man, Kenneth,' he said with great feeling, 'thae toilets are a godsend. They will aye be a memorial tae ye.'

As I've recounted earlier, part of my stipend had been paid in farmyard manure. With a memorial in the shape of a Public Convenience it was difficult to know what higher accolade awaited me!

I greatly enjoyed my time with the Highland District Council. With my contacts there, new avenues of service opened up through local Education Subcommittees, Health Councils and so on. I did not feel that these duties took away from my ministerial obligations. They were in fact complementary. In different ways I was still attending to the cure of souls. Sadly such service is now practically closed to the vast majority of ministers whose day to day parish duties leave them no time for anything else. Moreover the councillors' duties are practically full time.

I always took the view that the minister should be neutral as far as party politics is concerned and should not be actively involved in promoting any party. Like everyone else it is his duty to take part in the political process and to make up his mind which party he will support at the ballot box. He has to be independent of all groups within his parish especially any which might wish to bring pressure to bear upon him. I expect everyone knew that I am a Tory, after all, my mother would try to convince some of my colleagues of a pinkish hue that God is a Tory. Alistair Duncan Miller always supported the Liberal cause and stood as a Liberal Parliamentary candidate. When it came to the Regional elections I was keen to support Alistair and begged him to stand as an Independent. This he did and was elected with a large majority. We were pleased and proud when he became the first Convenor of the Tayside Region and delighted when he led the council to its first 'kirking' to Kenmore Church.

CHAPTER SEVENTEEN

400th Anniversary of Kenmore Kirk

In any human endeavour which has a routine, it is easy to get into a rut. As the Church's work is as routine as any with its weekly services, it is essential that this routine is punctuated by extraordinary and non-routine occasions. The congregation can work for and look forward to these high days, and after they are over draw strength and encouragement from them, as well as learning.

We were fortunate that in Kenmore we had quite a number of these occasions. I wasn't too many years in the place when we were asked to provide a live broadcast. At that time the radio always carried an evening service. We were all pleased and excited as it was to be the very first broadcast from Kenmore Church. The choir practised with great zest and we had a sudden influx of volunteers! At the normal services the praise for the broadcast was introduced so that the congregation could practise too. The minister hoped that his sermon would be worthy of the occasion. A week before the broadcast, the telephone engineers came to install the land-line and the whole parish was in a state of high anticipation. On the Saturday the producer, whom we knew, came to stay at the Manse. The morning service passed but everyone's mind was on the 'big one' yet to come. We were told the drill. The outside broadcast engineers would come in early afternoon to set up the necessary equipment in the vestry and to install and 'balance' the microphones and the congregation were bidden to be in their places an hour before the service was due to be broadcast. As the afternoon wore on and no engineers appeared the producer, now a worried man, eventually rang the BBC. He was reassured that the men had left but were doing some interviews first at the scene of a colliery disaster in Lanark. We waited. We went to the church where people were gathering. We waited. With some fifty minutes to go before going on air, we had a congregation, a choir, a minister and a sermon. We also had a producer but no engineers. With a heavy heart the said producer told the congregation that he would have to phone Queen Margaret Drive to tell them to prepare an alternative programme. Having told the congregation to remain where they were, for the service of God would go ahead as He did not need any outside help to receive us, the producer and I walked down from the church to the telephone kiosk. Just then two taxis roared into the square. Our engineers had arrived. Were our troubles over? Not a bit of it! The poor men had had a traumatic time at the disaster pit. They had set out for Kenmore but had decided they would require some food on the way. They had needed refreshment and had partaken of all kinds, so they were in good fettle. It was obvious that they needed help if we were to get on the air in time and it was very fortunate that we had various people, Jock Findlay, Jimmy Fraser, Jackie Moir and others with mechanical know-how, who gave much valiant assistance. With fifteen minutes to spare the microphones were installed and 'live'. It had not been the best preparation for our first broadcast but it was all very worthwhile when we received letters of congratulations and thanks from around the country. Best of all it was another help in knitting the community together in common purpose. We couldn't wait to be asked again.

We were fortunate that other high points punctuated the years. We were asked to provide a service to mark an anniversary of the Forestry Commission. This was very appropriate as the Forestry Commission at the time was one of the biggest employers in the parish. Another service commemorated the Battle of Britain and we had the pleasure of having the retired senior Chaplain of the Royal Air Force, Dr Hardie, sharing the pulpit. One year we had a series of broadcasts to mark the various seasons – the Ploughing, the Sowing and the Harvesting. One of these was interrupted by a very excited dog which burst into the church in search of her mistress. The said mistress had been our District Nurse over many years. She was of the Free Presbyterian tradition and had not taken too kindly to my more liberal approach in religious matters. She had, however, been an excellent nurse and we agreed to differ on church affairs. She had returned for a short spell as a relief and, as so often happens on these occasions, in the more relaxed atmosphere she became much more friendly, to the extent that we asked her to help us in the choir. She had a very good contralto voice and was of immense assistance. With all the cables being led into the church the doors could not be closed completely for the broadcast and the nurse's dog having escaped from her cottage made a bee-line for her mistress. In the middle of the first prayer the door crashed open, the dog slithered across the polished chancel floor and with a triumphant yelp leapt into the nurse's arms. Needless to say the nurse was mortified. With great presence of mind she rose and carried off the excited dog while the minister addressed the Almighty in measured terms, in his heart asking why such a thing should happen. All was well. We were assured that the commotion had not been picked up by the microphones and when all was over and the nurse reassured, we all felt that not only had we had the ploughing, the sowing and the reaping, we had come near to a sheepdog trial as well.

The outstanding event of my forty years ministry was undoubtedly the celebration of the 400th anniversary of Kenmore Church. In 1579 the people of the parish had petitioned Breadalbane to build a church at Kenmore. The building had been a place of worship extra to the Parish Church at Inchadney which, before the reformation, had been part of the 'vicarage' of the Dean of Dunkeld Cathedral. In 1779 the church at Kenmore had been refurbished by the then Marquis of Breadalbane and became the Parish Church. At this time also the graveyard was transferred to Kenmore along with the Market stance. These had been at Inchadney about a mile east of Taymouth Castle. In building his new castle and laying out the walled grounds of Taymouth the Marquis wished to be rid of the encumbrance at Inchadney.

The Kirk Session was persuaded that we should have a 400th celebration and plans were put in hand. I was very fortunate that in Colonel Neil Blair as Session Clerk and Mr Alistair Duncan Miller as Convenor of the planning committee, I had two men with vast experience of organisation in many fields. They made sure that everything was done efficiently. We had a special booklet prepared recounting the history of the church in the parish, which Miss Freda Hawkins researched and edited for us with her usual enthusiasm. Various events were planned. An exhibition on the history of church and parish was mounted in the library building and the Woman's Guild with the Kirk Session planned a big Sale of Work with an open air auction on the market stance in the village square. The Youth Club members, with adult assistance, mounted a pageant which I had scripted. This was produced in the Community centre and the scenes began with the prehistoric natives around the standing stones at Croftmoraig, continuing with scenes from various centuries – the death of Sybilla, the feud between the Campbells and the MacGregors culminating in the execution of Gregor Roy, the coming of Montrose and his Royalists through Kenmore in the middle of the seventeenth century, the visit of Robert Burns in 1787 and the visit of Queen Victoria to Taymouth Castle in 1843. It was a tremendous parish effort involving hundreds of people.

The week of special events marking the anniversary began with a service at which the Moderator of the Church of Scotland, the Right Reverend Robin Barbour preached. On the Saturday, the day of the Sale and Auction the heavens opened and it appeared as if all the planning might go for nought. The marquee on the village green threatened to buckle under the weight of rainwater. Sir Alex and Lady Douglas Home arrived at the Manse for lunch, the freshly picked strawberries from the Manse garden containing as much water as sugar. However, during lunch a clearance began to show and by the time that nicest of men, Sir Alex, opened the Sale and Auction, the rain had ceased and while it was not a bright summer day, hundreds of people thronged the square and all went well. Ian Thomson, himself a minister's son and head auctioneer of United Marts, kept the auction going with high good humour – even the minister found himself in possession of a lamb – a live lamb! As in all great undertakings it is in the peripheral minutae that the humour is to be found. It so happened that, as luck would have it, we had a visit from Isobel's ancient Aunt Florrie from Canada. She was a bright and elegant person who enjoyed the stir greatly. Being well into her eighties we wondered how she would stand up to the stress of the afternoon and in fact she found the heat in the marquee too much and she collapsed. With all the stress and strain of so much happening around us this was something that Isobel and I could have done without. As always, however, various members of the family coped with the situation and after being taken into the fresh air Aunt Florrie recovered quite quickly but was returned to the Manse to rest. The Sale and Auction eventually finished and we said our farewells to our invited guests the Douglas Homes, the Lord Lieutenant and his wife. As soon as we could, Isobel and I left the square and returned to the family and guests at the Manse, admitting to each other that we were absolutely exhausted – shattered beyond belief after the strain of the day and hoping that Aunt Florrie was not too bad. I made quick arrangements to provide the guests with a drink and was comforted to see that Aunt Florrie was holding court again. Isobel came in looking somewhat 'part-worn'.

'How are you Aunt Florrie?' she enquired solicitously.

Without answering the question the lady asked one of her own. 'What are we having for supper Isobel?'

I felt that the lady of the Manse came very close to committing murder just at that moment.

We had planned an open air Communion service for the final Sunday of our celebrations. There is a beautiful description of such a communion by the Bishop of Sodor and Man who had visited Breadalbane some time at the turn of the eighteenth century. He says in his diary of the visit that he had never witnessed such a solemn scene and it seemed right that in recalling all the centuries of Christian worship which had taken place in the parish of Kenmore that we should try to recreate the simplicity and solemnity of the occasion. We had special tokens struck. After the deluge of Saturday morning we were worried that all our plans would be thwarted but Sunday dawned sunny and warm. The people of all kinds and conditions, races and denominations gathered, in all kinds of garb from Sunday best to holiday shorts. When the hour of service came I led the Kirk Session, the elders bearing the elements, down from the church to the appointed place where a simple table had been set up. The late Stewart McDiarmid presented and once again, as in the scene depicted by the Bishop, the praise of God rose from the assembled faithful and mingled with the bird song. The loch shimmered in the sun, the infant Tay glided serenely by as it started its endless journeying to the sea and the hills and the mountain looked down upon us. The symbol of the Saviour's broken body was passed among the faithful, the Cup of Salvation was received with hope and joy. With so many, I was deeply moved, felt that indeed the Spirit of the Lord was among us. It was a day to remember always, a day in which the whole community was brought together in one holy and solemn purpose – to remember the dying Love of the Lord. It was a day too to remember all the faithful in the past generations who had kept the fires of religion burning in the hearts of the people. In thanking God for them we also sought His guidance for the future.

There were other great days within the life of the church when we had special services of various kinds. I was touched when the congregation honoured me on the occasion of my silver jubilee in the ministry and Isobel and I were presented with lovely gifts. The former Moderator, the Very Reverend John Fraser, preached at a special evening service, my brother Angus read a lesson and my brother-in-law Johnston McKay offered prayers. It was a very happy time and we were full of gratitude for the good years on Loch Tayside.

In 'refugee' year the Guild had a very high day when they were given permission by the commandant of Taymouth Castle Civil Defence School, Air Vice-Marshall MacGregor, to take over the Castle for a charity event. A fashion parade was staged with mannequins from the fashion houses bringing a gleam to many an eye. I was able to persuade the CO of the Scottish Horse to give us the services of the Pipe Band for a day and they played valiantly and movingly in the forecourt. Naturally, teas were served and altogether it was a tremendous success with hundreds of people milling around. My friend the Air Marshall feared for the safety of the noble pile. I teased him by suggesting that any destruction of the Castle of the Campbells while a MacGregor was in charge might have a certain poetic justice about it. Nice man though he was, he did not find such a thought all that amusing!

It has always been my belief that religion and the ordinary everyday living cannot be separated from one another, that the separation of the sacred from the secular is nonsense. Believing this I always tried to be part of the high days which were not church orientated. Where it was suitable I tried to involve the church in secular activities. Thus at the Coronation celebrations while the central event was the service in the church on the morning of the Coronation, the 'young' minister was to be found taking part in the afternoon sports and he and his family at the evening dance in a very overcrowded Holder Hall. I have a vague recollection of being knocked off my perch in the final of the pillow fight by one George Gartshore.

Then television came. Kenmore was chosen as the site for an outdoor version of the *White Heather Club*, a popular half hour programme of song and dance. For three perfect June days we played host to the cameras, the musicians and the dancers. Robin Hall and Jimmy McGregor were becoming more and more famous for their folk singing, Jimmy Shand was already a legend while Dixie Ingram and Isobel Jamieson had become household names through the programme. Some of the sweeping background shots were taken from the top of the church tower. We made friends of them all and were sorry when the excitement was over. We awaited the programme which was due to go out in the autumn of that year and we were not disappointed. The entertainment was first class and the scenic shots stunning and dramatic. Shortly after we had switched off at the Manse my phone rang. It was my friend and one time rigger, George Kew, telephoning from north east London where he lived. He had seen the programme.

'What are you doing up there Mac?' he asked in his best cockney, 'trying to get people into the kingdom of heaven. From what we've seen tonight you are already *in* the kingdom of heaven!' Dear George, he wasn't far wrong.

When the hotel at Kenmore was about to celebrate the 400th anniversary of its building, the owners wished to have some outdoor entertainment for guests and visitors during that summer of 1972. Their joiner and handyman, one of my elders, Sandy Mitchell, was commissioned to build a platform on the river bank behind the hotel. He 'volunteered' many of the members of the Sports Association to help him with this mammoth task and by the time the summer had come a very fine platform had been built. In cooperation with the Hotel company the Sports Association then agreed to run a series of concerts and we managed to obtain many now famous artists, who with good local talent provided splendid entertainment. Jimmy McGregor and Robin Hall, Jim McLeod and his dance band, Bill McCue, Jim Johnstone and his Scottish Dance Band, Alistair Gillies – all graced our platform on their way upwards to fame. The setting for these concerts was idyllic with the crowd sitting or standing in the natural amphitheatre on the sloping ground above the river. Often as Master of Ceremonies I was humbled by the amount of talent and the natural beauty around me.

The amount of effort put into all this by the members of the Sports Association was not altogether altruistic. The money raised by these events was donated to the Association. In the early fifties I had got together various local worthies in an effort to promote a Sports Day for the community. After one or two stuttering efforts we were able to advance to an annual Highland Games which took place in the Mains Farm Park which had been used by the local football team, Drummond Hill Rovers. When the Mains Farm Caravan Park grew in popularity it was obvious that the proprietor could no longer give the field for the event and we started looking for a more permanent Sports field which would be the property of the Association. Eventually the Taymouth Castle Hotel Company agree to sell the field to the west of Tomnacroich within the Castle grounds. Money was needed and while the annual Highland Games raised a little, the concerts in the summer were much more lucrative. Eventually with generous donations from the Mactaggart third Fund we were able to purchase the ground and have it properly levelled and landscaped. It was opened by the Convenor of Tayside Region, Mr Alistair Duncan Miller, in 1973 and has been the venue for the Highland Games and other sporting events since. Once again we were indebted to the District and Regional Councils for support and in return we happily gave access to the facilities to the local school. I have always felt that the best use of resources always can be made through cooperation especially in rural communities.

While the coming of television to the lochside might not rank as either a high day or a holy day, its introduction to Kenmore was in some ways unique. The late Sir John Mactaggart, the chairman of the Taymouth Castle Hotel Company, was keen to have television available to the hotel but did not want the village to be festooned with the unsightly aerials when the signal became available. He was most generous to Kenmore church and on this occasion offered the Kirk Session £500 with which to raise a 'master' aerial from which a signal could be piped in to Kenmore. The church would charge rentals for connections. Rightly the Kirk Session declined the generous offer, being of the opinion that they were not in being to be a broadcasting company, but not wishing to look a gift horse in the mouth Mr Duncan Miller (as Kirk Treasurer) and the minister agreed to look into the matter further. We took professional advice both as to the feasibility of receiving a signal and on the financial chances of success. Having satisfied ourselves on both counts we called a public meeting and a sufficient number of households agreed to receive a connection on the terms offered. With the £500 and with the agreement of the Forestry Commission, a master aerial was erected on Drummond Hill and the signal was duly 'piped' to the village. It was all a remarkable success. Kenmore village was the envy of all the other communities on the lochside. From the rentals the church benefited greatly. People were amused that the prime movers in this exercise, the minister and the Treasurer were outside the reception area and if we wanted to see anything special we had to seek an invitation from among the recipients. One of these was Mrs Menzies in Willowbank who 'ruined' the wee boys at the Manse by asking them down every Saturday afternoon to watch *Laramie* and other classic programmes of the black and white era. It was difficult to tear them away at bedtime.

171

CHAPTER EIGHTEEN

Surprise Visitors
to the Manse

One of the joys of living in a country Manse lies in the fact that there are often surprise visitors. These come in all shapes and sizes and from all levels of society. There are the social callers – friends from the past or friends of friends passing through and saying their 'hellos'. Men and women with problems which they found easier to discuss in the privacy of the Manse study rather than in their homes. Sad stories, unbelievable stories and stories of great courage and endurance. There was, of course, no magic formula that the minister could suggest which would ease all the troubles but I always felt that there were few who did not leave with a lighter step than that which they had when they arrived.

During the summer months we entered the silly season and had a constant stream of visitors from overseas seeking to trace their forebears. It was difficult to help them for all the church records prior to 1900 had been deposited in the Registry House in Edinburgh, nevertheless it was most interesting to hear the stories of families who had left the lochside because of economic pressures in the nineteenth century, had prospered in one of the then dominions but had always kept alive the link with Scotland. As with all groups of people, some were more gracious than others. I had one great success with a gentleman who came to the Manse and recounted his family history; I knew exactly from whence he had come. However, he too was full of ideas and told me that his forebears must have had considerable possessions on the lochside for they had been able to send their children to university and other places of learning. I told him that his forebears had been far more outstanding than mere landowners. They had in fact been meal millers whose application, thrift and vision, along with an unswerving belief in the goodness of God had enabled them to give their sons and daughters the blessings of higher education. My man was not impressed. Perhaps he dreamed of coming back to a landed inheritance on the lochside.

As well as would-be lairds however, we also had regular visitations from some of the 'knights' of the road. By the close of my ministry the welfare state had reduced the number of travellers on the road who in days gone by were called tramps. With the natural big-headedness of people living in Kenmore we always felt that we had a better class of traveller than other places. Ours, we felt, came not so much to beg as to persuade you that a little sharing of this world's goods would be as much of an advantage to us as to them.

One such was Davy, a man of small stature who told us that he had been 'on the road' for thirty years. He had served in the 'bantam' battalion during the First World War and on returning had resumed his work in the Govan shipyards. He was very unsettled, however, and one morning when he received a tax demand he flung the offending document into the nearest brazier and took to the road. While he must have slept rough on many occasions and carried all his worldly goods in a small hessian sack, Davy always managed to look neat and tidy. He would present himself at the back door of the Manse in excellent spirits, enquiring if he could occupy the little room above the steading for a day or two. Before taking up residence, however, he would be glad of a cup of tea as he had fasted most of the day, and Isobel would give him a meal in the kitchen. Davy drank his tea out of the saucer – a source of amazement to the wide-eyed little MacVicars now five and four years of age. Davy's conversation at this stage was always entertaining as he told his hostess and the boys of all his 'doings' since his last visit. While this was going on he would 'dunk' his biscuit in the tea, offering it to the boys who were enthralled, before taking a bite himself. This made the boys' rather fastidious mother wince but it was, in its way, a gentle communion of childlike spirits. My arrival on the scene did not interrupt the flow of conversation but usually changed its direction. After confirming that he could occupy the hill-house he would enquire if I had any 'penjins' and it was some time before we realised that Davy was referring to paperback books. Eventually he would depart to his 'retreat' with a good supply of Agatha Christie novels.

In his way Davy was a proud man. He did not expect something for nothing and each day when he came down for some water with which to make his tea, he would enquire if there were any chores needing doing. We were well supplied with firewood while Davy was about. He was of course more than ready to work for cash and in the springtime his arrival would be providential. He could use a spade well and did a tidy job but he had been on the road too long and he lacked constancy. One never knew when the thirst would come upon him and could not be denied. While staying in the hill-house he never touched alcohol of any kind but, sadly, there were limits to his endurance. The comical thing was that he could never depart without first making a row. Having been a good companion for many days, he would suddenly become cantankerous and fightable. On one such occasion Davy and I were digging in the walled garden. He was not communicative. To encourage us both I remarked that we'd soon have half the digging done.

'Whit dae ye mean, half done?' he enquired.

'Well,' I said, 'we've nearly finished this bit and we've only the other smaller plot to do.'

'Dae ye mean tae tell me ye're diggin' that ither bit?'

'Yes.'

'Well, ye can dig the bloody thing yersel,' was his vigorous response, and planting the spade in the ground with great vehemence he left the scene of our toil.

Knowing the drill well I came down to the house, made up his pay packet, and told Isobel that Davy would soon be leaving. Sure enough Davy would come down, more or less throw the key of the hill-house in at the back door, take his money and depart ungraciously without a word of farewell. We were always quite sad to see him go but were in no doubt that his first port of call would be the bar at Kenmore Hotel. Later that afternoon, just after three o'clock, which was then the closing hour, I happened to have business in the village shop. Obviously Davy had spent most of his hard-earned money and was now haggling with Jackie the shopkeeper. Davy was again back to his sharing theme and was trying to persuade Jackie that he would not miss a loaf of bread which was given in kindness. He in fact had persuaded Jackie, but was now pushing his luck by seeking further provision in the shape of a tin of meat. Jackie was unmoved and it was at this point that I arrived. Davy had forgotten, of course, the scene of the morning and greeted me as his great friend and supporter.

'Here is the man,' he said, turning to Jackie, 'who will confirm what I've been telling you – that man cannot live by bread alone.' I was glad that the shopkeeper and the minister had sufficient humour to see the man on his way with his loaf and tin of meat.

Davy came regularly for a year or two and then disappeared off the face of the earth. We often wondered what happened to the smart little man whose weakness lay in his itchy feet and a thirst that sometimes would not be denied.

Davy's place was taken by Sam, whose distinguishing feature was a malformed hand which was always hidden by a woollen mitten. He was a man with a very large chip on his shoulder. Rumour had it that he was of good family and when he was sober he was a very good worker and kept himself very tidy and spruce. In spite of his withered hand he was an excellent user of a spade but there was no denying the fact that he had a nasty temper and a cutting tongue. He was shown great kindness by Dave and Muriel who farmed at Balnasuim on the lochside, and on that farm Sam eventually had a caravan and settled down to a more static life. Although he had ceased to be a wanderer, Sam still had days when it was essential for him to journey to Killin or Aberfeldy. On such occasions Sam would be seen on the road, smart as a brush, in a neat blue suit and with shoes shining. Once in Aberfeldy however, all went downhill as Sam toured the various bars. By instinct he would start making his way home again to the lochside but it never occurred to him to make use of public transport. Thus it would happen that he would take some time to cover the six miles to Kenmore and the walk would have a great sobering effect. Reaching the bottom of what we called 'our' hill, Sam would realise that another nine miles to Lawers could not be contemplated without exploring alternatives. Sam would present himself at the door of the Manse and as was his wont with drink taken, he would assume a very high falutin' form of talk:

'Was your reverence contemplating visiting the parishioners in the West of his parish?'

'No, Sam.'

'What a pity! I had hoped to accompany him part of the way.'

'Would you like a cup of tea Sam?'

'If you are partaking yourself, I will join you.'

Over tea in the kitchen Sam's upper crust demeanour would continue. He would make deep philosophical statements on every subject but always came back to the practical issue of how a man of his years might cover the nine miles to Balnasuim. He well knew of course that in desperation I would drive him to his destination. While on the journey he would be filled with such gratitude that he would suggest that we stop at one of the hostelries en route so that he might buy me a drink. Though badly needing a drink, this offer was always refused. He would then go on, 'I would not offend you by offering you money for this journey but it would be my pleasure to make a donation to the church.'

Needless to say we never got further than the hand straying towards the wallet. Poor Sam! His latter years were spent in various homes for the elderly where for long periods he would be a model resident although he could never bring himself to have a relationship with the others. He was well liked by the staff but then he would have a 'blow out' and the social workers would have to move him on. Often I would get messages from Sam and would go to see him. His conversation was much different than in the old days but he had come to a real knowledge of his foolish ways yet knew that he could not quite overcome the craving. One year between Christmas and New Year he died in one of the homes in Perth. Such is the efficiency in the disposal of the dead who have no known relatives that Sam was cremated and his ashes disposed of before someone in the home came across a note among his few belongings requesting that Mr MacVicar at Kenmore should conduct his funeral service. I was sad that this last request was not granted but we remembered Sam in Kenmore and Lawers churches the following Sunday.

Perhaps our greatest friend among the travellers was Dochie Johnston. Duncan Johnston had travelled the roads around the lochside and beyond along with his mother Kate. They were tinkers and they lived the nomadic life, doing odd jobs and depending on the goodwill and warm hearts of the community. Before we came to Kenmore Kate had died and Duncan shortly afterwards married Rachel, the daughter of another tinker clan by name of Williamson. We first knew them when they visited the Manse shortly after the birth of their son. Isobel did not think the child was very strong but she was glad to see how well looked after he appeared, although she felt that he was too warm in the pram. It was with great sadness that we heard that the child had died and was to be buried in the cemetery at Killin. As they had no minister in Killin at the time the undertaker asked if I would take the funeral service at the grave. It was a day of rain. When we met at the graveside the mist was streaming down the shoulder of the mountain and the rain rattled down on the little white coffin. No one was present save the gravedigger and the child's parents. We asked that the soul of the child be kept in the shining places and that we who were left on earth might have peace. Between us we lowered the tiny coffin into the grave and I was completely undone. Dochie too sobbed loudly while the mother remained unmoved. It was the beginning of a long association with Dochie but we never felt the same affection for his wife.

Happier days were to come. The tinker family grew and still travelled up and down the lochside. On the foreshore below the Manse they appeared at regular intervals and Dochie would come to the Manse looking for this or that small offering of tea or sugar or paraffin, whatever. Sometimes he pretended to do some work in the garden but had little constancy. He always blamed his chest for his lack of energy and indeed he could always produce a wheeze which sounded terminal in its intensity. He maintained that his condition was due to the time which he had spent in the army. Like so many of his kind, having been lifted from the germ free air of a tinker's tent and placed in an environment where every kind of bacteria had a field day, Dochie's immune system was not geared to it and he took every disease that was going, culminating in a bout of pneumonia – or pewnomia as Dochie was inclined to call it.

As he had been invalided out of the services, I felt that there might be a case for some pension provision. Setting the claim in motion I kept telling Dochie that the chances were very slim but, to my great surprise, the claim received sympathetic attention and Dochie got an invalidity pension. From that day onward – although he was the only one – Dochie believed that the minister of Kenmore could work miracles. Over the years in saving him from various disasters he was confirmed in this view, especially on the occasion when he had foolishly bought an old banger of a car and had actually driven it to Killin. The police had to question him and when the charges were all enumerated the charge was not so much a sheet as a book. By this time Dochie and his family were living a more or less static existence in our steading and it did not seem to me a good idea for the head of that household to be sent to prison leaving the Manse folk to look after the rest. On the day of the trial I took it upon myself to write a letter to the Sheriff whom I knew, telling him that I would take a dim view of being left in loco parentis of one tinker wife with four kids. Giving the letter to Dochie I told him that when the Sheriff asked him if he had anything to say for himself he was to hand him the letter. Much to my surprise Dochie appeared in the evening filled with joy. He had not been sent to jail. Instead he had been fined.

'It was the letter that did it,' said Dochie. 'The Sheriff had been awful severe until he read it. After that he just laughed and said, "I better not send you to jail, Johnston."'

Needless to say Dochie had not concerned himself at that stage as to how he might pay the fine. Perhaps his faith in miracles was boundless. I suppose today I could have been in court myself for trying to pervert the course of justice – I've always felt however that justice and common sense should go together.

Having the 'family' in such close proximity to the Manse meant that we were privy to most of their doings. We were in fact forced to interest ourselves in many of them for Dochie saw no reason why we should not at least share the use of a telephone. Hardly a week passed without a request for us to make calls either to summon the doctor in the case of illnesses – or the police when visiting relatives or 'friends' became too obstreperous. Many of these crises were overcome without disturbing either the law or the medical profession. While Isobel would observe dryly that it would probably be easier for everyone if we transferred the telephone to the hill-house, she was always ready to take the childrens' temperatures. When the said temperature wasn't too hectic she would prescribe a half-aspirin and the doctor would be spared; when I had one of the boys in support I would take on the role of law enforcement officer and, armed with a stout cromag, would read the riot act to any warring factions. On most occasions such action would save the police budget. The only drawback lay in the fact that Dochie, having been far too meek and mild when faced with belligerent 'friends' would himself become aggressive when he thought he had the support of the minister. He would taunt the 'enemy':

'Ye'll no' fight noo when Ah've got the minister on ma side.'

There were two occasions however when direct action was almost our undoing. Dochie had arrived demanding that the doctor should be telephoned at once as the baby had been screaming all day. Angus happened to be home from the sea and he and his mother went to reconnoitre the position. Not too long afterwards they arrived back at the Manse with the baby who was indeed screaming. Isobel, while making up a bottle, was muttering darkly about the child's mother's mental state. It turned out that the child was suffering from starvation and when at last replete was more than willing to go to sleep. Isobel sat serenely with the sleeping baby on her knee while all the family cooed over the lovely child until our sister-in-law Jean who was visiting at the time and knew all about the ways of tinkers said quite firmly, 'You take that baby back now Isobel or you might find yourself with her for keeps.' So the mite was taken back to the parents' 'rersidence' where all was calm and Dochie and Rachel had taken refuge in sleep. Isobel, perhaps not altogether willingly, laid the sleeping child between them and departed. For Dochie this was possibly another miracle. The other incident happened on a Saturday night, or more accurately on a Sunday morning. There had been a wedding with a reception in the evening in the village hall and we had returned to the Manse about eleven o'clock. We had a guest staying overnight and she and Isobel, with Jean, soon went to bed while I finished the preparation for the following day. Being tired, this took longer than expected, and it was getting close to 1 a.m. before I eventually undressed and got into bed. No sooner had my head touched the pillow than there was a hammering on the back door just below our bedroom window. Jumping out of bed and flinging on a dressing gown I sped downstairs, tired, angry and anxious. I flung open the door and there, standing in the teeming rain, were the three daughters of Dochie and Rachel.

'What do you think you are doing?' I shouted at them.

The eldest spoke up. 'Ma faither's been murdered!' she said without emotion.

This was more serious than I had thought. I dragged the three sodden children into the kitchen and obtained further information. There had been a visitation from a 'Friend' and after drink was taken a fight had ensued, during which Dochie had received a mortal blow. I had the feeling that the girls were less perturbed than they should have been, but decided that there was no way I was going to get dressed, climb the hill in the rain to the hill-house and find out the true facts. By this time Isobel was up and about and took the children to the study where the wood burning stove was still warm. I then dialled 999 and was eventually connected to the police in Perth.

'Your name and address please,' said a cool voice. I gave the information requested and the voice said: 'Hullo, Mr MacVicar, how are you getting on?' I recognised a constable who had spent some years at Kenmore as our local 'bobby'.

'How's Mrs MacVicar?' he went on. I could not believe it was happening. It was 1.30 a.m. on a Sunday morning, Dochie was murdered and here I was carrying on a social conversation on the telephone. Returning to business however, the constable at last asked, 'What's wrong Mr MacVicar?'

'Dochie Johnston has been murdered,' I said.

'Och, it won't be as bad as that!' he observed.

'No, I don't expect it is,' was my answer, 'but you get a squad car up here as quick as you can so that we can find out.'

After some more pleasantries I rang off and viewed the three children now gently steaming in front of the fire, orphans of the storm. We awaited the cavalry.

An hour and a half later, with the whole parish asleep except the minister and his wife, the squad car arrived at the Manse door with all lights flashing. Two very smart young officers jumped out.

'What's wrong Mr MacVicar?' they asked. Wearily I told them that Dochie had been murdered.

'Och,' said they, 'it won't be as bad as that.' I couldn't argue any more. They went up to the hill-house and in a few minutes were back.

'Dochie has a good black eye,' they said, 'but they're all sleeping quite peacefully. Who was involved?' I told them who I thought would have been the culprit.

'Oh aye,' said they, 'he's sleeping under the hedge at the foot of your drive.'

'Well,' I said, 'lift him and put him in the cells. He'll get a fright when he comes to in the morning.'

'I don't think we can do that,' said the law. I was getting fed up by this stage.

'Of course you can – it'll do him good.'

'You don't understand, Mr MacVicar. Yesterday was the Pitlochry Highland Games and all the cells are full.'

With that we bade them farewell. It was now 4 a.m. We tumbled back into bed wondering what else could happen. I was glad that the sermon I had planned for the morrow had nothing to do with patience or forbearance.

By the time evening had come on the Sunday, Isobel and I were feeling a bit fraught. Isobel was wrath:

'I'm going up there to give them a round of the guns. This carry on has gone far enough.' I let her go knowing that no amount of raging would have the slightest effect. In a little while Isobel returned somewhat restored and amused.

'Dochie agreed with every word I said and could not have been more repentant. He hopes his reverence will have a good sleep tonight.'

He came near to the long sleep himself the following evening. It being Monday I had been slaving in the garden all day and was putting in a last 'push' in the evening. Lest any help might have been asked for, Dochie had absented himself from the scene during the day but now, in the gloaming, appeared at the fence above the walled garden. His pipe was going well and he was at peace with the world. I sweated and was unChristian enough to ignore his presence. Dochie, however, would not be ignored.

'Good evening, your reverence,' he said. A grunt from his reverence. 'I'm just pleased to see a hard-working man like yoursel' getting some recreation.' I suggested that a hard-working man like himself might have some recreation too if he had come to help me during the day. I then suggested that the affair of Saturday night had been beyond a joke. Once again he agreed with me on every ground but brought the whole matter to a conclusion with a reflection on the man who had given him the black eye.

'You know thae . . . .'(he named the family), 'you couldna expect anything better of them. They're no' like you and me at a'.'

After that observation I had nothing more to say.

Eventually Dochie and his family departed to a Council house with proper sanitation and facilities. We were glad to see them settled and the girls all grew up to be good looking women. Jean, who was ages with the elder girls, tried hard to interest them in the benefits of regular education but was not noticeably successful. We missed the coming and going and were quite sad watching individuals who had had a place in the community being sucked into a welfare culture in which their identity was lost.

CHAPTER NINETEEN

Household Helpmates
and Friends

Our parents were wont to tell us that the period when they were best off in material terms was before the First World War when, on a stipend of something less than £300 per annum, they were able to afford two maids indoors and a part time gardener. By 1950 the stipend of ministers had not increased all that much and the differential between household staff and ministers had closed significantly. On £450 per annum we had no chance of having any kind of 'live-in' staff. We were greatly helped however in having the Beadle's wife 'Gregor' who came on an hourly basis and was of the greatest assistance, not only in keeping the Manse spick and span, but also in keeping us posted on what was going on in the parish. The AWACS information gatherer – the spy in the sky – had nothing on Gregor. We also had a series of young girls who, having left school, had not found any permanent employment; Christine and Margaret, another Margaret and Joanne, they all had spells at the Manse and did all that was expected of them and were loved by the three boys. We were glad when they got more permanent and lucrative employment but were always sorry to lose them. We hope that they all have as good memories of us as we have of them.

The 'live-in' help in a Manse is beyond price, for they free the lady of the house to augment the work of the minister in the parish. Now I am well aware that ministers' wives should not be looked upon as unpaid assistants just as I am aware that some ministers' wives would be better having nothing to do with the parish! In the vast majority of cases however the wife's presence in the Manse, with the ability to give time to those who call there either by telephone or in person is something which is sorely missed nowadays when most of the ministers' wives are working or are so taken up with domestic chores and children that they have no time to give to anything else. For myself I know very well that Isobel was often in the front line of pastoral work and on these occasions was of infinite value not only to me but to the parish. Without the help which we had in the background she could not have done this.

The times when we were best off in this regard was when we had Edna, and later, Margaret. Both came to us in the most fortuitous circumstances. Edna Reid was a lady from British Guiana who, after having served in many of the aristocratic houses in London, came into the employment of the Misses Parker Ness at Letterellen. She was of a most dignified bearing – tall and elegant. Her grandmother had been born in slavery and somewhere among her ancestors was a Scotsman by the name of Reid. Edna was of the highest intelligence and it was most unfortunate that she had not had the benefit of higher education. When she became sixty and in receipt of the old age pension, Edna expressed the wish to return to her home and family in British Guiana. The Misses Ness understood her longing and made all the arrangements for her return home. By this time with our association with Letterellen, we had come to know Edna very well. She was a very devout Christian and attended church regularly. We were all sorry to see her go. As so often happens, Edna found when she returned to Guiana that life was not quite what she expected, and after a few months the Misses Ness got word from her telling them that she wanted her old job back. By this time they had already employed new servants and were unable to accommodate Edna. They came to us and asked us if we could possibly take her. While we could not pay her the full wage we could augment her pension and Edna approved the arrangements. There then followed three years in which our lives were well and truly managed by Edna. She was never a quick worker but rising as she did early in the morning and going to bed late in the evening she did not have to be.

While she worked Edna sang hymns which doubtless was very appropriate in a manse. She had a wide repertoire and it was not long until we could gauge from the hymns what kind of mood Edna was in. When all was going well the hymns of some of the evangelists could be heard on the stair: 'What a friend we have in Jesus!' was sung with devout sincerity. The more fraught she became the more 'high church' the hymns, starting off with some of Wesley, with the temperature rising she would go on to Lyte. Life was still bearable. When, however, the MacVicar family got beyond even Edna's patience threshold, 'Mother of God, Star of the Sea' was her solace. At that point it was as well for the family to retreat to a safe area. Edna had a very personal relationship with her

Saviour. During her time with us the Manse had no central heating and in winter conditions was a very cold house, especially in the early morning before the various fires had had a chance to spread some heat. Doing down the stairs in the winter time Edna could be heard telling her Saviour just how cold it was. It was a statement of fact to a friend with whom she was in constant contact. We found nothing strange in this but when we did not warn our guests, some of them got quite a shock. One very righteous man actually spoke to me suggesting that it was not good for the children, having such a blasphemous maid in the house. I was quite cross with him. I often wish he could have seen Edna and myself having a dance at Hogmanay. A glass of sherry did wonders for her rheumatism and soon restored the calypso movement of the Caribbean. Dear Edna, she introduced the children to bread making, she made wonderful ginger beer for the hot summer days and steaming hot vegetable curries. She enjoyed going on holiday with us and we had the great benefit of her constant attendance, loyalty and companionship. It was a sad day when Edna could no longer still the longing to go back home. Once again she returned to Guiana and for many years we heard from her. We were sure that at the appropriate time her friend Jesus would 'carry her through'.

Maggie was very different in many ways. She was neither tall nor elegant but rather round and walked with a definite roll. Maggie too had known 'service' having been with the great and good as a house table-maid. She had been with the minister of the United Free Church in Kenmore until she was forced to return to the croft to help her aging father. Eventually her father died and although she continued with what help she could get to work the croft, eventually it all became too much and she decided to give up. Maggie had had a hard life. Her parents never had much to come and go on. Everything Maggie had she had to work for and on the croft much of the work was backbreaking and unrewarding. The struggle for survival showed in Maggie. She could be very irascible, sometimes almost irrational in her opinions and in her actions. She had deep likes and dislikes and could not ever change her mind about anything. In her own words she would let things go from 'better to worse', and she would 'cut off her nose to spite her face'. Nor did she believe in beating about the bush as I discovered on the day on which I visited her having heard the news that she was thinking of giving up her croft.

'I've burnt my boats and given the laird my notice,' she said. I suggested that she had probably done the wisest thing and asked her where she would be able to get a house.

'That's just it,' she said. 'I've got nowhere to go and I wondered if I could get into your hill-house. Instead of paying rent I could work for Mrs MacVicar'.

All this came as a great surprise, for the idea of Maggie coming to the Manse had never entered our heads. I told her that we would not see her stuck as far as a roof over her head was concerned, but that I would have to discuss the arrangement with Mrs MacVicar.

'I'm not looking for any charity,' she said glaring at me, 'and I'll have to take the dog with me.' I left more shaken than she was with the turn of events.

And so Maggie and her dog came to the Manse and we discovered a new Maggie altogether. She never ceased to operate on a short fuse but a more generous and loyal friend no family could have had. It was soon evident that the hill-house arrangement could not last and we fitted out the larger attic in the Manse to take Maggie's furniture. We encouraged her to look for a more lucrative post and after a short time Maggie went to be housekeeper for Major Carmichael at Portglas. However, she still came to her attic bedroom at the Manse on her day off and our relationship continued to grow. We were sorry to lose Maggie's great help especially since our fourth child was on the way. Isobel was not very well and as some help was essential we managed to get an au pair girl from Holland. Dini duly arrived and hit Kenmore like a bombshell – a blonde bombshell. She was a big and well-made girl and must have been the first mini-skirt to come among us. Even the most innocent were confiding in me that they now knew the import of 'lead us not into temptation'. She was a happy and outgoing girl who dearly wanted to be friends with everyone. Sometimes Isobel and I worried about her choice of companions but it was soon evident that Dini was no innocent abroad and, for her tender years, had quite a strong sense of self-preservation. Dini loved going to the whist drives where she made quite an impression on all the males from sixteen to sixty. What they did not know as we knew to our cost, was that Dini had a boy friend who was an operator on the telephone exchange in London. Dini would spend hours talking to him, straining our patience to the limits.

It was just before the birth of our daughter Jean that something of a miracle came to pass. Isobel was unwell. The six months that

185

Dini was contracted to be with us was almost up. A crisis was looming. Maggie appeared on her day off. Marching into Isobel's bedroom she announced, 'Well, I've burnt my boats. I've put in my notice – nobody is going to tell me how to make a steamed pudding'. Isobel was speechless, but Maggie was in full flow. 'I'll just come back and work for you'. Isobel did not know what to say, but on my return the decision was soon made. No matter what it cost us we would have Maggie back on a permanent basis. It was the beginning of a twenty year association. We often had reason to bless the steamed pudding.

Unlike Edna, Maggie did not sing hymns either in the Manse or indeed in church. She was a loyal attender at divine service but would stand tight-lipped during the items of praise and no one could be more tight-lipped than Maggie when it suited her. We never knew whether Maggie could sing at all. During her life there had not been much to sing about and we like to believe that life was kinder to her in her latter years. She had never been used to children and there were many occasions when she and the boys operated under an armed neutrality agreement. Even that sometimes broke down when they riled her beyond the limit and more than once the rascals would be seen fleeing with Maggie in hot pursuit, the frying pan at the ready. Jean was born shortly after Maggie came to us and we were all besotted with the somewhat angelic girl who had been given to us. Her presence had a wonderfully humanising effect on the boys and she unloosed in Maggie all the tender and motherly instincts which had been restrained throughout her rather harsh life. Jean truly became the love of her life, could do no wrong and was always given first place. Certainly Jean gave great affection to her, an affection which lasted through childhood into adulthood, to the very end of Maggie's life on earth. It was a mutual admiration society with which the rest of us had to live.

After many good years in which we became very dependent on Maggie and felt that no one could make pancakes or potato scones like her, the time came for Maggie to retire. She moved into one of the 'pensioners' houses in the village and while still coming to the Manse for two or three mornings in the week, settled down to a very douce and comfortable way of life. It was good to see her enjoying life with all the harshness and the hardships behind her. Maggie, who had never to our knowledge played a ball game in her life, developed in her retirement a great passion for snooker and spent hours in front of the television following the fortunes of her favourites. Being Maggie she had a great liking for Hurricane Higgins with his cavalier approach to the game and to life, and despised Steve Davis with his douce and decent ways. We teased her about this and never missed an opportunity of extolling the virtues of the Londoner. Our remarks brought forth a irritated 'Huh'. When she went to her own house, Maggie retained her place in the Manse pew, would arrive at the church with her severe Sunday face on and would sit in her corner staring straight in front of her. Except on the day following Steve Davis's unexpected defeat in the world championship. Enter the lady of the Manse nodding a good morning to all in church. From experience she did not expect anything but the briefest of nods from Maggie (the church was not the place for socialising). However, as Isobel eased herself into her seat and graciously asked after Maggie's health the church echoed with the triumphant question, 'Where's your Steve Davis noo?'

While Maggie was with us it was quite unnecessary for us to read either the Dundee *Courier* or the *Sunday Post*. These were Maggie's sources of information and she read them from cover to cover. I was often most grateful to her for bringing to my notice some item of local news which I would have missed. The death notices were of particular interest to her and when they intimated the demise of someone known to her I would be given a resumé not only of the life which had ended but much detail unto the third and fourth preceding generation. Maggie lived to a good age and ended her days in the Abbeyfield Home where she made many friends. The boys helped to carry her to her grave and I found it difficult to take the service. We all had lost a very dear friend.

For special occasions we often had other help and among those who came to our aid was Bessie. Bessie was a farmer's wife and it soon became apparent that Bessie did most of the work on the farm. She was a cheerful soul which was all the more surprising when one considered the circumstances of her life. Bessie had a husband and a son – they were the loves of her life and they were both invalids. Bessie looked after them with the greatest devotion and as I was in the house of illness many times, I was privileged to see the commitment of this faithful woman. Bessie had a very cavalier way with the English language and if a word was close to the proper term that was good enough for Bessie. Thus she would complain to me about these young women with nothing on but a biniki. Or she would tell me of the sweet she had at the WRI dinner – 'Black Forest Gatoox', milk 'cartoons' were got from the shop. On one splendid day after a girl from Iceland had arrived in the village, Bessie confided in me, 'She's an atlantic you know!'

Bessie had a heart of pure gold and a faith which was a strength to more than herself. When, after years of weakness, her husband died, to be followed a few years later by the son, I went to weep with Bessie.

'What can I say, Bessie,' I said.

'I know how you feel,' she said, 'but last night when I went to bed I thanked God for everything. I know where they are and all their troubles are over. I don't need to worry about them any more'.

How many libraries of theology was that worth?

Bessie lived for many years after her men had died. She visited their graves every Saturday and held conversation with them as she placed the flowers. She took part in every village activity and no Ceileidh, Guild meeting or WRI were complete without Bessie's potato scones. She was in church every Sunday and loved Kenmore Church – 'It's a lived in church', she told me one day. She gave hours of voluntary help to every lonely soul around her and scattered her malapropisms with a light heart. 'I talk too much,' she would say laughingly.

No, Bessie, you never talked too much and when the tongue was stilled for good we felt bereft. Our comfort lay in the faith that the family in heaven was complete.

CHAPTER TWENTY

Epilogue to a Series
of Love Sories

There is so much that I *could* write about. Memories of the last forty-five years keep crowding into my mind. There are so many, however, which cannot be written about because the telling might react in a negative way on people who are still around. There are other memories, like the death of a child, or the sudden and accidental death of the young, or the wearisome dying of the not so young who long for peace. These give for thoughts which 'lie too deep for tears', and are not for sharing. I can confess, however, that I have often set out from the Manse to visit those struck by sudden tragedy, sometimes bearing the news of the tragedy to those unaware of impending doom, and wished that I could be spared the duty that lay before me. How often I found that some of the words of the Professor of Practical Theology were very true. He had once said in a class: 'Don't be too anxious when you go to visit in tragic situations. You will often find that the Good Lord has got there before you'. It is true.

To weep with those who weep saps the minister's emotional and physical energy but rarely, because of people's courage and faith, does it leave the minister in despair. He can come close to that, however, when he finds individuals who have no reason to weep when it comes to the parting. When there is no tender mercy what has life been like?

Very early in my ministry I took a funeral service for a colleague who had suddenly taken ill. All I knew of the deceased was that she had lived to a good age but had died in one of the local authority homes, which in an earlier age had been reserved for the aged destitute. I was sad for the old soul who had died in these circumstances. Imagine my surprise when I found at the graveside some dozen sons and daughters all looking quite prosperous. I conducted the service with, sadly, one or two unchristian thoughts entering my mind, for I kept wondering why a mother who had raised such

189

a large family had to spend her last days in the care of strangers. One of the sons was foolish enough to remark after the service that it was just as well that his mother was 'away', as she had not enjoyed her days in the home.

'Just as well,' I said with heavy sarcasm, 'when there was none of her own able to look after her'. With that I left them, hoping that the barb might have struck home. I doubt it.

So many memories! Being appointed a Chaplain in Ordinary to the Queen in Scotland was a great honour. Donning the red cassock was something I had not expected. Some were more impressed than others. The Christmas after my appointment I entered the church for the annual service of praise, resplendent in my new cassock, to be brought back to earth by the piping voice of a child: 'Here comes Santa now'.

When preaching in Crathie church the minister is a guest of the Queen at Balmoral Castle from Saturday to Monday. While I readily confess that I was more and more nervous the closer I got to Deeside, the truth is that these visits turned out to be the most relaxing and splendid occasions. No one could be more welcoming than the Queen and her family in their home.

I had a further taste of State Occasion when I was Chaplain to Lord Maclean in the second year of his duties as Lord High Commissioner to the General Assembly. Once again any anxiety which I might have felt in undertaking this duty soon disappeared before the kindness and understanding of Lord and Lady Maclean. The pomp which attends the Queen's representative during the Assembly week brings great colour to the city. Being old and wise in the ways of the Assembly made me useful to those of the household to whom the whole thing was a new experience. Sir Charles Fraser, the Purse Bearer, orchestrated everything with efficiency, grace and humour. Sometimes amidst all the parading and processing it was difficult to keep a straight face. On opening day we were about to process into the Assembly Halls; the banners were flying, the trumpets were sounding, there were the sharp words of command, the swords were glinting in the morning sun and the Heralds took up their station in their bright tabards. I was impressed by the scene when suddenly in my ear I heard the voice of one of the young officers in attendance – 'Padre, who is the guy dressed like the Ace of Spades?' I don't know how amused the Lord Lyon would have been to hear himself thus described.

On the Sunday there was, of course, the procession to St Giles for the morning service. I shared a limousine with the Earl of Errol, the Duke of Argyll and the Solicitor General for Scotland. All went well until after the service when we again got into our car. When the chauffeur tried to start it the engine refused to fire. Just for a moment I had a splendid vision of The High Constable of Scotland, the Keeper of Holyrood Palace, the Chief Law Officer of Scotland and the Queen's Chaplain giving a Rolls Royce a push start down the Royal Mile. Sadly it was not to be. As all will know the Royal Mile has a very definite decline from St Giles and with great *sang froid* the chauffeur free wheeled into position in the procession and started the car on its gears halfway down to the Palace.

One could go on but it is time to bring this particular book to an end. I have to ask myself why I wrote it at all. So many other people have had far more interesting and far more useful lives. I felt I had to do it to make a record of a life filled with good fortune and in this day and age when all the news seems to be of the bad variety, I felt that it might do something to redress the balance. I am also conscious that I conducted a type of ministry which was very different from that which will be conducted in the foreseeable future. Perhaps, however, from these past experiences, there may be some food for thought to help others plan for the future. Perhaps from the threshing floor of experience in the last forty years there are some grains of truth worth picking up.

This simple autobiography is a series of love stories.

The first is the love story with my parents and sister and brothers. I never was in any doubt that I had the best parents in the world nor knew anyone with better brothers or sister. The memory of my parents, with that of Archie and Rona, is bright and without stain. I am glad to say that at the time this book was being written, Angus, Willie and John were still very much alive. There are few subjects upon which we cannot have the most violent arguments. Our political views rarely coincide, but there are no men for whom I have such a deep affection and I could not be more proud of their various considerable achievements.

The second love story was with 28 Squadron which is a strange affection, for squadrons, unlike regiments, are not given to settled personnel. Many people both in aircrew and in groundcrew moved from one to another fairly frequently. For me it was different. I was with 28 Squadron for almost three years, most of which was spent on operational duties. During that time sadly we lost too many of our aircrew friends but there was always a core of pilots and of groundcrew who remained. Being a specialist unit and as much involved with the Army as with the RAF, we felt ourselves rather special, and there grew up a strong *esprit de corps* which proved invaluable in taking us through difficult times. In truth, though it may seem trite, we were brothers in arms and came to have a regard and affection for one another which was vital, real and valuable.

The next love story concerned the parishes and people to whom I was called to minister. Throughout these forty years there was no other place where I wanted to minister, even though in the first ten or twenty years I had opportunities to go to other places. Larger congregations and higher stipends were held out as inducements. It was very gratifying to be asked to consider some of the most famous churches in the land but, having given due consideration to the offers, Isobel and I usually found ourselves on the step at the front door of the Manse, looking up to Ben Lawers and across to the church at Kenmore. We were not going anywhere. Was this an innate selfishness? Were we being foolish? I don't think so. Loch Tayside was the kind of district in which I wanted to carry out my particular ministry. We will never know if the kind of relationship which was developed there could have been transferred to a town or city. What I *can* say is that I can count on the fingers of one hand the individuals during that forty years for whom I did not have any affection for most of them were very dear to me and I sought, in the Name of the Lord, to serve them to the best of my ability. I am well aware that that ability was limited but nothing was held back and never at any time did we regret rejecting 'the pastures new'.

Holding together all these love stories is the one which in human terms means most to me. I have been deliberately reticent regarding the personal relationships within my immediate family because I firmly believe that there are some things which are too intimate and sacred to be paraded in the public domain. It horrifies me to hear and to read about the details in the lives of those who seek the headlines by unveiling the secrets of their sexual and emotional lives. Who is interested? It is with the greatest sincerity and pleasure that I can write that without the love and the support of Isobel and the children there is nothing that I could have achieved in these last fifty years. They are my nearest and dearest and for me there is no one like them. Their love and affection, which is added to by that of four beautiful granddaughters, makes my life bright indeed.

I count myself supremely blessed that all of those who have played a pivotal role in my life, from my parents through to brothers, sister, wife, children and grandchildren have all sought to serve the Lord and have all striven to uphold the teaching and the influence of the church.

So these love stories constitute my life and they have been bound together and given a shining brightness by the greatest love story of all – that of our Father in Heaven giving His only Son to be the Saviour of the world.

The church of course has been at the centre of my life for these last fifty years and now that I have been away from the active ministry for some time I have been able to formulate some views regarding the church and the ministry, always reminding myself that it is easy for the retired in any sphere to become an instant expert. There is always the temptation to hark back to the fantastic 'good old days' when ministers (righteous beyond measure themselves) ministered to a believing and righteous people. These days never did exist, but, on the other hand, the church has now entered a very difficult period when in Scotland, large numbers of people have no belief at all, see no reason for any belief and ignore the church. Many more admit to a belief in God but have no time for the church. In an age when all authority is not only questioned but often despised, there is little hope that the church can exercise any authority. The reasons for this state of affairs are manifold but in our country at least the searching after a material heaven, here and now, has taken precedence over everything else. There is also the liberalisation of social convention which has been matched by a liberalisation of Christian doctrine in some spheres. Such liberalisation leads to a period when people are less secure in their outlook and beliefs.

In this regard one thinks immediately of Sunday observance. In days past we in Scotland were restrained and restricted on a Sunday by the belief in the sanctity of the Sabbath day. We spoke of Sunday as being the Lord's Day. Even the laws of the land ensured that people behaved differently on a Sunday. The majority of Christian people would assert now that Sunday is not any more the Lord's Day than any other day of the week and every day belongs to the Lord. Sadly, however, in an imperfect world too many have mistaken a more liberal interpretation as a licence to do everything else on a Sunday except the essential of worshipping God and renewing their spirits amid the strains and stresses of life which do not change even with material success. I have great hopes that things will settle down in this regard as more and more people begin to realise that the re-creation of their minds and spirits is even more essential than their physical recreation. The church's main task is to maintain itself so that it is there always to play its part in that re-creation. The worst thing that can happen is for the church to try to bring about a return to Sabbath observance by narrowing doctrine on the subject and I am sorry to detect within the ministry of the church just such a desire to return to the old days when the church exercised a strict discipline and had a code of practice for every circumstance.

This is much the same reaction as we see in Russia on that country's political scene. With the liberalisation of Russia there is a good deal of chaos and hardship. The old communist diehards are harking back to the 'good old days' when the Politburo exercised a rigid authority. 'At least,' say they, 'we had some law and order and everyone had something to eat.' In the same way in the church today there are many longing for a return to the old ways, and the old thinking. 'At least,' say they, 'we knew what the church stood for.' It is foolish however to think that a return to a narrow and legalistic doctrine will restore the church to its former position of authority. There are some of us who believe that it was the church's authoritarian attitude which alienated many in former days and, where exercised today, is still alienating people who might be kept within the fellowship.

One cringes to think of the folly of trying to maintain an authority where blinds were drawn for the Sabbath, where whistling on a Sunday was a heinous offence, when no book save the Bible could be read, when it was all right to be as drunk as a skunk on a Saturday before midnight as long as nothing was consumed until after midnight on a Sunday. What kind of God finds this kind of behaviour necessary? It is not much wonder that men and women with widening horizons and broadening experiences began to question the religion and the church which could maintain these conditions? Much of this doctrine was based on the interpretation of the Bible and here too I am sorry to observe that some of our ministers today are tending to return to a fundamentalist interpretation of the Holy Scriptures. 'The Bible says . . .' becomes the final argument.

The Bible is, of course, the most sacred book. Without doubt it contains the Word of God most graciously in the accounts of the life and teaching of Jesus Christ. The Old Testament contains the history of an emerging people chosen to cradle a belief in the one true God. The story of their struggles, their visions and their culture contains much which is eternally true. The letters of Paul, the greatest Christian missionary, deal with the emergence of the Church of Jesus Christ and there is much in these letters which is vital to the church today. As we interpret the Bible, however, it seems to me that we must always bear in mind how the Bible came to us in its present form; how it was written by human hand; many of the original documents lost by human folly; much regained in the most haphazard way and finally given form by the arbitration of human minds. While recognising the Power of the Holy Spirit in all this, it becomes very clear to me that it is at least unlikely, in view of the constant human element, that every word is necessarily a word from God for our day. Abraham's idea of God is very different from that proclaimed by Jesus Christ. The discipline required by a nomadic people three thousand years ago and interpreted by Moses in the Ten Commandments may not be the same kind of discipline required at the close of the twentieth century in a completely different cultural situation. The teaching of the prophets in their own political situations may not have the same relevance in ours. The advice of Paul to a church in a culture which still countenanced slavery may not always be applicable to the concerns of our church. Even the teaching of Jesus as put forward by the Gospel writers comes in the first instance from second or third hand. At least two of the writers could not have known Jesus. It is more than likely that while the reporting from an oral tradition may be very accurate, these writers might easily have put a gloss on some of Jesus' sayings to suit their own biases or prejudices. When all this is considered we can still say that contained in the Bible is a great deal for our guidance, our comfort and our salvation. It is a cause for continuing gratitude that much of the Word of God is contained in it. There is so much in it which will strengthen our faith and assist us in developing a relationship with our God. It is not helpful, however, to pretend either that the Bible contains the cure for all our ills or that it is the sole vehicle by which the Word of God is given to us. It would be a strange God who would indicate some two thousand years ago: 'Well, that's it - that's my word. It cannot be detracted from or added to.' To suggest this is a blasphemy, because we know that many men and women, by their word and by their speech and by what they were in their lives have transmitted God's word to us. They have been the proof of a living

Saviour. The word has been made flesh in the lives of the faithful and the greatest remembrances of a long ministry are of the men and women who having known the saving Power of Jesus Christ have revealed that Word in their lives.

A fundamentalist approach to Scripture inevitably leads to an extremist theology which too often leads to people deluding themselves that *they* know what God's will is while it is hidden from others. There is some truth in what the man said: 'the devil can quote scripture for his own purpose', and we have seen only too clearly how every fringe sect can find quotations from the Bible to support their beliefs no matter how ridiculous. They have demeaned the greatest story ever told and those who adopt a fundamentalist belief in the Bible do the same and often hide the true word from God. We must always be on our guard that we do not hide the greatest truth that the greatest story ever told is a continuing narrative, as is the saving of mankind through the Risen Christ.

The ministry which suited me best was the ministry of one to one. I enjoyed preaching and while numbers do not matter too much, it was always uplifting to preach to a full church. It gave me a great thrill to institute projects and see them through to fruition in the organisations. My work as Presbytery Clerk and in the Committees of the national church gave me great satisfaction, in spite of the tedium of the journeys to Edinburgh and return. However, it was in the one to one relationships that I had the greatest delight and satisfaction when, in joy or sorrow, in good days and bad, the parishioner and the minister could be one in bringing situation and circumstance before God. Now in the days of huge congregations and wide charges, the minister is so busy baptising, marrying, burying, organising, that he has little time to listen to the individual or his particular problems. The minister on a Sunday is so often rushing from one service to another that he has no time to talk to anyone.

Having been a vice convenor of what was known as the Unions and Readjustments Committee of the Church, I have to accept some responsibility for much of the change which has come over the church in the last fifty years. For many reasons it had to happen. In Scotland because of disruptions, schisms and divisions, there were far too many churches. Apart from anything else the church could not afford the ministers it had if they were to be paid a decent stipend. When it came to closing churches there was much unhappiness.

Congregations which were able to support themselves saw no reason why they should be united with another church down the street. This was a natural feeling but was in fact a kind of congregationalism which had no place in a national church. The strong had to be persuaded to support the weak. In financial terms these 'weak' ones were often those in rural areas where, in spite of innumerable unions and linkings still could not, in post-inflationary times, support a minister on their own. There were innumerable meetings and much unhappiness and there is no doubt the church was scarred. There was, however, much readjustment which was inevitable and much too which was good for the church. I always blessed my predecessor at Kenmore for bringing about the union of the two churches there in 1931. At the time and for many years there was some bitterness but it was the right thing to do and I reaped the benefits. So it has been in other places. Unfortunately the main exercise took place at a time when because of many factors there was a general loosening of people's attachment to the church and too often the stresses attendant on readjustment were used by some to sever their church connections. Soon a vicious circle developed. There was less support for the church in membership and while the remaining membership valiantly increased the income of the church they could not keep up with inflation. This led to further pressure for more readjustment. So it went on.

It may be too early to say but there is a growing feeling that the slimming down process has gone too far. As a national church we are no longer ministering to all the people, but like every human organisation the church can only do what it can afford. If the membership of the church is serious in its desire to proclaim the Gospel to the people of Scotland, then they must give sufficiently to maintain more ministers. Finance is not the only factor but the provision of more ministers needs more money. I am sure that the provision of a ministry with the ability to have a more personal approach to people would be of enormous help in reversing the decline of the church in Scotland. When one considers that in my own Presbytery of Dunkeld and Meigle the number of ministers preaching the Gospel and being shepherds to their flocks has dropped from 83 in 1915 to 15 in 1995, it is not surprising that there has been a steady decline in church membership and that many of the flock have been lost for the lack of a shepherd.

A great deal has been made about the part the laity can play to make up for the shortage of ministers, and a great number has decried the 'cult of the ministry'. While I give way to no one in my admiration of the committed layman or woman, it has been my experience that without a minister who is a true enabler and teacher and leader within a community, no amount of lay participation fills the gap. This I believe to be true in all charges – it is certainly true in the rural communities. No number of meetings or conferences can replace the work of the minister taking his faith and beliefs into the circumstances and situations of individual people. The minister must be there to represent Jesus Christ, continuing the ministry as He saw it in bringing good news to the humble, binding up the broken hearted, proclaiming liberty to captives, comforting all who mourn.

This is the essential ministry. It does not matter too much if strict discipline is observed. It doesn't matter too much about purity of doctrine and less the strict adherence to church law and practice. What matters is that the minister, knowing his own dependence on the compassion and Love of Christ, should go out reflecting in what he says, in what he does and in what he is, something of that love and compassion. This is the proclamation of salvation for which so many souls are longing.

After forty years I began to feel less able to do all the things I wanted to do. Yet another readjustment had taken place and Kenmore and Lawers was linked with Fortingall and Glenlyon. I undertook to take on the extra responsibility for one year but the extra services and the increased workload confirmed what I had suspected, that the time had come to give way to a younger person. It was a strange time. I told my Kirk Session of my intention to retire well ahead of the date, so that the congregations could get on with the preliminaries for calling a successor. In retrospect I am not convinced that this is a good idea. Both minister and congregation feel that the final months are a marking time. The show is over but the players are still upon the stage.

The final month came, however, and we had wonderful services in Kenmore Church. First we had a celebration of Holy Communion to which most of the members came. Very keenly I felt that we were joined by a great host of the church in heaven, the faithful and true who have found their peace with God. We were indeed surrounded by a great cloud of witnesses. Then came the final service with a packed church. As one member put it, 'full to the neck'. People came from far and near to be present. People with whom I had wept and people with whom I had rejoiced; Church people, people whose church connection was tenuous; people whom I had been able to help and others who for one reason or another I had had to rebuke. They were all there along with the cloud of witnesses. It was a very moving occasion but as I said at the close of my sermon, 'Why should I be sad? I've had forty wonderful years of service in the ministry. I've been given health and strength to do the Lord's work. I am surrounded by my nearest and dearest and so many who have given support and sustenance far beyond any deserving. Why should I be sad? Instead let us rejoice and be glad'.

We closed the ministry by singing with gusto, 'Lift up your hearts – We lift them to the Lord'.

And that was that. The congregation gave us a wonderful farewell party in Taymouth Castle. Beautiful gifts were given to Isobel and myself and Alistair Duncan Miller and Douglas Hutchison, the two senior elders, spoke in the most generous terms. It was a particular pleasure that it was Bessie McDonald who presented the gifts. The entertainment for the evening was quite fabulous, with Jim McLeod and his Scottish Dance Band, Bill McCue and Mary Sandeman. I'd had a relationship with them all when they were making their way in the entertainment world. All having reached the top of their professions they came back for this special occasion and entertained us royally. We also had young Donald Campbell as our personal piper for the evening.

Everything comes to an end and as we said our farewells at the top of the great staircase, one youngish widow who had suffered much, kissed me and said, 'We couldn't have got through it all without you!' That meant more to me than all the plaudits.

So it was over and we felt emotionally and physically exhausted. After a holiday, however, the family got down to considering what we might do in thanksgiving for all the kindness shown to us over the years. In the end we decided that we would offer a window to the church at Kenmore. In consultation with an artist, Anita Pate of Haddington, the design showed in one 'light' some of the things which gave us happiness – the view to Ben Lawers, the Manse, the children playing on the lawn, with the symbols of other activities which had been part of our lives. In the other 'light' were depicted the things which made life worthwhile; the open Bible, the Church and the Cross. The window is of plain glass so that people can look into the church and those inside can look out to the trees and the hills. This was particularly significant to me, for I have always felt that the Church and the world must be One. Two texts in the window expressed our feelings. From the Book of Psalms: 'If I take my flight to the frontier of the morning, Thy right hand will hold me fast', spoke of God's kindly Providence over us all, while the other from the Gospel expresses the faith which sustains us all: 'The light shines on in the dark and the darkness has never mastered it'.

Thanks be to God.